Chartered
Public
Relations

Chartered Public Relations

Lessons from expert practitioners

Foreword by Professor
Anne Gregory FCIPR

Edited by
Stephen Waddington
Chart.PR, MCIPR

CIPR   CHARTERED INSTITUTE
OF PUBLIC RELATIONS

KoganPage

LONDON PHILADELPHIA NEW DELHI

Publisher's note

Every possible effort has been made to ensure that the information contained in this book is accurate at the time of going to press, and the publishers and authors cannot accept responsibility for any errors or omissions, however caused. No responsibility for loss or damage occasioned to any person acting, or refraining from action, as a result of the material in this publication can be accepted by the editor, the publisher or any of the authors.

First published in Great Britain and the United States in 2015 by Kogan Page Limited

2nd Floor, 45 Gee Street
London EC1V 3RS
United Kingdom
www.koganpage.com

1518 Walnut Street, Suite 1100
Philadelphia PA 19102
USA

4737/23 Ansari Road
Daryaganj
New Delhi 110002
India

© Chartered Institute of Public Relations, 2015

The right of each commissioned author of this work to be identified as an author of this work has been asserted by him/her in accordance with the Copyright, Designs and Patents Act 1988.

ISBN   978 0 7494 7372 3
E-ISBN   978 0 7494 7373 0

British Library Cataloguing-in-Publication Data

A CIP record for this book is available from the British Library.

Library of Congress Cataloging-in-Publication Data

CIP data is available.

Library of Congress Control Number: 2014047416

Typeset by Graphicraft Limited, Hong Kong
Print production managed by Jellyfish
Printed and bound by CPI Group (UK) Ltd, Croydon, CR0 4YY

CONTENTS

12   Is public relations evolving into reputation management? 156

Julie McCabe Chart.PR, MCIPR

PART III   The application of best practice in markets – an analysis of the application of public relations in different markets   171

13   Engineering the future? Using influence to benefit society   173

Anne Moir Chart.PR, MCIPR

14　Defining the defence communicator　189

Clare L Parker Chart.PR, MCIPR

15　The evolution of UK public relations consultancies from 1984 to 2009　216

Jane Howard Chart.PR, FCIPR

PART IV International – the impact of the globalization of markets on public relations 229

20   A critical review: The four models of public relations and the excellence theory in an era of digital communication   290

Stephen Waddington Chart.PR, MCIPR

FOREWORD
The shift to professionalism in public relations

I know it's bad form to start a Foreword with a negative, but to quote my fellow Chartered Institute of Public Relations (CIPR) colleague and friend Dr Jon White, sometimes it does seem like our profession is like a car stuck in the mud. The wheels are spinning round, but we aren't gaining much forward momentum. Lots of activity, frantically busy, great new communication tools to play with, but is our profession earning respect and are we any nearer to achieving what seems to be public relations nirvana, a place in the boardroom?

The answer is yes and no. The evidence is that we are gaining some traction. The latest CIPR State of the Profession[1] survey shows that we are continuing to grow and international studies indicate that growth is about 12 per cent. Compared with earlier surveys more of us are reporting directly to CEOs and boards and hold more executive places on boards. Sir Martin Sorrell in one of his rare interviews with *PR Week*[2] has recognized that public relations has an increased and important role to play and has enormous potential, but says we need to get over our feelings of inferiority. We would also have to admit that in the eyes of 'the man on the Clapham Omnibus' and of the media we remain the practitioners of the dark arts, spin-doctors and purveyors of something short of the truth.

How then are we going to make the breakthrough that makes a difference and be recognized as a profession that is valuable and makes a positive difference? My personal view is that if you act as a professional you will eventually be recognized as one. To my mind professionals should belong to their profession. They join their professional body to show that they are bound by a code of ethics and to make a public commitment to professionalism. Joining a professional body also, in my view, brings an obligation to contribute something.

It is not just an exchange relationship that goes something along the lines of, 'I pay my money and I want to get value in return, especially the badge of respectability'. A professional body *is* the members of a profession and unless professionals contribute and drive it forwards, it will stultify and become irrelevant. An important statement made by this book is that professionals can contribute to their profession by writing on topics that demonstrate its breadth, depth and contribution. This is a book that fellow professionals can learn from.

There are a number of characteristics of a profession. First, it has a distinct body of knowledge that professionals need to know and act upon and that is taught by qualified individuals. Second, it has a defined set of skills which require expert training to achieve proficiency. Third, continuing professional development is necessary to stay current and competent to practise; fourth, it has a code of ethics which sets standards to guard the public interest and fifth, it is a requirement that those who practise the profession achieve a certain standard before they are accepted into the various grades of membership. There are other characteristics, but these five are fairly standard. When I signed the documents which were submitted to the Privy Council so that the then Institute of Public Relations could be considered for a Royal Charter, I had to check and double check that these bases were covered and we went through fiery hoops to prove it.

Reviewing the contents of this book and understanding that the authors of these chapters are all Chartered Practitioners, demonstrates very clearly that the Charter is now being enacted and that the profession has made substantial progress. These chapters are the edited versions of the submissions made by the authors for their Chartered examination. There are chapters here on theory, which expand the body and boundaries of knowledge, on current skills and practice and those needed for the future. The authors of these chapters have signed up to a code of ethics which is enforced, they have also signed up to continuing professional development and had to reach a high standard to obtain Chartered Practitioner status, submitting themselves to study and examination by their peers.

But this book is more than a series of essays written for examination: the essays provide a chronicle of the progress of our profession. They show how it has changed and how it has embraced a diverse theoretical and academic base. They demonstrate not only a much broader and deeper range of activities, but an ability to be critical and analytical of their use. They show how it has become more strategic, global, aware of its ethical obligations and more self-critical and reflective. These are the hallmarks of professionalism; of a maturing and more confident profession. It is essays like these that give me great optimism. This book shows public relations practitioners taking their profession seriously and when that happens, others will too.

Professor Anne Gregory FCIPR

1 CIPR (2014) *The State of the Profession*, CIPR, London.
2 Rodgers, D (2014) Sir Martin Sorrell on PR's place in the new wave of integration, *PR Week*, 9 October.

ABOUT *CHARTERED PUBLIC RELATIONS: LESSONS FROM EXPERT PRACTITIONERS*

One of my primary goals as president of the Chartered Institute of Public Relations (CIPR) in 2014 was to realign the organization with its vision and purpose.

I hope that the year will be characterized as a period when the CIPR reasserted a commitment to professionalism as set out by the founders of the Institute of Public Relations (IPR) in 1948, and committed to statute through its charter in 2005.

A key component of this work is to clearly set out the journey for members leading to Chartered PR Practitioner accreditation.

Chartered Public Relations: Lessons from Expert Practitioners published on the tenth anniversary of the CIPR's Charter, is an important contribution to this effort.

The Chartered Practitioner status is pitched by the CIPR as 'a benchmark for those working at a senior level and a "gold standard" to which all PR practitioners should strive to reach.'

The first stage is a questionnaire that probes your career, expertise and knowledge.

Stage two is a 3,000 to 4,000 word paper. The paper 'must be an original piece of work and should demonstrate the attributes defined as essential to chartered practitioner status.'

The final stage is a formal interview about your career and paper.

Chartered Public Relations: Lessons from Expert Practitioners is an anthology of some of the essays that successful Chartered PR Practitioners have produced over the past five years as part of their chartered process.

Some of the papers have been updated for publication. In each instance the author has included the publication date and details of any changes that have been made to the original paper.

My objective as the book's editor is to celebrate the work of Chartered PR Practitioners and create a substantive piece of work that can act as a showcase to encourage other practitioners to achieve the status.

The project will also make a valuable contribution to the community of public relations practice, and the advancement of public relations thinking worldwide.

The book tackles five critical areas of the development of public relations as it shifts to a more professional approach:

- The shift to the open organization – the application of public relations within every area of a modern organization.

- Developing areas of practice – an exploration of the opportunity in developing areas of public relations.

- The application of best practice – an analysis of the application of public relations in different markets.

- International – the impact of the globalization of markets on public relations.

- Reflections – an examination of the fundamental theories of public relations and their application to modern practice.

The CIPR has a stated ambition to rapidly grow the community of Chartered PR Practitioners and celebrate the work of this important community as a mark of the shift of public relations towards a clearer statement of professional standards.

If you believe as I do that the public relations industry needs to make the shift from a craft to a profession then you should sign up to continuing professional development (CPD) via the CIPR and start your own journey to Chartered Practitioner.

I hope that *Chartered Public Relations: Lessons from Expert Practitioners* inspires you to start your journey to Chartered PR Practitioner accreditation.

I owe several people my thanks for their help with this project. Phil Morgan, deputy chief executive, was instrumental in making this project a reality along with the team at Kogan Page.

Margaret Clow coordinated the project and proofed early drafts. This is the third book we've worked on together and her patience and professionalism working to tight deadlines is much appreciated. Thank you Margaret.

My thanks to the community of Chartered PR Practitioners that submitted their papers and helped make this project a reality. Thank you all.

Professor Anne Gregory initiated the then IPR's application for Charter, worked to prepare our application and signed our submission to the Privy Council when she was President in 2004. She received the Charter from the Clerk to the Privy Council as Past President in 2005. It's entirely fitting and appropriate that Anne kindly agreed to contribute the foreword to the book. Thank you Anne.

I'd also like to recognize the contribution of the then Director General, Colin Farrington, and lawyer Michael Stewart for their work in helping the Institute to achieve Chartered status.

Finally, thanks to the board, council and staff at the CIPR that supported the work of the CIPR during my year as president.

Stephen Waddington, Chart.PR, MCIPR
President 2014, CIPR

BECOMING A CHARTERED PUBLIC RELATIONS PRACTITIONER

Achieving the status of a Chartered Public Relations Practitioner is a validation of your skills, qualifications and experience by the only chartered body for PR.

Under the CIPR's Royal Charter, individual chartered status gives you the equivalent standing as experienced professionals in other industries. This benchmark of professional excellence and integrity represents the highest standard of knowledge, expertise and ethical practice.

As well as reflecting your breadth of experience and your academic achievements, chartered status demonstrates your commitment to life-long learning. It shows that you keep pace in a fast-moving profession, updating your knowledge and skills through CPD.

The three-stage application process enables you to self-evaluate and reflect on your professional journey in PR, identify the challenges and opportunities ahead, plan for your future and drive your career forward.

The benefits of attaining chartered status are:

- Demonstrate to your peers that you have met the rigorous criteria set out for chartered status.

- Enjoy greater influence within your organization and in the profession.

- Gain a professional competitive edge and enhance your career prospects.

- Reassure prospective employers and clients that you practise to the highest standards.

- Chartered Public Relations Practitioners are entitled to use the designated logo.

Who should apply?

To apply for Chartered Public Relations Practitioner status, you must be either a Member (MCIPR) or Fellow (FCIPR) **and** hold one of the following:

- CIPR Diploma in Public Relations – a postgraduate qualification;
- or a Master's degree from a recognized university course;
- or be a CIPR Accredited Public Relations Practitioner.

You will be asked to provide evidence of your relevant experience and current CPD participation. To retain chartered status, you will need to remain a CIPR member and maintain your CPD record.

You can begin a new application at any time. The application process has three stages:

Stage 1: Statement of experience

You may find it helpful to print and review before submitting.

Stage 2: Written paper (3,000 to 4,000 words)

The scope of these is broad and reflects the diversity of public relations work:

- reflect critically on the profession;
- consider the contributions of public relations to society with value beyond mere financial reward;
- explore the value of a code of conduct in practice or the attitudes and ethical policies that would need to be evident to create a role model for the profession;
- celebrate innovation, influence, strategic development or change initiation;
- give examples of how public relations has made you proud of your skills and knowledge, and why others' use of it has made you feel concerned, embarrassed or even ashamed;
- describe what public relations is when someone practises it with knowledge and expertise at chartered level.

You will be asked to demonstrate the following qualities:

- **Ethical practice**. Understanding of how ethical dilemmas arise and how to respond to them.

- **Leadership contribution to the PR profession and to your organization**. Capacity to offer leadership to others through mentoring and professional development.

- **Strategy ability to develop PR strategies**. These need to fit the business needs of your clients or your organization, based on grasping the link between business goals, strategy and communication. Understanding of the wider political, economic and social environment that shapes a communications strategy. Application of appropriate methods of research, planning, measurement and evaluation. Proven skill in building and managing the reputation of your clients or your organization.

- **Learning ability to create a learning environment for yourself and for others**. High degree of self-awareness.

- **Innovation capacity to create strategies that overcome challenges**. Ability to think creatively and to stimulate others to do so.

- **Communication**. Proven skill in communicating new concepts to clients and colleagues. Capacity to communicate under pressure, particularly in crisis situations. Ability to operate effectively within different organizational structures and cultures.

You can also choose a subject area of your own, as long as it provides the best illustration of your suitability for chartered status.

Stage 3: Interviews

A panel comprising two Chartered PR Practitioners undertake a review and invite you to a face-to-face interview. Remember you will need to have your statement of experience and your essay paper to hand. There will be a member of CIPR staff in attendance as an observer.

Sukhjit Grewal
Director, Professional Development and Membership, CIPR

PART I
The shift to the open organization
– the application of public relations within every area of a modern organization

Putting citizens at the heart of public relations
Public relations and public value

PAUL MYLREA CHART.PR, FCIPR

This paper was originally written in August 2009. Substantial revisions have been made to the original text for this book to reflect developments in media, technology and practice.

If public relations is the 'planned and sustained effort to establish and maintain goodwill and mutual understanding between an organization and its publics',[1] then at the heart of public relations is a detailed understanding of who those publics are, how they think, and what they consider important.

This focus is no longer an optional extra. We live in interesting times, with economic, technological and political developments all combining into a perfect storm. The economic downturn has meant stark choices on government priorities. Shifts in technology and society mean the opportunities to engage with the public are more diverse than ever before. Yet there remains deep public scepticism about the political process.

This public scepticism also extends to public relations, putting communicators – particularly in the public sector – at the heart of the storm.

In such a climate, public relations could be seen as discretionary rather than a central part of service creation and delivery.[2] With the economic downturn putting pressure on public sector budgets, it is vital to demonstrate that public relations *is* an essential service. The challenge, therefore, is to demonstrate effectiveness.

Measuring effectiveness is not simply a question of working out whether public relations efforts are successful at reaching their publics. What is needed is the ability to demonstrate that there is a true dialogue going on. Public relations needs to demonstrate it is adding value through this dialogue.

At the heart of the debate is this question of value. All too often, value is confused with cost – with the cheapest option being therefore the 'best' value. Yet value is a much broader concept that needs to take into account what the public itself considers valuable.

In a paper written for the Cabinet Office Strategy Unit in 2002, Gavin Kelly and Geoff Mulgan wrote: 'The third main source of public value (after outcomes and services) is trust, legitimacy, and confidence... if levels of trust in public institutions increase over time this is a source of value even if it does not flow from improved services or outcomes.'[3]

If trust is a source of public value, then the central aim of public relations to 'establish... mutual understanding between an organization and its publics' is about the creation of this value. For, as Rhodri Davies of another think tank, Policy Exchange, said: 'A crucial part of the role of public sector managers is to engage in meaningful dialogue with citizens and service users... Outcomes must be agreed with citizens through meaningful engagement. Only then can we be sure the outcomes we are striving for are the right ones.'[4]

This focus on outcomes is more complicated when these outcomes are not easily measurable. In demonstrating take-up of government benefits, for example, it is relatively easy to compare methods of engagement and select the most cost efficient. In cases where the public outcome has a demonstrable value – in, for example, reducing the cost to the state of health problems caused by obesity or smoking, or cutting the amount lost through benefit fraud – it is also easy to measure the return on investment of public relations spending.

It is far harder when trying to demonstrate a shift in attitude that has no immediate costable outcome or quantifiable change in behaviour. That was the challenge facing the communications team at the Department for International Development (DFID) when I was Director of Communications between 2007 and 2010.

Our challenge in DFID was to increase support for the action to reduce poverty in the developing world. The challenge has a basis rooted in statute and given added impetus by a range of parliamentary and civil service reports. The 2002 International Development Act laid down that 'The Secretary of State may... promote, or assist any person or body to promote, awareness of global poverty and of the means of reducing such poverty.'[5]

If this authority seemed optional, the urgency of boosting support for development was underlined in 2007 by a Capability Review, which argued that:

'The Department (for International Development) needs to build up the ways in which it demonstrates its accountability to the UK taxpayer. In particular, it should more explicitly and publicly explain how development fits within the wider UK interest and global policies.'[6]

The International Development Committee of the House of Commons reinforced this further in its 2009 report, saying:

'If DFID is to take effective action to combat these trends it needs to be able to draw on reliable information which provides a meaningful insight into public opinion.'[7]

Underlying all this is a belief that true dialogue with citizens is at the heart of a healthy state. DFID's 2006 white paper, Making governance work for the poor, for example, emphasized the importance of creating a dialogue between the public and governments in the developing world in order to ensure that development outcomes were achieved. 'Accountability,' the white paper said, is 'the ability of citizens, civil society and the private sector to scrutinize public institutions and governments and hold them to account.'[8]

DFID was already held to account in public by parliament and its committees. But as spending rose to meet the government's commitment to devote 0.7 per cent of Gross National Income to international development, so the need to publicly argue the case for it grew.

That is why from 2007, DFID embarked on a concerted and strategic effort to deepen its understanding of the beliefs and values of Britons towards poverty in the developing world.

On the surface, public support for action to reduce global poverty seemed strong. In DFID's 2008 tracking poll, 74 per cent of the public were concerned about poverty in developing countries, roughly the same as in the previous year despite the economic downturn.[9]

Yet this support, while widespread, was far from guaranteed. The poll showed that only 22 per cent said they were 'very concerned' about poverty compared to 27 per cent a year previously. As Simon Maxwell, the former Director of the Overseas Development Institute, said: 'Support for international development is broad but shallow – vulnerable to how people feel about prospects at home.'[10]

Although DFID had conducted annual polling since 1999 to measure the public's perceptions of development issues and the government's participation in reducing global poverty, this did not give a detailed enough picture to engage in relevant and meaningful dialogue. In 2008, therefore, DFID decided to use desk research and qualitative focus group analysis to inform a quantitative survey. The survey was then analysed to create audience segments.[11]

The segments that emerged provided rich information for DFID's communications team. The five groupings – active enthusiasts, interested mainstream, distracted individuals, family first sympathizers and insular sceptics – helped refine our understanding of both core supporters and our most trenchant critics.

For example, almost a third of active enthusiasts – the most supportive group – said they did not know much about the lives of people in poor countries, while 40 per cent of the interested mainstream – the second strongest group of supporters – claimed to know little or nothing at all. Seven in 10 distracted individuals believed that nothing seems to get better in the developing world no matter how much was spent.

Other findings demonstrated the general lack of knowledge about global poverty and what was being done to reduce it, as well as a general sense of helplessness and a widespread concern about corruption and waste.

The segmentation also gave us deeper insights into the means to reach these groups, showing, for example, that while television remained the most important channel where people are exposed to global poverty, the internet was becoming the main route to find out more once interest is awakened – even for relatively sceptical groups.

These were just some of the top line findings. Yet even these had an immediate impact on our strategic communications choices, confirming, for example, the decision to revamp the website and provide engaging information in accessible videos to bolster understanding and support among our active enthusiast segment.

Insight into the dynamics driving family first sympathizers – who were not likely to give money to charities but did get involved in Red Nose Day, often through school events – helped us develop successful youth communications. For example, a campaign run jointly with Save the Children and the *First News* newspaper on children in conflict gathered more than 230,000 signatures from young people across the country.[12]

The analysis was the first ever segmentation model of the UK public's engagement with development. Its importance was not just in helping communications professionals within DFID identify key barriers to understanding and engagement, but also in providing detailed evidence to people across the DFID of the way people in the UK felt about development.

It was unsurprising if people working in a specialized and often highly technical area of international policy did not fully appreciate how ordinary people see the same issues, particularly if much of the work is carried out overseas, out of sight and in some cases beyond the imagination of many people in the UK.

Yet an inability to communicate the work of DFID to taxpayers in ways that engage, inform and enthuse led to what was called an 'ignorance gap' about 'what aid does, can and should do, and what aid might be able to achieve in theory and the impact it has in practice'.[13]

While technical experts, development specialists and multilateral bodies heaped praise on DFID for its model of development assistance and its impact, few taxpayers knew it even exists. The then Secretary of State, Douglas Alexander, described the department as the government's 'best kept secret'.[14]

Changing this, however, was not going to be possible simply by getting DFID's Communications Division to shout louder. We had to start explaining to people across the department what establishing a real dialogue actually meant, and what we needed from them in order to communicate effectively with the public.

The segmentation, therefore, provided the basis for a dialogue with other parts of DFID. In an organization that prided itself on evidence-based policy-making, demonstrating the evidence base for strategic communications choices helped establish the professionalism of the approach and create a framework for internal dialogue. It answered general feedback from across the department that while they understood the need to communicate, they did not really understand what we wanted or what good communications looked like.[15]

Detailed analysis of the results continued to be fed into the 2008 departmental communications strategy, Communications Matters.[16]

We also discussed the results with others who shared our concern about the level of support for efforts to reduce global poverty, working, for example, with development charities to deepen our understanding of public views and attitudes. Sharing existing research and cooperating on new analysis would, we believed, benefit everyone working in this field.

These insights fed into the white paper produced by DFID, Building Our Common Future[17] in 2009 and in particular to the decision to launch a new logo – UKaid – to identify where Britain's spending on international development was being used to alleviate global poverty.

The segmentation provided hugely valuable insights into what was likely to build opposition to development – excessive use of numbers and statistics, a failure to address concerns about corruption, and excessive emphasis on the scale of the problem – and early insights into how we could deal with this.

But we still did not know enough about what makes people shift their attitudes and beliefs on international development. And although we knew who takes action, we did not know enough about the drivers that encourage people to act.

Did this matter? Researchers supported our intuitive sense that it did. This was not about research for research sake, or even about boosting our own professional credibility. It was about avoiding unintended consequences from nuances in meaning that only become evident too late, as well as being about effectiveness.

Jennifer van Heerde and David Hudson of the School of Public Policy at University College London have, for example, argued that simply 'accommodating citizens' preferences'[18] in communications is likely ultimately to lead to disengagement – the very opposite of what we were attempting to achieve.

Instead, they argued, communications should be used to engage citizens in a dialogue which actively shapes their preferences. The challenge is 'to make the citizens realize what sort of people they are and what is right to do because they are what they are'.[19]

The implications for public relations – in particular in the public sector – were profound. If the public was to see action on global poverty as part of their identity, it has to be achieved through this dialogue. Far from being government 'spin', the public relations needed to establish a two-way dialogue with the public that informed policy, created engagement and generated public value.

Without public relations, the risk of public disengagement – and further, corrosive scepticism of the political process – would grow. In his foreword to a 2009 study of Make Poverty History, the mass campaign in 2005 to get international action on international development, Professor Frank Webster underlined this: 'Nowadays, more than ever, politics involves mediation. Most people in the West do not directly experience abject poverty, contemporary war, or even much the adverse effects of climate change. Even in formal political affairs, it is rare for electors to debate with representatives face-to-face. Public engagement requires communications.'[20]

These communications needed to be guided by professional and evidence-based insight – whether described as insight into audiences, customers, service users, beneficiaries or the general public – if they were to establish mutual understanding and create trust.

This theme has continued after the 2010 elections. Government communications under the coalition government has been about a renewed role for public relations as advertising budgets reduced and total communications spending fell from £881 million in 2009/10 to just £410 million in 2013/14.

Practitioners have increasingly turned to public relations for cost-effective solutions. Cost as a factor of constrained budgets, and effective because in a social, digital, networked world mass marketing was no longer effective in reaching a number of niche audiences.

Government PR campaigns have been targeted at specific audiences: for example, getting small businesses to expand, selling British trade and tourism through the GREAT campaign, reaching out to visitors to the 2014 World Cup with the FCO's 'Know Before You Go' campaign, or the Breaking the Silence campaign on the effects of male rape.

It is interesting that even after a change of government, the commitment to spending 0.7 per cent of GDP on development aid remained policy. In January 2013, in a review of international development policy, 'It also reaffirmed its commitment to spend 0.7 per cent of the UK's national income on overseas aid by the end of 2013 – and to put this pledge into law.'

It added: 'This government believes that helping very poor people in other parts of the world to achieve a greater measure of prosperity is not just the right thing to do, but the smart thing to do.'

Was this the result of the earlier work to understand public perceptions on development? That is too much to claim. Yet, it is hard to believe that the government would continue with a policy that it believed was universally unpopular.

Public relations, therefore, is not an optional extra. It is at the heart of that elusive concept of public value. As well as continued work to deepen our understanding of the drivers of public attitudes, we need a wider appreciation of this both inside and outside the profession. Across government, there needs to be a deeper understanding of the value of dialogue as an essential component of policy formation, while public relations practitioners need to demonstrate a robust evidence base for their work.

Notes

1   CIPR definition of PR, CIPR [Online] http://
    www.cipr.co.uk/direct/careers.asp?v1=whatis [accessed 09/08/2009].

2   'While DFID's budget continues to increase under the 2007
    Comprehensive Spending Review settlement, the 2009 Budget imposed
    a requirement on all government departments **to find additional efficiency
    savings. In DFID's case this will amount to £155 million in 2010–11.
    The department has identified savings in the following divisions:
    ... A £10 million cut in the budget of the Communications Division, to
    be achieved by "more effective, focused central communications work
    and more efficient use of web and social media networks"... We reiterate
    that it would be regrettable if "efficiency" measures actually made the
    department less effective.'** (bold in original) Extract from International
    Development Committee, session 2008–09, Fourth Report:
    Aid under Pressure, section 4, pp 80–82, HMSO, London [Online]
    http://www.publications.parliament.uk/pa/cm200809/
    cmselect/cmintdev/179/17907.htm [accessed 09/08/2009].

3   Kelly, G, Mulgan, G and Muers, S (2002) Creating public value: an
    analytical framework for public service reform, Cabinet Office Strategy
    Unit, October 2002 [Online] http://www.cabinetoffice.gov.uk/media/
    cabinetoffice/strategy/assets/public_value2.pdf [accessed 10/08/2009].

4   Davies, R (2009) The battle over 'value' and 'outcomes' – who decides?
    [Online] http://www.publicservice.co.uk/feature_story.asp?id=12394
    (Updated 7 August 2009) [accessed 07/08/2009].

5   *International Development Act 2002* (Part 1, Section 4, point 2),
    HMSO, London [Online] http://opsi.gov.uk/acts/acts2002/
    ukpga_20020001_en_2#pt1-pb1-l1g4 [accessed 09/08/2009].

6   *Capability Review of the Department for International Development
    2007* (Chapter 6, Area for Action 4, p. 23), Cabinet Office, London
    [Online] http://www.civilservice.gov.uk/Assets/Capability_Review_
    DfID_tcm6-1058.pdf [accessed 09/08/2009].

7   International Development Committee report (2009) *Aid Under
    Pressure: Support For Development Assistance In A Global Economic
    Downturn*, Fourth Report of Session 2008/09, HMSO, London
    [Online] http://www.publications.parliament.uk/pa/cm200809/
    cmselect/cmintdev/179/179i.pdf [accessed 08/08/2009].

8   DFID white paper (2006) *Making Governance Work for the Poor*,
    Chapter 2, 2.2, HMSO, London [Online] http://www.dfid.gov.uk/
    Documents/publications/whitepaper2006/wp2006section2.pdf
    [accessed 06/08/2009].

9 Figures taken from TNS UK Ltd (2008) *Public Attitudes Towards Development*, report prepared for COI on behalf of the Department for International Development [Online] http://www.dfid.gov.uk/ Documents/publications/public-attitudes-to-development-2008.pdf [accessed 09/08/2009]. Figures from 2008 are not directly comparable with 2007 as new questions were included, the order changed and our audience segmentation included. However, the figures for overall support remain roughly comparable, and this is substantiated by other reports such as the *OECD Policy Insight* publication of December 2008 on the impact of the economic downturn on public support for development, Zimmerman, R (2008) The fallout from the financial crisis (5): the end of public support for development aid?, OECD, Paris [Online] http://www.oecd.org/dataoecd/56/35/41804623.pdf [accessed 06/08/2009].

10 Maxwell, S (2008) ODI opinion: doing development in a downturn, Overseas Development Institute, London [Online] http:// www.odi.org.uk/resources/download/1902.pdf [accessed 07/08/2009].

11 DFID/Ipsos MORI (2008) DFID Citizen Segmentation Report, August (Internal Report) DFID/Ipsos MORI, London.

12 *First News* (2009) Conflict children [Online] http:// www.firstnews.co.uk/conflictchildren/ [accessed 10/08/2009].

13 Riddle, R (2005) Aid Effectiveness: what's at stake for heads of communication, Notes for a presentation to the Annual Meeting of Informal Network of DAC Heads of Information/communication, 4 March 2005, Paris [Online] http://www.oecd.org/dataoecd/ 10/23/34571661.pdf [accessed 10/08/2009]. Cited in Beaulne, P (2008) Communicating international development results, MA submission, University of Leicester.

14 Quoted in Hasan, M and Macintyre, J (2009) The politics interview, *New Statesman*, 16 July 2009 [Online] http://www.newstatesman.com/ uk-politics/2009/07/alexander-afghanistan-brown [accessed 10/08/2009].

15 This is a summary of feedback from participants at DFID's Senior Civil Service AwayDay, summer 2007, and further conversations with Directors as we developed DFID's Communications Strategy.

16 DFID (2008) *Communications Matters* (Internal Document), [Online] http://www.dfid.gov.uk/Documents/publications/commsstrategy.pdf [accessed 10/08/2009].

17 DFID white paper (2009) Building our common future, HMSO, London [Online] http://www.dfid.gov.uk/About-DfID/Quick-guide-to-DfID/How-we-do-it/Building-our-common-future/ [accessed 10/08/2009].

18 Van Heerde, J and Hudson, J (2008) The righteous considereth the cause of the poor? Public attitudes towards poverty in developing countries, *Political Studies*, **58** (3), pp 389–409 [Online] http://davidhudson.files.wordpress.com/2008/10/van-heerde-hudson-public-attitudes-towards-poverty-in-developing-countries-0710081.pdf [accessed 10/08/2009].

19 Goldmann, K (2005) Appropriateness and consequences: the logic of neo-institutionalism, *Governance: An International Journal of Policy, Administration and Institutions*, **18** (1), pp 35–52, cited in J van Heerde and D Hudson (2008).

20 Professor Frank Webster was the head of the Department of Sociology at City University, London, from 2008–12. His comments are taken from his Foreword to Sireau, N (2009) *Make Poverty History: Political communication in action*, Palgrave Macmillan, London.

Plus ça change, plus c'est la même chose for public relations?

ALAN SMITH, CHART.PR, MCIPR

This paper was originally submitted in August 2009, revised in February 2010 and updated in August 2014.

When I originally asked this question in 2009 ('The more things change, the more they stay the same for public relations?') I answered by saying, 'Maybe, but probably not.'

I think that assertion, that our profession would not stay the same, should not, and indeed was about to enter a new era of leadership and professionalism, remains true.

I made it in response to the challenges and huge opportunities coming at that time from social media specifically, and the internet generally. At the time those challenges and opportunities were still forming. Twitter ruled and Facebook was only just making its mark.[1] Neither Instagram nor Pinterest existed as commercial products (both were launched in 2010).

From today's perspective, it's clear that social media have changed the PR profession forever. That much is irrefutable.

But what of the other points I made at a time that now seems so long ago but which is still fewer than five years? About the role of the professional? About where we sit in a new communications landscape? About competitors? And what are the opportunities for public relations professionals in today's connected world that go beyond social media? After all, public relations was never solely about media relations. That new media now exist doesn't change that.

I re-read my paper expecting (hoping) that minor edits would do the trick in preparing it for this book.

Not so. Looking back to a past view of the future in which we now live can be a little surreal.

I sought to discuss something of what might happen, based on my observations and experiences at that time. It deliberately drew no certain conclusions, although much of what I discussed has happened, some of it far beyond where we might reasonably have expected back in late 2009.

One thing that *has*, I think, changed in the past five years is the sense of cause and effect that defined formal public relations practice in its modern form for the previous 80 years or so.

So I've dipped in, selected passages from the original paper, and comment on them here. In doing so I hope to refresh it, pose some of the questions in new ways, and perhaps pose new questions for the first time.

Changing some context

When I wrote the original paper I was an in-house corporate communications director for a global software company based in Sydney. Today I work with a social analytics start-up company (also based in Sydney). Although I remain a public relations professional, I now do much more than tell our story to the market, media and prospects. I advise on taking marketing and communications positions to market for our clients and work alongside data analytics experts, programmers, and social media hotshots.

The entire premise of the company (DIGIVIZER) simply didn't exist in December 2009. The concepts of bringing together the social web, big data and CRM in real-time (which is what we've done) were barely coalescing. My role is now about using public relations expertise and experience across a much broader canvas than even social media, to embrace messaging and positioning in a new world of crumbling intermediaries, of direct engagement with influencers, customers and prospects.

Perhaps for the first time in a long time the public relations role has morphed to be exactly that – the management of direct relationships with the public on a large scale.

Even more, it's about conversations, not shouting. Back in 2009, I wrote:

> 'What the Internet, and all the social media constructs that now plug into it, are about are conversations. This is a very different mindset from briefing conventional media and relying on them to convey a message, or briefing audiences through other conventional channels.'

At the time I made the comment that phrases such as 'conventional' and 'social media' served only to continue the myth that these were somehow discrete. I was right when I said that all of these channels were blending and blurring. Today, that blending and blurring has been replaced with a true continuum that requires us to understand and advise on the right balance of channels for any given communications assignment. It's a role that the PR professional can and should own, but we face new competitors, something I touch on later.

I also cited Seth Godin's book *Meatball Sundae* in the context of shouting (seeking to make yourself heard, usually through advertising) and the need to seek and gain permission to have sensible conversations with audiences.[2]

Any PR professional operating today that seeks to win an argument by shouting the loudest, or by attempting to do so without the permission of the audience, will fail. This *has* changed the way we do our work, and it has made us more professional in the way we act and in how we advise clients or colleagues. This has happened for two reasons (which had not yet taken hold in 2009): we can talk directly to audiences, and they make it very clear if they don't like our approach.

While probably now taken for granted, this has been an important shift in the past five years.

Cutting the strings

In December 2009, I wrote:

> 'The stereotype of the invisible PR person pulling the strings of the spokesman is going to dissolve before our eyes.

> 'This is, in my opinion, a good thing, for a number of reasons. Our collective feet will be held more firmly to the fire if we are the person whose face is on show (and in the new media world, it will likely be our face).

> 'We will actually have to know what we are talking about, so that we can have these conversations ourselves, relying less on setting up interviews with experts. Our ability to interpret our clients' or our employers' messages will have to become much more acute and honed.

> 'Simply to be able to scale public relations operations to cope with the multitude of conversations that will now need to take place means that the public relations counsel will need to do much more of the talking.'[3]

We have I think indeed become more accountable in a much more direct way, with our colleagues and certainly our audiences. It's interesting to compare the continuing heritage media approach of citing unnamed spokespersons with the social media approach of naming them. The immediacy and the connected nature of these new channels mean that, right or wrong, the world knows about everything very, very quickly. We now have to be absolutely certain that the moment is right, and that our arguments, that we now present personally, pass muster.

And we all experience a news cycle measure in minutes, not days. I expressed the opinion at the time that:

> 'A resurgence will occur in the value assigned by clients and employers to the counsel provided to them by public relations professionals. The consequences (and fear) of "getting things wrong" in this newly amplified way, and for many organizations the uncertainty of this new world, mean that public relations professionals will be turned to much more.'

Has this happened? I'm not sure. The outdated notions of 'getting the CEO into the press' and the expectation that any given communications project is somehow bound to succeed still lingers in many quarters.

At the time I had recently attended a social media seminar and had been amazed at how many of the audience worked for companies clearly still banning any interaction using new media. They were clearly struggling to convince their management of both the value and inevitability of this new way of communicating. There was frustration almost mixed with anxiety, even fear. That they were there at the conference was a great opportunity for them to arm themselves with what, in essence, was a kit bag of techniques. What were fascinating were the 'old-world' aspects of their various organizations.

Those attitudes have certainly changed and one consequence of the connected world has been a renewed understanding about the benefits of communications, and their power. The complexity of interaction with audiences, across all aspects of public relations programme execution, has also increased.

It's also the case that enlightened organizations are taking a more strategic approach to communications, bringing together corporate comms, services, sales and marketing into a unified whole.

Then and now: what has changed, what might still change?

In my original paper, I compared the first decade of the 21st century with the birth of modern public relations following the first world war, and the emergence of practitioners such as Edward Bernays. I drew on his book *Crystallizing Public Opinion*, published in 1923.[4] He drew a distinction between what he called a public relations counsel and a press agent. This comparison remains truer than ever since 2009. Bernays defined and therefore distinguished the public relations counsel as *someone adding value by being able to provide counsel in both directions*, between the client or employer, and the channel and audience.[5] In my view PR professionals are those who *do* add value and do so beyond previously narrow confines of what public relations might have been. And this goes beyond the disruptive effects of the social web and a real-time connected world.

This adds a new dimension to what we do. In essence, most of what most of us have done historically has been to communicate in one direction, outwards. For sure, if we created an event, a dialogue between people took place, but only in that room, only in that paper, only in that language, only in that country.

Now, the message is outside the venue almost before we've finished, it's available across national borders, translation engines give you the gist in seconds. One single blog, one single social comment, one single statement on camera which then appears on the web, can change everything.

Simply being an expensive distributor of material is simply no longer enough, nor sustainable as something defining public relations value. The internet and the social web have allowed the development of an almost-confusing range of services that let PR teams manage processes without the need for expert advice on the way through, and do so worldwide. These services seek to automate part of what many still do, and what many of us used only to do.

This has changed the value of evaluation. There is now simply no excuse for not knowing the results of our work. Where the *real* value lies though is in the *interpretation* of the data, and its currency.

The internet is what has driven this, *not* because it's another communications channel, or set of channels, but because *it changes fundamentally the way we connect and communicate.*

What about the media?

Back in 2009, I said:

> 'From where I'm sitting, I'm not sure the media are coping. When I asked one of our consultancies what their opinion was about the state of the... media, their response was, "they are circling the plughole".'

I think I got that right, and it probably wasn't hard to predict. Of course, media disintegration has gone much further than their mere collapse in the face of the internet onslaught. The UK's Leveson

Inquiry, Murdoch's subsequent closure of the *News of the World*, the launch of *The Guardian* overseas as web-only editions, and much more, have accelerated the effect.

The ability to continue to provide value that is unique has, in the past four-five years, rewritten the media landscape, both for us in the PR profession and for those in heritage and new media outlets. All of us are now confronted with many influencers seeking payment for articles, yet audiences refusing to assign this paid-for output any credibility. Here in Australia, blogging agencies have appeared with rosters of well-credentialled writers acting as writers-on-demand. In effect they are a new breed of journalist. But old-style media paid journalists to be on staff to then seek out and write stories. An empty page at the end of a news day resulted in a shortened newspaper, but the journalist still got paid (at least for a while).

Today's new blogging agencies only write on demand, and only then for a fee. Their business model is that nothing appears without payment explicitly for it to do so.

We have a new set of challenges.

The answer to the conundrum of trying to charge for credible content when many can now get all that they need for free remains unclear in the long-term.[6]

Once again, this presents new opportunities for public relations professionals. Once again, this is not about finding outlets that can provide bulk coverage. It is about finding the *right* outlets that connect you to like-minded individuals.

It's also about understanding that influencers are now more diverse, more dispersed, and by no means attached to historic media outlets. At DIGIVIZER for example, we search out, analyse and map influencers for clients based on their influence as defined by client inputs and complex analysis of their networks and the relevance of those networks (and not just on dumb volume).

All this is now taken for granted. Back in 2009, serious blogs, once rated by readers and companies, still stood out as being unusual. I quoted one specialist blogger in 2009, electronics writer Brian Bailey,[7] who made it clear even then that what he wanted was information and insight that was relevant to his audiences, so that he could add value by writing useful and serious articles to help his readers understand more about the market in which they worked, and the vendors on which they relied. He needed to reply implicitly on public relations functions in organizations, but he was quite prepared to set out the rules of engagement that went along with the right to earn his trust.

In short, the perfect definition of an influencer. As Bailey also said:

> 'Stop sending the press releases... start sending me announcements
> about significant... advances and the contact people that I can talk
> to for more information if and when I need it. Then I may blog about
> you...'

In 2009 we still talked about journalists and media. Today, we have to grapple, understand and engage with influencers, journalists and many more interpreters.

And surely the job of the public relations professional remains to interpret messages for the right audiences through the most appropriate channels.

Goodbye to the good old days

In 2009 I included schematics representing the new environment as it was then appearing, and compared it to the old. Take a look at them and see what you think from the perspective of 2014/15.

Figure 2.1 represents the old world, certainly the world in which I started my career in the early 1980s. We created messages which we interpreted and presented to a segmented audience, through fairly direct and relatively easily managed channels dominated by the media.

Our interactions were with direct audiences, and we could look them in the eye, usually literally, and get the feedback from the body language. Although our intentions were to spread the word, we picked individuals and groups off one by one.

FIGURE 2.1   Diagram 1: the good old days

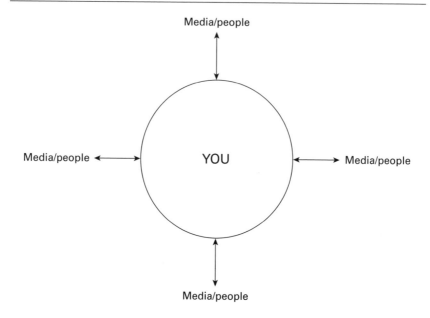

Now take a look at Figure 2.2. The world has changed dramatically. The interactions and conversations have become more numerous and less under any given set of controls.

The internet allows these groups and individuals to communicate around the circle, at once, without any reference to us, and often without us realizing what's happening. Everything gets noisier. In the context of public relations, the planned bit is now a lot looser, the messages can be bent out of shape more easily, and the audiences may never be known to us.

In fact, I think this second diagram is too simple: each of the points around the outer circle, the media/groups, and the noise, has its own additional 'audience ecosystem' circling off the edges of the diagram, into the distance. Figure 2.3 is closer to the future (as it then was, the present as it now is).

The power is in the connected conversations with those whose influence really does count, and with genuine advocacy built on enthusiasm and credibility established with these audiences.

FIGURE 2.2 Diagram 2: it just got noisier

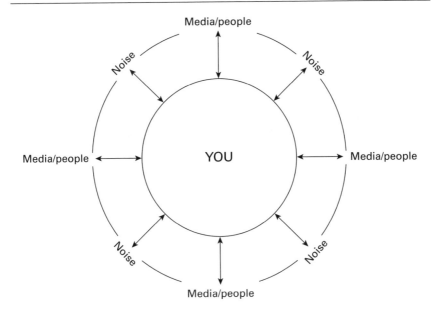

FIGURE 2.3 Diagram 3: the complicated truth

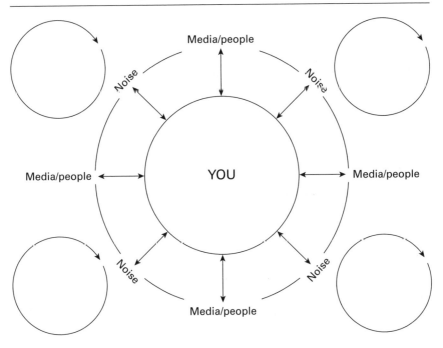

In fact, if we are successful in our work, this debate will be large in volume, supportive in tone, and significant in its effect. But even if we are not active, *the debate can now still take place, and still have similar effects, almost completely beyond our control, and almost certainly not on our terms.*

The structure of public relations consultancies and in-house teams

I thought that dramatic mistakes were being made in 2009 in the way in-house teams and, especially, PR consultancies were starting to structure their groups or organizations.

I saw the grafting on of discrete groups, to create the New Media Team or the Social Media Group. By creating such distinct groups, the implication was drawn that this was a discrete set of tasks and skills, to be deployed perhaps at a premium cost or fee.

What was wrong with this approach was that, as Seth Godin would say, it's grafting the meatball onto the sundae. We should not be 'old school' or 'conventional media'. We must be 'relevant media', or better still, 'relevant channel' experts.

It is not an appendix to what we do. It *is* what we do.

And it continues to this day. Take a look at the recruitment websites or LinkedIn. See how many digital specialist roles are advertised. See how few communications strategy roles are advertised. We run the risk of missing the context our clients and companies so desperately need, and the communications wisdom that applies across all available channels.

Our skills and expertise still need to assess the balance that needs to be struck on behalf of clients or employers. We have to know how our audiences get their information. Who do they turn to? How do they define 'value'? What are the feedback mechanisms? How will we know what's being said, and where? How quickly can we respond? Figures 2.2 and 2.3 above attempt to show how complex and entrenched this has indeed now become.

Where to from here?

As I said at the time, if only we knew. Exciting, isn't it? Still! The early steps we were considering at the company I worked for in 2009 now seem obvious, and have passed into conventional wisdom.

They worked because we were relevant, credible, and transparent, creating content of interest couched in language relevant to our audiences. That still applies in the pursuit of professional public relations excellence.

One example was the creation of a seed programme for a new product. Alongside media relations programmes with specialist print media, we instigated a programme in which we identified external influencers to receive one of the products to experience and then discuss in-print or online.

Our intent was to side-step much of the traditional print media in favour of engineers, bloggers, enthusiasts and others who we felt might want to play with, and talk about, a new product.

What was different was that, once we'd vetted these people for engineering competence, we left them alone. The intent was to let them be as objective as they saw fit. We did not seek to influence the experience, or to influence what they wrote. We couldn't. They wouldn't let us. And we didn't want to. If someone had a negative experience, that reflected badly on the actual features of the product, something we actually wanted to fix.

It was, we felt, ground-breaking stuff. It was unfamiliar territory for us, and it was exhilarating.

In my original paper, I wondered rhetorically whether it would work. Looking back on it from 2014, it seems still to be a reasonable template for today's public relations professional.

My original conclusions also still seem relevant and pertinent. The elephants in the room do still seem to be: if everyone can communicate with everyone, who needs public relations professionals?

If media change out of all proportion, or even disappear, what might public relations professionals do?

If every piece of formal communication can be critiqued in seconds by people they don't know, how do public relations professionals manage the communication process?

If broadcasting and communication are now meshing and blurring to produce something quite new and distinct, how do public relations professionals change to remain relevant and valuable?

As I said at the beginning of this paper, things may change, and I still don't think they will stay the same. And in any case, and as I said then, predictions are merely a metaphor for attempting to second-guess the future.

What I didn't see were the new competitors – content managers, evaluation consultants, digital exerts and more, all encroaching on the space previously held by the public relations professional.

Better that we define our own futures on our own terms, before someone else does.

Professionalism is about attention to detail and delivery of results, about adding value that a client or colleague can't find elsewhere. Value is always at a premium, and always sought. We have no option but to be professional.

I'm sure we'll rise to the challenge.

Notes

1   See http://mashable.com/2009/12/30/facebook-2009/ for a reminder.

2   Godin, S (2007) *Meatball Sundae: How new marketing is transforming the business world (and how to thrive in it)*, Portfolio (US)/Piatkus (UK). See in particular the following pages in the UK edition: pp 59, 62–63, 64, 66, 69–70, 127, 181, 183.

3   Godin (2007), p 127.

4   Bernays, E L (1923) *Crystallizing Public Opinion*, Boni and Liveright, New York.

5   Bernays (1923), p 57.

6   At the time I quoted Shoebridge, N (2009) Putting paid to online charging, *Australian Financial Review*, 17 August 2009, p 41.

7   http://www.chipdesignmag.com/bailey/2009/08/05/no-more-press-releases/

Death or rebirth?
A digital future for PR

03

MATT APPLEBY CHART.PR, FCIPR

This paper was originally written in August 2009. Minor revisions have been made to the original text for this book to reflect developments in media, technology and practice.

My career has developed in parallel with the social changes brought about by the mainstream acceptance of the worldwide web. I joined my first PR consultancy in 1996 – it was another year before I was allocated my first corporate email address and web access.

It is logical therefore to use the Chartered Practitioner process to build my knowledge and expertise in social media. It is clear that its impact on the present and future development of our profession is relevant within the wider context of the CIPR's professionalization programme – it has changed society, challenged the media and led to new models of professional practice.

The impact of social media

There's little question that we're experiencing '...the greatest evolution in the history of PR' (Brian Solis cited in Breakenridge 2008, p xvii).

But while many question whether we're on the brink of the death of PR, I'd argue we're seeing its rebirth.

Ten years ago *The Cluetrain Manifesto* (Locke *et al*, 1999) set out the founding principles of what would become today's web 2.0. It introduced the concept that 'markets are conversations' and the shift from monologue to dialogue, control to engagement as models for corporate communication. It went further in identifying the shift from the corporate to the human, from markets/audiences to communities/individuals.

Even though it's a decade old, its principles are a good starting point to explain the movement that has put the individual at the centre of online life and eroded concepts of markets, users and consumers. This humanization of communication has deep implications for not only how we identify and reach the people we seek to engage, but also what we say to them.

Our behaviour in this socialized online world is very different, we seek to gather in communities, to find like-minded individuals and we want to share, talk and create with them. And the crucial point for PR is that many people are already there and their numbers are growing by the day.[1]

If this is how and where people are living their lives, this is how they are expecting companies to behave. Consumers want direct communication from and with brands, but on their own terms. They want easy access to information, to be able to ask questions and to expect a quick response. They want to hear a voice from within the company and to believe they can trust that voice.[2]

If you get it right, they become a highly motivated community of advocates for the things that they love. Get it wrong and it could haunt you forever.

As Niall Cook (2008) says, 'The ground rules for participation are still undefined and open to interpretation' (p 119). It may be a work in progress but, there are a set of clear guiding principles that flow from the interpretation of market as conversation: listen, engage, measure. I think once we understand these and their implications, we're ready to start the journey. And start we all must.

Even where organizations don't think they're ready to use social media, the traditional media are all already engaged so they have to consider how best to manage this situation. As they increasingly see the conversations that are happening about their industry/product/ business without their participation, the need for a guide through the jungle will become increasingly clear to them.

The case for us in PR to engage is even stronger, much too strong to ignore. The debate rages online about how we best adapt and strong communities have emerged to share nascent best practice through using the channels and techniques themselves. It's interesting to see PR and journalists having this debate and doing it so publicly.

More and more people's first port of call for news is online and the most trusted source of 'news' is more likely to be a friend than a media outlet. Readerships of national and now regional newspapers have been in steady decline for decades and the internet has made a significant dent in the amount of TV that we watch. The audience that is in front of the TV is increasingly fragmented across devices and channels or is timeshifting content to suit their own schedules.

And even though it still maintains a vital position of influence in society, the role of offline media for PR is increasingly defined by its impact as a driver of traffic online. If you're watching TV you're likely to be doing it with a laptop on, if you're reading a paper on the train to work you'll have internet access on your iPhone. What we can still achieve through offline channels is converging with, and adding value to, our online activity.

It's not just consumption that's changing, it's attitude: 'The people formerly known as the audience wish to inform media people of our existence, and of a shift in power...' says Jay Rosen, professor of journalism at New York University, on his blog (Solis and Breakenridge 2009, p 85). They are viewers and directors, listeners and broadcasters, readers and writers.

As more media moves online, there's another shift in the relationship with PR. The mutually beneficial aspect of the journalism/PR symbiosis has been built around our ability to supply appropriate content to help the media fill space.

Online, the space expands to fit the content, not the other way round. From the media's perspective we may be able to help by providing an interesting story or brokering a relevant interview but why should they then include the video, image or links that we also provide? They don't need to fill the space – why should they not expect us to pay? There's an increasingly grey area which is blurring the lines between online editorial and paid-for content.

Does it matter? Do people now care about the source of news as long as that source is disclosed?

As businesses increasingly embrace the idea that they are effectively also media/publishing companies and invest in developing their own online content, we're seeing people happy to consume a mix of news from companies, online and offline media, friends and complete strangers.[3]

While this is an evolving dynamic between the media and PR, the biggest changes to practice are coming from the social media activities that remove the third party – the engaged, white-of-their-eyes, person-to-person participation.

The evolution of PR practice

The growth of social media and changes to traditional media is having a major impact on how we practise PR. 'Nothing will ever be the same again; the advent of an online world means that almost every aspect of the PR discipline needs to be rethought' (Phillips and Young 2009, p 8). That's quite a gauntlet to throw down.

The principle at the heart of what's changed according to Brian Solis is that we've lost the 'public' from public relations and we need to get it back or risk being left out of the conversations that will happen without us (Solis and Breakenridge 2009, p 79).

It has led to a fundamental reappraisal of the way in which PR practice is having to adapt in order to remain effective in the digital domain. Our ability to listen, engage and measure are all dependent on new and emerging strategies, tactics and tools. Phillips and Young define it well as the move from 'reputation management' to 'relationship optimization' (Phillips and Young 2009, p 4).

There are several implications from this shift in definition – your reputation is no longer yours to manage; control has moved to those with whom you share relationships; and our role as PR practitioners is about building and capitalizing on connections for our clients (rather than on their behalf).

We are being challenged to guide our clients into relationships in which they have to directly engage. We become facilitators for the conversation, creating the strategy, writing the engagement policies, listening and researching, steering clients down the right path to effective engagement then measuring the outcome.

This process of leading clients to engage themselves creates the risk that they do not see the value in continued PR consultancy services. As our role evolves we have the opportunity to move towards higher strategic ground. As Fazer Seitel puts it: 'PR professionals can be much more focused on strategy because the internet enables them to be less of the "paper pushers" and more of the strategic thinkers who counsel C-level executives' (cited in Breakenridge 2008, p 240).

If PR is the discipline that understands the principles, implications and applications of social software it is well placed to perform a wider management consultancy role in advising companies and organizations on strategies for its commercial exploitation.

We have to be able to make our voice as advisers heard in new parts of organizations – in customer service or new product development, say – as a result of what communities are saying.

This opens up new opportunities for PR practitioners to widen the scope of services they provide.

Where customers prefer other customers as sources of information and there's no hiding place for bad service or products,[4] delivery has to meet the promise or there's a legion of people waiting to tell you and an audience of potential millions. The use of social media as a customer service tool may seem like a novelty now (in 2009), but will come to be expected by consumers. Professional communicators can add value in managing these customer engagements and relationships – and mitigate the risk of badly handled negative interactions.

The changing structure of organizations provides additional opportunities. Where the barrier between an organization and its public is becoming more porous, social media is subverting traditional hierarchies.[5] If the entire workforce is now a *de facto* marketing department, the need for effective internal communication is paramount. There is a huge potential opportunity here for PR practitioners to make a strong case for investment in internal communications or risk undoing the good work done by any externally-facing activity.

There is also a skillset that PR people have in helping businesses and organizations to identify the news (and wider content) that they have and then turning it into something of interest to others.[6] This would seem to be a further opportunity for PR to advance.

The PR profession's ability to create great ideas and compelling content is arguably its strongest advantage as it competes with other disciplines to develop commercial opportunities from social media.

The advantage of building an army of consumer advocates[7] through online conversation overcomes the structural fragmentation and decline of traditional media channels in terms of reach and delivers more compelling, genuine word-of-mouth content. Or to put it another way: 'Social media is like word of mouth on steroids' (Kagan 2009).

Content and conversation are all important once we get used to the idea that control has passed from marketer to consumer: they own the brand now, not the marketing manager. The command and control model has had its day. 'You might want to think less about "marketing" and more about "findability"' (Defren 2009, p 39).

Brian Cross, director of Fleishman-Hillard's Digital Group, says: 'PR 2.0 teaches you that you don't target audiences – you draw an irresistible bull's-eye on yourself, on your brand... You just have to make yourself as attractive as possible so that they find you' (cited in Breakenridge 2008, p 268). It's a case of finding the right communities then making sure that you or your clients can contribute something positive in order for them to welcome you to join.

This also means a reappraisal of the way in which we measure and evaluate campaigns. It presents a challenge in demonstrating effectiveness against a new set of metrics. 'The key today is not volume but influence: that is how deeply into the networks did the story reach and for how long did it set the agenda in online "conversations"' (Phillips and Young 2009, p 132).

The impact on the individual practitioner

All of these changes to how we practise are naturally having an impact on how we evolve as individual PR practitioners – social media managers, community engagement officers, or whatever else we may come to be called.

We have to carve out a new role, genuinely participating[8] on a personal level in the communities with which we seek to engage. They will expect it: 'We know some people from your company. They're pretty cool online. Do you have any more like that you're hiding? Can they come out and play?' (Locke *et al*, 1999).

It blurs the line between 'PR person' and 'person' as authenticity and transparency play such a key role in effectiveness. Gone are the days when becoming part of the story was a major barrier to success for a PR professional.

We have to get used to the idea that what we do is evolving (despite those who would read PR the last rites) and that we must all personally adapt and develop a stronger culture of continuous education and learning.

Several issues flow from the necessity of transparent participation: the value of our own personal brand online is more important; the ethics that guide our behaviours are more significant; and ultimately we stand or fall on whether we are trusted by the people with whom we engage.

If we are expected to participate more openly, it exposes us to greater personal scrutiny. We will be judged on the impact of our personal blogging, recruited on the basis of our social media following and valued against the online company we keep.

If we expect our people to participate, we will hold them to higher standards of personal behaviour. In a smartphone world, what goes on tour, no longer stays on tour. It's important to retain the personal and remain human, but we are going to need to find a balance for what will be tolerated by employers and, by extension, clients.

If we assume that we offer full disclosure of who we are, people should be prepared to engage with us on a personal level even where we are representing the interests of a client – as long as we are genuinely participating and have something of value or interest to contribute.

The impact on the emerging profession

As the body that represents individuals in PR, the CIPR has a valuable role in supporting the evolution of practice and practitioners.

Firstly, if PR is to emerge from the shadows, and PR people are to become respected and trusted in the communities which they join, the protection of our collective reputation becomes increasingly important. Trust is an even more important commodity in this new environment – we have our heads above the parapet when we participate more openly.

Members will need constantly updated guidance on social media ethics, disclosure and emerging best practice within a culture of continuous learning. We need to ensure that ours is the discipline that is seen as best placed to operate in the social media space and fight off the land grab from advertising, digital and others.

Overall, we need to see a greater understanding and public respect for the growing professionalization of PR practice.[9]

Death or rebirth?

In accepting that the world around us has shifted fundamentally, it's a seemingly easy leap to write off PR as we know it. Because of its transparency, immediacy and inherent honesty, social media has thrown a spotlight on bad PR practice, but there's a very real danger of throwing the baby out with the bathwater.

> 'In today's Web 2.0 world, traditional methods of communication won't reach your audience; much less convince them.'
>
> – *Breakenridge (2008), cover*

Brian Solis argues too that PR is broken,[10] that we've stopped connecting with the people we seek to reach and that social media in particular gives us the chance to change. The argument for PR 2.0 is critical of 'old PR' when in a lot of cases it's describing what we would all agree are bad PR practice eg badly targeted media pitches, overly adjectival releases, meaningless ghosted quotes.

The extreme is useful if it shocks people out of their fear and inactivity and it certainly helps to make the case to clients, but we must keep social media in context. There's still a massively important place for using media channels, creating experiences and building good 'old-fashioned' relationships with stakeholders.

It is also a real chance to divert a river through the PR stables and there's no hiding place anymore for poor practice – it means that operating professionally and to the highest standards has to become the absolute minimum expectation for effective PR, whatever channels we use.

But it's even truer when we move into the less familiar territory of bypassing our traditional mediators in the media (or elsewhere) – when we lose the third party to endorse/filter what we say. Not only do we have to reframe the relationship that we have with 'traditional' media as it adapts to the new social media world order, but we have a unique opportunity to open a direct dialogue with the people and communities that matter to us and our clients.

We are in the midst of an exciting collective experiment as we relearn and reshape our profession to adapt to constant change – from the impact of social media on society and the media, through to the evolution of professional practice. PR is far from dead and by joining the conversation we can ensure a healthy future.

2014 update: five years on

Looking back after five years, the debate about the future of the PR, its definition of profession and the nature of the agency model has moved on – and the forces driving change in 2009 have only accelerated.

Five years ago, we were preoccupied with making the case for social media within communications campaigns. That has certainly moved on as we've seen continued growth in social media usage; the emergence of powerful new networks; media fragmenting further and in some cases moving away from print; and consumer media consumption habits evolving across multiple devices.

PR has seemingly won the battle (so far) to be seen as the discipline most naturally suited to managing social media, but it's a distinction that's becoming increasingly irrelevant. While PR practitioners naturally have the skills to create great content and tell the human stories around an organization, the separation between, for example, PR, advertising, digital and data teams is breaking down in favour of practitioners who can work across paid, owned, earned and shared channels. We need to ensure as PR professionals that we have the skills and expertise to work in this more integrated way.

As we saw five years ago, we're also seeing the emerging opportunities for PR professionals from the growing importance of internal communications and employee engagement. We have a significant role and responsibility to be advising organizations at the very highest level as they move to become more social businesses.

For me, one of the most significant positive changes since 2009 has been stronger professional leadership on the issue from the CIPR. The creation of its independent Social Media Panel has developed guidance on best practice and given the Institute its 2014 president, Stephen Waddington. Changes to the CIPR's governance have put it in a stronger position to lead on key issues such as the promotion of CPD, a stronger academic underpinning of PR practice, and improving the wider public understanding and reputation of the emerging profession.

All of which might suggest that PR is in rude health. But the death debate continues.

At the time of writing, a new book by Robert Phillips, *Trust Me, PR is Dead*, is about to be published and the pre-publicity is proving provocative. It's raising interesting issues particularly around the agency model[11] and a move towards what the author calls 'public leadership' to replace public relations – 'activist, co-produced, citizen-centric and society first'.

My concern with the 2009 'PR is dead' literature was that it used what were already largely outmoded/obsolete practices as its evidence that PR was broken. The current debate seems to some degree to be in the same camp – there needs to be a recognition that massive progress in the evolution of PR has already been made.

Of course, if PR can't continue to add value to the organizations it serves, if its methodology fails to keep pace with disruptive technological change and if it doesn't retool itself to respond to new opportunities, it will quickly perish.

But social media has been a positive force on the profession. It has done much to address the myth that PR equals media relations, it is helping to kill off the bad PR practices which lead to proclamations of its death and is driving a positive culture of continuous education and professional development. And, through the CIPR's reforms, improved links with universities, and initiatives like the #PRredefined project, it has provoked a long-overdue re-evaluation of what it means to be a PR professional.

In a recent editorial, *PR Week*'s editor-in-chief, Danny Rogers, wrote about 'an overriding structural and existential challenge'[12] which threatens the future growth of the PR industry. It's a rallying cry for the change still to come.

It's an artificially restricted debate, to talk about change just in the context of the PR industry, when it's much more relevant and interesting to look at the future direction of those we still currently call PR professionals. The people who will work in multi-disciplinary integrated teams across all channels and platforms with experts (and expertise) in data, planning, research, sociology, psychology, management consultancy, creative services and so on.

This is the reinvention and rebirth which can secure a vital future for PR practitioners and for a more integrated, valued and expert profession to emerge.

Further reading

Anderson, C (2009) *Free*, Random House Business Books, London.

Breakenridge, D (2008) *PR 2.0*, FT Press, New Jersey.

Cook, N (2008) *Enterprise 2.0*, Gower Publishing Ltd, Hampshire.

Davies, N (2008) *Flat Earth News*, Chatto & Windus, London.

Defren, T (2009) *Brink* [Online] http://www.shiftcomm.com/downloads/SMMarketingebook-SHIFT_Communications.pdf [accessed 4 August 2014].

Green, A (2014) *#PRredefined*, Tangent Books, Bristol.

Kagan, M (2009) *What the F*ck is Social Media: one year later* [Online] http://www.slideshare.net/mzkagan/what-the-fk-is-social-media-one-year-later [accessed 4 August 2014].

Locke, C, Searls, D, Weinberger, D and Levine, R (1999) *The Cluetrain Manifesto*, Basic Books, New York.

Phillips, D and Young, P (2009) *Online Public Relations*, Kogan Page, London.

Phillips, R (2015 forthcoming) *Trust Me, PR is Dead*, Unbound, London.

Solis, B and Breakenridge, D (2009) *Putting the Public Back in Public Relations*, FT Press, New Jersey.

Notes

1 For example, Facebook registered 1.32 billion monthly active users as of 30 June 2014, see: http://newsroom.fb.com/company-info/ [accessed 4 August 2014].

2 Breakenridge (2008), p 190.

3 'Today, socially networked consumers decide what is newsworthy and relevant to them,' Breakenridge (2008), p 124.

4 'People in networked markets have figured out that they get far better information and support from one another than from vendors,' Locke *et al* (1999).

5 'Marketing will no longer be the preserve of the marketing department. If every employee has the capacity to talk to people in the market, what will this mean for the "official" spokespeople, or even the CEO... Customers want to see inside your organization, they want to talk to the people who make it what it is; they want to hear their stories,' Cook (2008), p 11.

6 As Todd Defren puts it 'think random acts of content', Defren (2009), p 18.

7 'Essentially social media empowers customers to effectively sell and represent your brand as a powerful and influential surrogate sales force,' Solis and Breakenridge (2009), p 157.

8 Mark Brooks quoted 'You ARE the company these days... You can't hide behind a brand anymore,' Breakenridge (2008), p 124.

9 As my favourite of the Cluetrain theses has it: 'Elvis said it best: "We can't go on together with suspicious minds",' Locke *et al* (1999).

10 Solis argues that: 'In the new game of PR, messages are dead, pitches are dead and people no longer comprise one audience. There is no market for messages or pitches, only how something benefits those who you're trying to reach through the culture of the communities in which they participate,' Breakenridge (2008), p 267. Was there ever truly a market for this? PR practice now has to operate to the highest standards and it has the opportunity to be improved through the lessons and principles of social media – to increase its reach and effectiveness.

11 'The company of the future is a de facto social movement; its communications function comprising a series of highly connected community organizers, each with a dedicated area of expertise. There is no longer the need for conventional CSR – "purpose" becomes part of a shared manifesto – nor for external PR consultancies: the modern corporation can rid itself of them and happily be its own expert media,'

http://unbound.co.uk/books/trust-me-pr-is-dead/updates/the-sunday-times-social-movements-and-public-value

12 'So now is the opportunity for those with earned... and owned... media skills to completely rebrand their business alongside endeavours to reinvent themselves according to today's transforming media, they may finally need to cast off those two deadly letters – P and R' (Rogers, D (2014) *PR Week*, July/August, p 5).

Freedom of Information

Is it changing the way we do PR?

SUSAN FOX CHART.PR, FCIPR

04

This paper was originally written in August 2009. Minor revisions have been made to the original text for this book to reflect developments in media, technology and practice.

What is Freedom of Information?

The Freedom of Information Act 2000[1] came into force on 1 January 2005. It gives people the right to know: anyone can ask, in writing, for information held by a public authority. The authority must respond within 20 working days and supply the information if they have it, unless one of the Act's exemptions applies (there are 23 sections of the Act, and the public interest test applies to most). If the authority refuses to disclose the information, the requester can ask for an internal review. If the authority still refuses, the requester can complain to the Information Commissioner's Office (ICO). If either party is unhappy, they can appeal to the Information Tribunal and ultimately, on a point of law, to the High Court, Court of Appeal and Supreme Court.

All public authorities have a duty to provide advice and help to people making requests,[2] and are required to produce a publication scheme – a guide to the information they hold.

The traditional PR[3] role of gatekeeper of information is therefore challenged by the Freedom of Information right to know. Equally, the traditional PR role of supplier of information to the public is strengthened by the requirement for a Publication Scheme. The risks to reputation of releasing information that would otherwise not come out are balanced by the opportunities of demonstrating openness and accountability.

Why it matters

Volumes

Over 100,000 public authorities are subject to the Act, which is fully retrospective. Central government received over 51,000 Freedom of Information requests in 2013, and the increase has been on average 6 per cent a year since the launch of the Act.[4] The ICO received over 5,000 complaints during 2012/13, an increase of 10 per cent over the previous year.[5]

Around 27 per cent of CIPR members work in public sector organizations which would be subject to the Act.[6]

Users

While the Act does not allow public authorities to ask why requesters want the information, some research has been done to identify the main users:[7]

- Journalists
- MPs/elected representatives
- Campaign groups
- Researchers
- Private individuals
- Businesses

These groups are also important to PR departments as audiences, stakeholders or customers. Journalists are one of the most significant groups of serial Freedom of Information requesters, making 10 per cent to 23 per cent of requests and accounting for about 20 per cent of internal reviews. It is estimated that between 40 per cent and 70 per cent of journalistic articles rely in some part on Freedom of Information.[8]

Public awareness

Public awareness of the right to know is high, with 86 per cent aware of the right.[9] They are highly aware of how this right can be used:

- 89 per cent know they have the right to see what public money is spent on;

- 88 per cent know they have the right to find out what type of information is available from Government and other bodies;

- 86 per cent are aware they can ask for environmental information.[10]

And people are exercising their right. About 80 per cent of organizations received at least one request, with around 28 per cent of organizations getting more than 500 requests a year.[11]

Reputation

The public sees the link between Freedom of Information and reputation: 78 per cent agree it increases confidence in public bodies and 73 per cent agree it increases trust.[12]

While the public's awareness of their right to know is high, organizations' awareness of that right has slumped from 92 per cent in 2007 to 79 per cent in 2013, the lowest on record; this is coupled with lower awareness of the legal obligations of organizations.[13] Organizations are also less inclined to agree that it increases trust (61 per cent, down from 81 per cent in 2007).[14] They do not recognize the PR opportunity Freedom of Information presents, with only 59 per cent agreeing it improves knowledge of the organization externally – a sharp drop from previous years.[15]

This is significant, as public relations is the result of what you do and what you say, and what others say about you.[16] Freedom of Information means that the door is opened, and what you do is open to scrutiny – it goes to the heart of an organization, and puts reputation management centre stage.[17] The reputation damage that MPs and the House of Commons experienced following the expenses issue is a result of what they refused to release, what they did release and what it revealed of their behaviours and actions, coupled with a misunderstanding of what mattered to their publics.

As Julia Clark writes in Ipsos MORI's *Understanding Society*: 'In the same way that it is easier to believe the worst about a public service you haven't used, it is also much easier to distrust someone you know little about. The way for politicians to push past this crisis is for them to re-connect with their constituents.'[18]

Freedom of Information puts PR professionals in a good position to influence an organization, and a communications director as part of the senior management team can make a great contribution to the organization's integrity.

Democracy

Freedom of Information has caused information to be released on a wide variety of topics, including the Iraq war, restaurant inspections, speed cameras, arms sales, the 1911 census and experiments on animals. Democracy and Freedom of Information are seen to be closely linked:

Richard Thomas, former Information Commissioner:

'It is not an extravagant claim that FOI can now be seen as a feature of 21st century democracy.'[19]

Christopher Graham, current Information Commissioner:

'With 10 years' experience of the Freedom of Information Act, it's clear that FOI is a driver of accountability, transparency, and openness – and, as such, of efficiency and innovation in service delivery too.'

Gordon Brown, former Prime Minister:

'I believe we should do more to spread the culture and practice of Freedom of Information... This is the public's money. They should know how it is spent.'[20]

David Cameron, Prime Minister:

> 'I think that it has actually been a good thing. What we are seeking here is more transparency, so that people can see who is meeting and who is doing what.'[21]

The Phillis Review of government communications:

> 'Openness, not secrecy... is of fundamental importance. This is the key to improving Government communication'.[22]

Freedom of Information and PR

Freedom of Information in practice

Responsibility for responding to information requests is spread across many different jobs in public authorities, including PR. The biggest group is information manager, officer or head of information,[23] followed by dedicated Freedom of Information staff. Communications staff, lawyers and corporate services staff are also sometimes responsible.

Authorities are becoming less positive about the Act: just 73 per cent say the Act is needed (down from 91 per cent in 2008) and 53 per cent saying it is a burden (up from 42 per cent in 2008).[24] Around 12 per cent feel that having to respond to media, commercial and research requests is a disadvantage of the Act.[25] There is a challenge for PR staff to convince their colleagues of the importance of good media and public relations.

The consensus is that Freedom of Information is a valuable tool for investigative reporters, who describe a 'noticeable' or 'huge' difference to their reporting.[26] Jeremy Hayes[27] says: 'There is definitely a club of investigative reporters who have made themselves adept at making FOI requests' and 'For many journalists, the volume of new information has proved considerable and productive'.

However, the time taken to respond to requests and deal with complaints has meant that Freedom of Information is of little use for short-term news stories. The Constitution Unit of the UCL observes that 'FOI works only when the number of requests for information is not too high'.[28]

Opportunities

High public awareness, frequent use by journalists and campaigners and the benefits of Freedom of Information give PR staff grounds to embrace the Act and integrate it into their approach. Research by UCL shows that there is evidence that Freedom of Information is improving transparency, accountability and public understanding of decision-making, but that it has not yet led to a better decision-making process, increased public participation or – crucially for PR – an increase in trust.[29]

Resistance to releasing information can often lead to protracted bad publicity (as with MPs' expenses), where releasing the information proactively might have a more positive impact on reputation. Knowing your audiences and anticipating their interests and needs is a more important PR skill than ever.

The old mindset of PR playing the gatekeeper is a thing of the past. Information is still power but the power is now often in the hands of the public. PR departments need to face the fear and lead their organizations in developing a proactive and open mindset.

The UCL Constitution Unit notes 'Restrictions on FOI could... be balanced by more proactive disclosure of information on websites'.[30] Publication Schemes can be used imaginatively, anticipating interests and presenting information in interesting and accessible ways. The MOD Publication Scheme, for example, released information on UFOs via the National Archives, who said the documents were being made available 'after several requests made under the Freedom of Information Act'.[31]

Journalists view internal reviews as 'another means for delaying the release of information'.[32] PR departments can help by knowing what requests have come into the organization, and contacting the journalist early on to establish a dialogue, understand the story and provide information proactively.

Guidance for PR practitioners

As well as handling requests on behalf of their organizations, PR departments are likely to be the subject of requests themselves, for example for costs, contact reports, strategies, plans, drafts, policies and lines to take. Many organizations will take care over what is written and how it is recorded: seeing your email published on the web can be a sobering experience.

Commercial organizations holding information on behalf of public authorities are also subject to the Act: contractors should not expect (and public authorities should not give) any guarantees of confidentiality. The Information Commissioner ordered the UK Atomic Energy Authority to release information about meetings with its PR firm, ruling that the 'information provided in confidence' exemption[33] did not apply.[34] Leeds City Council was ordered to release market research responses, which were held by a research company on the council's behalf.[35]

While disclosure is the default position, there are some exemptions which PR practitioners should be aware of. Section 22 allows an authority to withhold information if it is intended for future publication, although the public interest test must be applied. For example, the Information Commissioner agreed with the Pesticides Safety Directorate that they were right to withhold lists of safety studies on two pesticide ingredients as they were to be the subject of future publication.[36] If, in the opinion of a qualified person, releasing information would be likely to inhibit the free and frank provision of advice or exchange of views, or would be likely to prejudice the effective conduct of public affairs, then the exemption at Section 36(2) could be applied, subject to the public interest test.

There is little guidance on Freedom of Information for PR practitioners. The Ministry of Justice website has 'Working assumptions' on press releases and communications, which offer useful practical advice to the government media relations officer.[37]

The CIPR Code of Conduct supports the aims of the Freedom of Information Act, stipulating that members must work within the legal and regulatory framework of the profession, and emphasizing transparency and honesty.[38] Its legal web pages refer you to guidance on the Information Commissioner's site and its skills guide includes Top Tips on Freedom of Information (see appendix).

The current context

Growing into it

In an article in *PR Week* 12 years ago, before the Act came into force, Sir Bernard Ingham wrote: 'Journalists are primarily interested in revealing secrets, not in what is freely available. But I do believe that a Freedom of Information Act can have a beneficial effect on PR practitioners', adding that management would have to accept that information about their activities would become routinely available.[39]

It appears he may have been wrong on his first observation: journalists are still using and quoting the Act as a source of investigative material. However, I believe he was right in his second prediction: that it is having a beneficial effect on PR.

Public sector PR practitioners are moving forward and leaving the gatekeeper role behind. Using Freedom of Information to further the reputation of the organization will reap more benefits than fighting it and trying to hide bad news. Websites like **www.whatdotheyknow.com** make it all the more transparent. This site guides users through information requests, providing a template. It publishes requests, and reports on the status and details of responses: the issue for public authorities is no longer what information is released, but how they do it. Founder Tom Steinberg said:

> 'We're... in a post MPs' expenses era when transparency has gone, temporarily, from being only of theoretical interest to literally the most contentious issue of the moment.'[40]

Good Freedom of Information practice should be a badge of honour, an opportunity for PR staff to build Freedom of Information into corporate governance, corporate social responsibility and audit reporting.

Getting the balance right is important. The ICO's view is that openness is the default position. However, communications professionals know that a website is not an archive, and that too much information can be as confusing and as obfuscating as too little. Freedom of Information requests can be time-consuming, and requests are rarely the same; people want information interpreted for them. The challenge is to judge when a few requests become a trend, which information is most useful, and to present it in flexible ways, anticipating demands.

While an organization may not have foreseen (or wanted) the disclosure of certain information, the PR professional can help by setting the disclosed information in context.

Blurring the lines

Freedom of Information gives rise to new dynamics in PR: open versus secret, gatekeeper versus influencer and interpreter. With other dynamics, they are blurring the lines and challenging PR's status quo:

- internal v external
    - blogging and tweeting mean your internal information isn't contained for long.
- personal v professional
    - staff have a personal presence on social networking websites, blurring with their professional identity.
- print v web
    - the drop in print publications is more than met by instant online information.
- press officers v citizen journalists
    - press offices no longer control the message.
- timed v constant
    - event attendees are Tweeting, Facebooking and blogging as your speaker is addressing the audience; work is being critiqued in a 24 hour multi-channel flow.
- news v topical
    - social media encourages reuse of material once it becomes topical, so you can link to an old blog post or a previous news release; news no longer needs to be new.
- published v promoted
    - there's no longer a way of publishing materials without promoting them: the website is the expected channel and it is international and searchable with handy alert feeds.

- technical specialists v core skills
  - PR professionals need to master cross-cutting skills such as engagement, insight and strategy, and no longer pigeon-hole themselves into channel specialisms such as press office or publications.
- PR, advertising, marketing v communications
  - distinctions between the traditional communications disciplines are less clear, certainly in the public sector: the different means of getting messages across to audiences are blending into one communications profession, with the emphasis on cross-cutting skills.

The PR profession is developing a new way of working. The emphasis is moving away from timed, controlled communication and isolated channels, towards judgement, flexibility, dialogue, multi-channels and speed. The public will take a bigger role in determining the agenda. UCL observes: 'The old order of Westminster-centred politics and press is gradually breaking up. New media and direct democracy are presenting new challenges. With the proliferation of platforms and outlets, politicians have to work harder to get their message across. So far new media have created more opportunities than threats to the traditional model.'[41]

Conclusions

Freedom of Information is just one of many recent innovations which is changing the traditional role of PR. The profession is having to move away from timed, controlled communication to a more responsive, integrated and flexible approach, with the public determining more of the agenda.

Freedom of Information is certainly challenging the traditional role of PR as gatekeeper, and as such can be uncomfortable. However, it also offers opportunities to gain a reputation for openness, trust and accountability, putting the PR professional in a good position to influence how an organization is run. This is being recognized in some areas, as PR staff use the Act to release information in interesting ways, or as an early alert to topics their stakeholders show interest in. The duties of PR staff are changing, with at least as many PR staff as lawyers having responsibility for handling Freedom of Information requests. However, there is little practical advice and guidance on Freedom of Information for the PR professional.

Public authorities are beginning to consider how they release information, rather than whether it should be released at all, but Freedom of Information hasn't yet increased general trust in public authorities. Persistent refusal to release information has been seen to damage reputation: there is still an opportunity to change the mindset and to consider proactive disclosure of information close to the public's interest.

Organizations have been slow to realize that Freedom of Information can be a tool to improve relationships with the public, and there is an opportunity to build it into corporate strategy, as part of reporting, audit and corporate social responsibility arrangements.

In conclusion, I find there is evidence that Freedom of Information is changing the way we do PR and that (in conjunction with other changes in communication) it will change PR even further in the future. As professionals we need to welcome this as an opportunity and consider how we would like the PR and communications profession to develop.

Appendix

Freedom of Information uberchecklist for PR professionals

- Build Freedom of Information into communication plans. Consider 'What would be released under Freedom of Information?'

- Get to know your Freedom of Information officer. Set up a system so they tell you when a journalist has made a request, and work closely with them on the best way and best time to disclose information.

- Prepare additional information to supply useful context where necessary.

- Check Freedom of Information requests regularly to identify what's interesting your stakeholders, and who they are. If you spot a trend, make the information available on your website. Consider making a feature of regular or growing topics for request.

- Work closely with your Freedom of Information officer to ensure your website offers the right information, and that it's up to date and easily accessible.

- Coordinate Freedom of Information work with media enquiries, Parliamentary Questions and social media monitoring – they often cover similar issues at the same time.

- Contact journalists when they've made a Freedom of Information request. Junior journalists often make a request instead of going to the press office – offering help can be beneficial to both parties.

- Poorly worded questions don't make good or accurate stories – give the journalist some help to specify what information they really need.

- Consider what will be best for your organization – releasing the information on your website as soon as you get a request, or managing the story through the journalist who requested it.

- The Act is retrospective: consider the skeletons in your organization's cupboard – make it part of your risk assessment process, and identify mitigating actions.

- Include Freedom of Information performance in your Annual Report and corporate audit schedule.

- Keep your files up to date, tidy and easy to access; stick to your retention schedules, and weed your files out regularly. It makes responding to requests much easier.

- Train your staff in good records management and in email writing and note taking skills.

- Have a contingency plan – your organization may not want to release the information, but you may be ordered to release it. Consider how you'll handle it.
- Check out **www.whatdotheyknow.com**
- Keep up to date with the latest Freedom of Information news in your sector.

Notes

1 The Environmental Information Regulations 2004 also came into force on 1 January 2005. These implement European Directive EC/2003/4 and replaced the 1992 regulations. They give individuals the right to access environmental information. They are broadly the same as the Freedom of Information Act, with the main differences being that requests for information can be verbal, that they cover anybody carrying out a function of public administration, and there are fewer exemptions, all of which are subject to the public interest test. In 2013, the INSPIRE regulations gave the public the right to view spatial or geographic information held by public authorities covered by the Environmental Information Regulations that hold one or more spatial data sets, and by any person or organization holding special data on behalf of a public authority. In this document, the term 'Freedom of Information' is used to cover both the Freedom of Information Act and the Environmental Information Regulations.

2 Freedom of Information Act 2000, Part I, S.16 (1).

3 I use the term 'PR' to denote a broad spectrum of communications activities, such as might be found in a public sector PR department, including media relations, online communications, internal communications and staff engagement, campaigns, market research, stakeholder engagement and public affairs, issues and crisis management, branding and corporate identity, event management, publication production, Corporate Social Responsibility.

4 Freedom of Information Statistics – implementation in central government, Ministry of Justice, 24 April 2014 [Online] https://www.gov.uk/government/uploads/system/uploads/attachment_data/file/305525/foi-act-2000-statistics-implementation-in-central-government-2013-q4-annual.pdf

5 Information Commissioner's Office, Annual Report 2013/14, p 15.

6 CIPR, State of the Profession Survey 2013/14 [Online] http://www.cipr.co.uk/sites/default/files/J9825_CIPR_StateOfTheProfession_2014_V10_AW.pdf

7 Independent Review of the impact of the Freedom of Information Act, a report prepared for the Department for Constitutional Affairs, Frontier Economics, October 2006, pp 27–38.

8 Hayes, J (2009) A shock to the system: journalism, government and the Freedom of Information Act 2000, working paper, Reuters Institute for the Study of Journalism, May, p 48.

9 Prompted awareness of the right to request information held by government and other public bodies, Information Commissioner's Office Annual Track 2013, Individuals, Opinion Leader, June 2013, p 29.

10 Prompted, Information Commissioner's Office Annual Track 2013, Individuals, Opinion Leader, June 2013, p 30.

11 Information Commissioner's Office Annual Track 2013, Organizations, Opinion Leader, June 2013, p 31.

12 Information Commissioner's Office Annual Track 2013, Individuals, Opinion Leader, June 2013, p 36.

13 Unprompted, Information Commissioner's Office Annual Track 2013, Organizations, Opinion Leader, June 2013, pp 27 and 25.

14 Information Commissioner's Office Annual Track 2013, Organizations, Opinion Leader, June 2013, p 30.

15 Information Commissioner's Office Annual Track 2013, Organizations, Opinion Leader, June 2013, p 30.

16 I use the CIPR definition of PR: 'Public relations is about reputation – the result of what you do, what you say and what others say about you. Public relations is the discipline which builds and maintains reputation, with the aim of earning understanding and support and influencing opinion and behaviour. It is the planned and sustained effort to establish and maintain goodwill and mutual understanding between an organization and its publics.'

17 See my article (2006) Making the most of the Freedom of Information Act, *Profile*, Jan/Feb.

18 Clark, J (2009) Public reaction to the expenses scandal, *Understanding Society*, Ipsos MORI, Summer.

19 Richard Thomas, former Information Commissioner and Visiting Professor, Northumbria University, 'Open Government is good Government', Newcastle, 20 September 2007 [Online] http://www.ico.gov.uk/upload/documents/library/freedom_of_information/research_and_reports/northumbria_text.pdf

20 Gordon Brown, Statement on Constitutional Renewal, 10 June 2009 [Online] http://www.number10.gov.uk/Page19579

21 House of Commons, 13 July 2011, *Hansard* column 327 [Online] http://www.publications.parliament.uk/pa/cm201011/cmhansrd/cm110713/debtext/110713-0001.htm#11071354001792

22 House of Lords, Select Committee on Communications, First report of the session 2008–09, Government Communications, 26 January 2009, paragraph 49 [Online] http://www.publications.parliament.uk/pa/ld200809/ldselect/ldcomuni/7/7.pdf

23 Information Commissioner's Office, Freedom of Information three years on, Continental Research, December 2007–January 2008, p 12. The sample was 522 people with day-to-day responsibility for Freedom of Information, across a range of types and sizes of public authority in England, Wales and Northern Ireland.

24 Information Commissioner's Office Annual Track 2013, Organizations, Opinion Leader, June 2013, p 30.

25 Information Commissioner's Office, Freedom of Information Three Years On, Continental Research, December 2007–January 2008, p 30.

26 Holsen, S *et al* (2007) Journalists' use of the UK FOIA, *Open Government: a Journal on Freedom of Information*, 3 (1), p 13.

27 Hayes, J (2009), pp 10, 48.

28 Constitution Unit (2008) Constitutional futures revisited, press notice, Constitution Unit, UCL Department of Political Science, 13 November.

29 Hazell, R, Worthy, B and Glover, M (2008) The Impact of FOI: the evidence, UCL Constitution Unit, Government Information Policy Seminar Series, 19 November.

30 Constitution Unit (2008) Constitutional futures revisited.

31 Files released on UFO sightings, BBC online, 14 May 2008 [Online] http://news.bbc.co.uk/1/hi/uk/7398108.stm

32 Holsen, S *et al* (2007), p 11.

33 Freedom of Information Act 2000, Part II, S.41.

34 Decision Notice FS50123005, 16/06/2008 [Online] www.ico.gov.uk

35 Decision Notice FS50118044, 10/04/2007 [Online] www.ico.gov.uk

36 Decision Notice FS50094226, 05/02/2007 [Online] www.ico.gov.uk

37 Ministry of Justice [Online] http://www.justice.gov.uk/information-access-rights/foi-guidance-for-practitioners/working-assumptions/foi-assumptions-press

38 CIPR Code of Conduct [Online] www.cipr.co.uk

39 Ingham, B (1997) *PR Week*, 18 July.

40 BBC (2009) news, 11 August [Online] http://news.bbc.co.uk/1/hi/technology/8194859.stm

41 Constitution Unit (2008) Constitutional futures revisited.

The future practitioner

05

CATHERINE ARROW CHART.PR, FCIPR, FPRINZ

This paper was originally written in August 2009. Minor revisions have been made to the original text for this book to reflect developments in media, technology and practice.

It's a slow road to the future – or at least, it would seem so if you are in public relations. While the technologies that drive communication processes have developed at a rapid pace, on revisiting my Chartered Practitioner submission from 2009, it would seem the pace of change in PR has been relatively sedate.

That's not to say that progress hasn't been made. At the time of writing we are weeks away from the World Public Relations Forum in Madrid, which has the theme 'Communication with Conscience'. PR and leadership, along with the potential development of global credentials are on the agenda. The research colloquium will bring our practitioners and academics closer together. These were all areas I examined (and hoped for) in my submission, which looked at how PR needed to move on from purely relationship development to the role of organizational conscience; at how our professional associations needed to support new learning; how practitioners themselves must rethink their responsibility and contribution to the profession and what, collectively, we must do so future practitioners are not left waiting anxiously at the crossroads of modern practice, uncertain of the road ahead.

But, five years on, there's still more to do. We are about to experience device jumps that take us away from barrier technologies like the smart phone to wearable technologies that integrate with the Internet of Everything. These technological changes present huge challenges for practitioners but the most difficult transition will be navigating complex social shifts and societal changes, helping our organizations operate with honesty and transparency, cementing the contribution of public relations to societal good.

'The critical responsibility for the generation you are in is to help provide the shoulders, the direction, and the support for those generations who come behind' – Gloria Dean Randle Scott.

This submission examines the role of the public relations practitioner in the context of today's operational environment, explores the need for change in the relationship between professional associations and members and highlights areas where development of both role and rationale is required in order to cement the societal contribution of the public relations profession.

Practice makes perfect

'Act in a wide variety of unpredictable and advanced professional contexts.' – *CIPR Diploma Syllabus*

Financial meltdown, climate change, piracy on the high seas and on the web, food shortages and nations struggling to repay staggering amounts of debt. Just some of the 'unpredictable and advanced professional contexts' that public relations practitioners face each day. The public relations profession has evolved from its initial practice models (Grunig 1984) with the most rapid changes evident in the last twenty years (Sison 2007).

As the old century gave way to the new, practitioners not only questioned their role, they sought to renew and update the definition of their purpose, a process which continues to this very moment, with the recently formed Canadian Public Relations Society definition offered up for debate, translation and adoption at a global level.

The role of the practitioner has been subject to much intellectual and academic scrutiny, from Holzhausen's imperative activism, to L'Etang's systems for change. Gregory (2008) has consistently examined the nature of the practitioner's role, with particular emphasis on the competencies necessary to meet the complex challenges faced by practitioners. Internationally, the four definitive roles suggested, and mostly agreed on in the West (Dozier 1992) have been challenged (Taylor & Kent 1999), as the role of public relations in developing countries is perceived differently in each hemisphere.

Alongside this research and discussion, there is a growing movement, backed in part by academia, which may act as a catalyst for a complete reframing of the profession from one concerned with building relationships to one in which the practitioner acts primarily as the organizational conscience, internal and external advocate and agent for change.

Research initiated in the early 1980s by Broom around public relations' roles identified four distinct roles – the expert prescriber, communication facilitator, problem-solving process facilitator and communication technician. Subsequent research by Dozier (1992) boiled this down further to two roles, the communication manager, covering expert prescription and problem solving, and the communication technician, whose sole focus is tactical implementation. Later research (DeSanto and Moss 2004; Moss, Newman and DeSanto 2005) highlighted five elements plus technical implementation, all of which, while certainly of interest and relevant, centred on the management of the communication process, rather than public relations function which centres on the building and sustaining of the 'public' relationships that afford individuals and organizations their 'licence to operate'.

As far as competencies and skills are concerned, there is obviously an overlap between the communications manager and the public relations practitioner, but the public relations practitioner must have a wider competency/skills base in order to facilitate the effective identification, instigation and maintenance of key relationships – of which management of the communications process is one element.

For as well as dealing with complex challenges and environments, the practitioner is faced with a complex process; the relationship itself. While Grunig and others have identified the various types of organizational relationships likely to be built, the process divisions of the relationship have not, certainly in academic terms, been clarified. From the practitioner's perspective, three key elements exist: understanding, communication and action. Each element requires a set of skills and competencies which, together, allow the practitioner to undertake the boundary spanning activities required in professional practice. However, as our societal and environmental circumstances have shifted as a result of a complex set of drivers – including but not limited to the advent and growth of virtual relationships and networks – so too have the practice models available to practitioners worldwide.

As other disciplines increasingly adopt public relations methodologies in order to further relationships in their organizational sphere, so practitioners have been developing new competencies, primarily through accelerated learning and ethnographic approaches, that add new dimensions to their operating capacity.

The fall of many of the world's leading financial and corporate structures in the last two years has precipitated the need for an organizational conscience which sees the practitioner continuing as the 'eyes, ears and voice' of the organization, but increasingly the 'values-setter'. By developing an understanding not just of the organization but of the communities that intersect with its operations, the practitioner is aware of and alert to the changes that the organization needs to make internally in order to survive and grow within the external environment. While Grunig's two-way symmetrical model is laudable as far as facilitating dialogue is concerned, even the most professional of practitioners is still implementing regurgitated values, set elsewhere in the organization.

Practitioners in the 1980s – myself included – were often actively involved in the drafting of mission statements and organizational objectives. These were most frequently centred on the organization, not the communities it served, despite protestations from public relations counsel. Mission statements were, for the most part, one-way communications and did not respond to recommendations, changes or feedback from any public, other than perhaps the shareholders. Organizations set out to achieve stated goals and, despite inclusions that alluded to the 'customer' being central to the process, any dialogue between the organization and its affected publics was unlikely to change the actions undertaken; a somewhat ironic situation given that actions define the nature of the relationship. Communication unsupported by action or understanding cannot maintain the licence to operate.

The utilization of social media channels has allowed many practitioners to experiment within this new environment. Direct evidence can be now be produced as to the need for change within the organization. Lone voices, which would once have been confined to the 'letters to the editor' column, now combine with force and intensity, allowing the 'chief listening officer' to present evidence to the board, directors or members of parliament; that without change, without better serving the public interest, without compassion, the organization will fail. Additionally, as direct communication between the traditionally perceived organizational leaders and communities becomes the norm – whether that is facilitated by blog or network – the practitioner becomes the organizational navigator, smoothing the relationship pathway so that the organization and publics journey together, rather than one or the other left trailing behind.

Many companies have now had active experience of this journey. In New Zealand, Cadbury has found itself altering course in response to stakeholder demands. New telecom entrant 2degrees has met with a cool reception, despite an expensive pre-warming of the marketplace, because its actions failed to meet the considerable expectations it generated using traditional and more recent communication channels. Fonterra, the country's largest multinational, is still picking over the wreckage of the Sanlu baby milk scandal of 2008, although in that case it was a complete failure of understanding, communication and action.

As Taylor and Kent observed in 1999:

> 'By questioning assumptions we become aware that new frameworks of public relations theory and practice are needed, that the public relations profession cannot simply export Western theories and explanations to foreign contexts, and what works at one stage of national development or in one economic context does not necessarily work in others.'

In training and working closely with more than 2,000 practitioners (at all levels) over the last 10 years, it has become increasingly evident that the academic models of public relations practice are not keeping pace with the reality of practice faced daily by those in the field. Assumptions are made based on historical evidence and then researched. This research then forms the basis of educational provision and the standards created to inform and equip practitioners, even though some of the content and 'body of knowledge' has been outstripped by time. Also falling behind are the definitions and descriptors used by the very professional associations charged with representing members-in-the-field, for example, the CIPR gives 'reputation' considerable visibility throughout all representative collateral, when in reality, the relationship, the community and the dialogue are at the heart of daily practice for many, many members. In examining Brazilian public relations, Molleda and Ferguson (2004) identified four very different roles for the practitioner – ethics and social responsibility, employee well-being, community well-being and government harmony. Wu and Baah-Boakye (2004) cite various studies including Holtzhausen (2005), Rensburg (2003), Wu, Taylor and Chen (2001) that suggest political and societal changes in a culture can change the way in which public relations is practised. Setting these assertions against the turbulent societal, economic and technological changes that have occurred in western countries since 2005, coupled with the ethnographic interaction with a 'sample size' of over 2,000 practitioners on both sides of the world, it is possible to conclude that the practice model currently being enshrined in academic research is, in reality, an historical model and that urgent research is necessary into the present and active model of practitioner experience.

Such research should investigate:

- The extent to which the practitioner is not only working alongside the organizational leadership, but is leading the organization.

- The instance of organizational change initiated and implemented by the public relations practitioner as a result of listening and understanding community engagement.

- Examples of practitioners determining and establishing organizational values acceptable to stakeholders and appropriate for implementation.

- Where such methods are identified, the measurable contribution to relationship, organizational and community outcomes established.

Practice by association

'Change is the law of life. And those who look only to the past or present are certain to miss the future.' – *John F Kennedy*

If practitioners are caught in a maelstrom of change, the professional associations representing them may well be about to find themselves in the eye of the storm. The challenge to professional associations has been evident for some time, particularly the associations that do not provide either a 'licence to operate' or compulsory education programme for their members, with benefits resting on networking, education and voluntary attainment of qualifications (Arrow 2007; Traverse-Healy 2005).

The professional association has been thrown into sharp focus and content analysis of member and potential member observations on network based 'association style' sites such as LinkedIn, Melcrum Communicators' Network, various Facebook and other social network pages, reveals considerable questioning among individual practitioners as to the value and benefit of belonging to a national or international public relations association. Add to this the many free web-based educational resources, blog-based 'how-to' guides, exchange and social networks where virtual cards can be exchanged and working relationships built and many of the traditional elements of a professional network can seem threatened or irrelevant.

Public relations is an unlicensed discipline in most countries around the world. In the six countries where it is regulated by law, the operation is often overseen by government, which in turn is viewed as political control of information (Molleda and Moreno 2006). In Nigeria, a licensing law was passed, recognizing the profession and putting accreditation in the hands of the professional associations (Molleda and Alhassan 2009). The research reveals that the law is welcomed and the respondents' belief is that it will improve the standing and credibility of the profession in that country.

In the UK, the process of accreditation has progressed to the point of this, and other similar, submissions. Ultimately, accredited Chartered Practitioners will exist, but such accreditation remains voluntary. Similar schemes, such as the Accreditation in Public Relations, which is widely recognized as an international accreditation, operate in a number of countries, including South Africa, Australia, New Zealand, USA and Canada but again, participation, although recommended and desirable, is voluntary. In most countries around the world, anyone can put a sign over the door or a site on the net reading 'public relations practitioner' and set to work unequipped with the knowledge, experience or ethical framework with which to do so; a sad fact of life which consistently acts to the detriment of our profession.

Codes of conduct and codes of ethics have been created by the majority of professional associations but despite their existence, a critical view of the enforcement of such codes is frequently made by external parties (Anderson 2009), with enforcement often a challenging experience due to the imprecise definitions of key terms such as 'the public interest'. Additional discrepancies, such as inconsistencies in approach to measurement and evaluation (Arrow 2009), the definition of public relations (Arrow 2008a) and the body of knowledge itself all add to the difficulties of demonstrating member benefits. Whilst most associations offer 'benefits' in the form of cheap insurance or supplier discounts, it can surely be argued that the main benefit to members should be professional recognition, credibility and quality assurance.

As trust is a vital component of the relationship sphere, perhaps the role of the professional association has to be more firmly focused on building trust between the profession and all external communities. To this end, there is a need to explore whether a global licence to operate, compulsory national accreditation or registration and/or compulsory qualifications should be introduced. Working together to address the issues raised by the emerging networks previously described, through bodies such as the Global Alliance, it should be possible to find not only solutions to the challenges posed by emerging technologies, but some of the fundamental professional questions that remain unanswered.

In countries where public relations is still an emerging or developing discipline, the professional association is vital as a rallying point for practitioners. For example, in his study of public relations in the United Arab Emirates, Kirat states:

'Professional associations are also making moves to make the profession of PR in the UAE more credible, more professional and more effective.

The profession is badly needed to meet the challenges of economic, political and cultural globalization.'

In discussing the issue, Kirat stresses that while public relations faces huge challenges everywhere in the world, it is particularly important that it is present and practised in a professional manner in the Middle East, as he believes the region's future generations depend on building understanding, respect and trust.

Similar observations can be found in studies of public relations in Bosnia (Kent and Taylor, 2007), Taiwan (Wu and Taylor 2003) and Colombia (Molleda and Suárez 2005).

So where is the need for change in the member-association relationship? Traverse-Healy spoke on the subject in 2005, saying:

'...for us as a profession the clock is ticking. Society deserves that we vigorously reaffirm our ideals and forcibly articulate our public policies ... a priority task as individuals and for our national associations is to help the enquiring public distinguish between good and bad practice – between ethical and unethical behaviour.'

He developed his argument further, suggesting this priority task must also help the public distinguish between accredited practitioners and the self-acclaimed practitioner – arguing there was cause to believe that what might be considered acceptable ethical behaviour by self-styled communicators may not be the same for those who have undergone an accreditation process.

Such action does not just mean change on the part of the association. It requires a commitment from members to actively participate in professional development programmes, accreditation processes, the lobbying of governments to have public relations acknowledged in its own right – indeed, a change in the statistical categories operated under United Nations guidelines would be a good first step (Arrow 2008b) as we can then accurately count the number of active practitioners worldwide, which then makes evaluating their collective contribution a more manageable task. Members must feel driven to participate in the process if only because, in the long term, compulsory registration and qualification would be absolutely in the interests of the many publics we serve. The associations will in turn need to raise the volume on their activities. Larger associations, with more funds and more resources, are better equipped to undertake action on behalf of their members and here, bodies such as the Global Alliance need to step forward and help smaller, developing associations undertake the same level of activities as their bigger neighbours (Global Alliance 2007, 2009). Our changing environment prizes collaboration and effective cross-border collaboration is certainly something from which all public relations associations will benefit, as will the members.

Role forwards

In concluding this examination of the role of practitioners and their professional associations, it is important to add some indicators as to the current and future direction of public relations as social conscience or ethical compass for the organization.

Sison, in her 2007 paper, explores in some depth the notion of the practitioner as the organizational conscience and as co-creators of culture. It is not a new notion and has been put forward by many academics and practitioners over the years, including Holtzhausen, Grunig, Bowen and Fitzpatrick and has been opposed by others including L'Etang (2003). Sison's research differs in that she examines how practitioners become the organizational conscience through the development of values, with her study concentrated on the involvement of Australian practitioners in the development and implementation of value and culture in their workplace.

Lieber's (2008) discourse on the moral developments within public relations take this discussion further, emphasizing that as unethical behaviour by an organization can resonate around the globe, it is imperative that the practitioner is empowered to take both a moral and ethical stand within their organization.

Interestingly, if such a stand was taken to its logical conclusion should the organization be resistant to ethical operation – a practitioner whistle-blowing on the organization in the public interest – then the practitioner would be simultaneously in breach of and adhering to the majority of ethical codes.

While once upon a time such a situation might seem impossible, if the practitioner is setting values and acting as the ethical conscience for the organization, such a situation actually becomes a distinct possibility. Something perhaps to be addressed by associations in the here and now, with a wary eye to the future? Equally, the social media environment demands absolute transparency from an organization. Failure to tell the truth or obfuscate the facts results not only in instant and far-reaching reputational damage but in a failure of trust and engagement – and ultimately the relationship. How then does the young practitioner deal with a situation in which immediately telling the truth conflicts with the clause in the code of ethics which forbids confidential information to be revealed?

In explaining the social media environment to clients and organizations, it has become apparent that once the organizational leadership understands the implications of direct, unfiltered channels they either opt to become a closed system or an entirely open one. Where they opt for an open systems approach, the first step is generally organizational change. Understanding the reality of transparency, the rapidity of engagement and speed with which trust can be undermined has resulted in each instance in change – most frequently navigated by the public relations practitioner or facilitator. This means not only equipping the practitioner with the skills necessary to advise and train others but also providing them with the skills necessary to deal with the complexities of change.

Lieber's study yielded tangible data that a duty to society rationale is, in fact, a part of everyday public relations and in his discussion he comments:

> 'While research and dialog (sic) on ethics seems commonplace for today's public relations, it is important to note that such efforts remain neophyte at best. Only recently have decades old industry codes transitioned to ethics being centrepieces in both public relations practice and curricula.'

Lieber's forecast was that public relations was facing a future where its 'biggest days' of growth and maturity were still to come and that more research into ethics was essential to create a better understanding of a field where, he considered, generalized ethical codes and standards could no longer apply.

Our responsibility, echoing Gloria Dean Randle Scott, is to help provide the direction and the support for those who come behind us.

While great progress has been made by the public relations profession, the future really is in the 'here and now'. Our speed of change and rapidity of engagement must match that of the environments we now operate within, so that we don't leave our future practitioners waiting anxiously at the crossroads of modern practice.

Further reading

Anderson, J (2009) Media 7 interview, Ethics & PR, Series 3, episode one [Online] http://tvnz.co.nz/media7/s3-e1-video-2863235 [accessed July 2009].

Arrow, C (2007) Where next for professional associations? PR Conversations [Online] http://www.prconversations.com/?p=355 [accessed July 2009].

Arrow, C (ed) (2008a) What is PR? PR Conversations, publication download [Online] http://www.prconversations.com [accessed July 2009].

Arrow, C (2008b) What's my name – and what's my number? PR Conversations [Online] http://www.prconversations.com/?p=378 [accessed July 2009].

Arrow, C (2009) Measuring the social web, Oceania Centre for Social Media [Online] http://oceaniacentreforsocialmedia.weebly.com/research.html [accessed July 2009].

Botan, C and Taylor, M (2004) Public relations: state of the field, *Journal of Communication*, 54 (4), pp 645–61.

CIPR Diploma Syllabus (2009) Chartered Institute of Public Relations (CIPR) [Online] http://www.cipr.co.uk

DeSanto, B and Moss, D A (2004) Rediscovering what PR managers do: rethinking the measurement of managerial behavior in the public relations context, *Journal of Communication Management*, 9 (2), pp 179–96.

Dozier, D M (1992) The organizational roles of communicators and public relations practitioners, in *Excellence in Public Relations and Communications Management*, ed J E Grunig, Lawrence Erlbaum Associates Inc, Hillsdale NJ.

Global Alliance (2007) PR landscapes, South Africa [Online] www.globalpr.org

Gombita, J (2009) Introducing a new, maple-infused definition of public relations, in both official languages, PR Conversations [Online] http://www.prconversations.com/?p=561 [accessed July/August 2009].

Gregory, A (2008) Competencies of senior communication practitioners in the UK: an initial study, *Public Relations Review*, **34** (3), pp 215–23; DOI: 10.1016/j.pubrev.2008.04.005; (AN 33527720).

Grunig, J E (1984) Organizations, environments, and models of public relations, *Public Relations Research and Education*, **1**, pp 6–29.

Grunig, J E and Hunt, T (1984) *Managing Public Relations*, Holt, Rinehart and Winston, New York.

Grunig, L A, Grunig, J E and Dozier, D H (2002) *Excellent Public Relations and Effective Organizations: A study of communications management in three countries*, Lawrence Erlbaum Associates Inc, Mahwah NJ.

Holtzhausen, D (2000) Postmodern values in public relations, *Journal of Public Relations Research*, **12** (1), pp 93–114.

Holtzhausen, D and Voto, R (2002) Resistance from the margins: the postmodern public relations practitioner as organizational activist, *Journal of Public Relations Research*, **14** (1), pp 57–84.

Kent, M L and Taylor, M (2007) Beyond excellence: extending the generic approach to international public relations. The case of Bosnia, *Public Relations Review*, **33**, pp 10–20.

Kirat, M (2006) Public relations in the United Arab Emirates: the emergence of a profession, *Public Relations Review*, **32**, pp 254–60.

Lee, J, Heath, R and Bowen, S (2006) An international study of ethical roles and counsel in the public relations function, conference papers, International Communication Association, 2006 Annual Meeting, pp 1–37.

L'Etang, J (2003) The myth of the 'ethical guardian': an examination of its origins, potency and illusions, *Journal of Communication Management*, **8** (1), pp 53–67.

Lieber, P S (2008) Moral development in public relations: measuring duty to society in strategic communication, *Public Relations Review*, **34**, pp 244–51.

Marquis, C, and Battilana, J (2009) Acting globally but thinking locally? The influence of local communities on organizations, *Research in Organizational Behavior*, **29**, pp 283–302.

Meintjes, C and Niemann-Struweg, I (2008) The professionalism debate in South African public relations, *Public Relations Review*, **34**, pp 224–29.

Molleda, J C and Alhassan, A (2006) Professional views on the Nigeria Institute of Public Relations' law and enforcement, *Public Relations Review*, **32**, pp 66–68.

Molleda, J C and Alhassan, A (2009) Professional views on the Nigeria Institute of Public Relations' Law and Enforcement, paper presented at the annual meeting of the International Communication Association,

Sheraton New York, New York City, NY [Online]
http://www.allacademic.com/meta/p14314_index.html
[accessed July/August 2009].

Molleda, J C and Ferguson, M A (2004) Public relations roles in Brazil: hierarchy eclipses gender differences, *Journal of Public Relations Research*, **16** (4), pp 327–51.

Molleda, J C and Moreno, A (2006) Transitional socioeconomic and political environments of public relations in Mexico, *Public Relations Review*, **32**, pp 104–09.

Molleda, J C and Suárez, A C (2005) Challenges in Colombia for public relations professionals: a qualitative assessment of the economic and political environments, *Public Relations Review*, **31**, pp 21–29.

Moss, D A, Newman, A and DeSanto, B (2005) What do communications managers do? Refining and refining the core elements of management in a public relations/communication context, *Journalism and Mass Communication Quarterly*, **82**, pp 873–90.

Sison, M (2007) Public relations as conscience: practitioner involvement in organizational value setting, conference papers, International Communication Association, 2007 Annual Meeting, p 1.

Suddaby, R, Cooper, D J and Greenwood, R (2007) Transnational regulation of professional services: governance dynamics of field level organizational change, *Accounting, Organizations and Society* **32**, pp 333–62.

Taylor, M and Kent, M L (1999) Challenging assumptions of international public relations: when government is the most important public, *Public Relations Review*, **25**, pp 131–44.

Traverse-Healy, T (2005) A personal perspective, IPRA Congress, Istanbul, 26–28 June 2005, plenary session.

Wu, M and Baah-Boakye, K (2004) A profile of public relations practice in Ghana: practitioners' roles, most important skills for practitioners, relationships to marketing, and gender equality, *Journal of Public Relations Research*, **16** (4), pp 327–51.

Wu, M and Taylor, M (2003) Public relations in Taiwan: roles, professionalism and relationship to marketing, *Public Relations Review*, **29**, pp 473–83.

Wu, M Y, Taylor, M and Chen, B (2001) Exploring societal and cultural influences on Taiwanese public relations, *Public Relations Review*, **27**, pp 317–36.

Communications shared services in the public sector

06

An idea whose time has come or a passing phase?

SALLY SYKES CHART.PR, FCIPR

This paper was originally written in January 2011. Minor revisions have been made to the 2011 text so as to reflect developments in media, technology and practice.

In the current search for value and duplicated communications spend in the public sector, the concept of shared services has recently attracted attention from practitioners, local authorities and commentators. In this submission for Chartered Practitioner status, I will explore what is meant by shared services, including a brief exploration of its origins in sectors other than public relations and communications, followed by a discussion of the applicability of shared services to a professional function.

This submission is designed as both a discussion of this innovative area for the PR profession and to demonstrate the qualities of a Chartered Practitioner. These include a critical reflection on the state of the PR profession, the contribution of PR to society and how the profession is developing at a strategic level.

I will draw upon my experience in the private sector as the leader of a UK-based shared services communications hub, serving 12,000 employees in the pharmaceutical sector and as an international communications director in the Europe, Middle East and Asia (EMEA) region of a major medical devices manufacturer. Now, as a leader in a public sector communications team and a senior civil servant, I take an active interest in how the shared services concept has made the transition from private to public sector. I am also grateful to those public sector and local authority colleagues who have shared their experiences via trade journals and conferences. This has been very helpful to understand how different models of shared services are emerging and working in practice in the public sector.

In considering the relevance of shared services to communications and public relations, I acknowledge at the outset that the diversity of sub-functions, which may be present in a 'PR or Communications Department' is significant and so I use the terms Communications and PR in the broadest sense, rather than to denote particular activities. And although by no means exhaustive, the scope of functions included would run to media relations, internal communications to employees, corporate communications, corporate reputation and brand, community relations, stakeholder engagement, online and social media, speechwriting and crisis communications.

No discussion of the role of the Communications and PR Department, even in the context of shared services, would be complete without exploring the degree to which organizations value the function. This also encompasses measuring PR and communications outcomes and benchmarking, which are deemed to be among the prerequisites for successful shared services. Shared services have been significantly enabled by the growth in supporting information technology, allowing remote location of operations whilst still retaining connectivity, speed and automation of processing information, global and virtual working and the development of more consistent and homogenized systems for business processes.

PR and Communications in the modern business world cannot function without technology; the internet and social media are fundamentals of business communication, often in the remit of PR professionals.

The fundamentally changing nature of communications between organizations and people is well documented, not least in the seminal *Cluetrain Manifesto* (Locke, Levine, Searls and Weinberger 2009) with its pacy debunking of traditional marketing methods and introduction of the notion of markets as on-going conversations between consumers, companies and the makers of products. Citing self-reliance as one of the top 10 virtues of the web based world, they observe the following about individuals' willingness to do things for themselves. Self-service via the web is a fact of business, consumer and personal life:

> '...people figure out that they have to do things for themselves.
> Indeed they want to do things for themselves. This is a well known
> phenomenon of customer support: People would rather find the answers
> from your website than have the answers delivered to them by picking
> up the phone.'

(p 203)

For PR and Communications, online communications are replacing more traditional channels internally and externally as the primary means of information delivery and, crucially, dialogue – accelerated by cost pressures, but also delivering new dynamics into the relationship between citizens and those who provide public services. Although not exclusively housed in the PR and Communications departments of public sector organizations, organizations' websites are often managed within the communications teams. Increased reliance on web based information and self-service tools for both employees and users of services has focused attention on the web as a means to drive efficiencies and has shifted it to a critical role as part of business infrastructure.

Reporting as the UK government's Digital Champion, Martha Lane-Fox concluded:

> 'Both my report and the Government's initial response, argue for
> a Channel Shift that will increasingly see public services provided
> digitally "by default". Shifting 30 per cent of government service
> delivery contracts to digital channels has potential to deliver gross
> annual savings of more than £1.3 billion... I believe the government

should take advantage of the more open, agile and cheaper digital technologies to deliver simpler and more effective digital services to users, particularly to disadvantaged groups who are some of the heaviest users of government services.'

In the field of online and digital communications we have potentially a fertile area for communications shared service development. It is also an area where comparing and benchmarking costs and statistics on usage, downloads, meet preconditions to set out on the shared service journey, such as the ability to measure and benchmark. Moreover, social media tools offer the ability to connect with citizens on a personal level.

Following discussion of the benefits and applicability of shared services to communications teams in the public sector, I hope to draw some conclusions on the lessons learned by early adopters and from the literature.

The growth of shared services in staff functions

In researching this submission, I found limited information on the application of shared services to the field of communications and PR. This made me interested to explore the issue further and hopefully contribute to the development of the PR profession by seeing how a tried and tested approach for other professions could be applied to communications and PR. In my researches I found a specific shared services text very useful. Dating from 2000 during the early stages of shared services development, the book *Shared Services – Mining for corporate gold* (Quinn, Cooke and Kris 2000) charted the progress of some of the large US, British and global conglomerates on their shared services journeys.

The authors date the usage of the term 'shared services' from the early 1990s, they identify it as an initially corporate American phenomenon, which quickly spread as a multinational movement because of its purported cost savings (20–30 per cent is quoted) and cite its initial applications in finance and transactional processes.

Shared Services – Mining for corporate gold is primarily a non-theoretical text, designed for organizations seeking to implement shared services. The text was useful in making links between the challenges that centralized professional functions have and identifying organizational characteristics, which hinder or help the development of shared services. These chimed with my own experience of setting up a shared services function for communications. The authors use a generic description of 'staff groups' to describe what one might typically see as the business's support functions. These would include, for example, finance, HR, purchasing, legal and communications. In my experience, communications are organized as either a **centralized corporate group** (usually reporting to a communications professional) or **devolved** with communicators supporting business units and reporting to the head of the business (not normally a communications professional) or a mixed economy of a central **corporate team with embedded communicators** supporting business units (usually geographic or subsidiary product led divisions) and often acquiring, over time, distinct specialized knowledge.

In this latter model, some organizations also operate so called **matrix management** where the communications leader is jointly accountable to the corporate head of profession **and** their business unit leader. Dual reporting brings the challenges of serving multiple stakeholders and two bosses. In the public sector, the challenges are nonetheless complex, but are different because they relate to enacting policy determined by elected politicians and providing service levels to the public. Public sector communications have to be seen in their related political context.

In their comprehensive overview of PR theory and practice, with contributions from many of the UK's most respected PR academics and practitioners, *Exploring Public Relations* (Tench and Yeomans 2006) outlines the following distinctions between political communications and the public policy communications, thus:

'The context of public sector communications is also political. Political communication arises from political parties with the objective of putting across the party's views to the electorate. Policy communication arises from the policies decided by elected politicians, with the support of policy officials who advise on implementation.'

(p 578)

The communication team is also likely to include specialists, but this time within sub-disciplines in PR and communications such as public affairs, media relations, and internal communications. PR and communications teams also augment their internal capabilities by buying in consultancy expertise.

Quinn, Cooke and Kris (2000) outline some historic perception and operational issues facing staff groups generically, which they argue shared services helps to break down. They say (Chapter 1) that:

- Staff groups are monopolies and monopolies are always resented and reviled;
- Decentralization is passé – line managers favour it even when it does not make any sense;
- Staff roles suffer from wearing two hats: corporate enforcer and friendly service representative all rolled into one.

Quinn, Cooke and Kris also observe, somewhat presciently 10 years ago, that:

> 'The public sector and government is a huge arena for change where corporate staff functions represent big ticket items in an ever decreasing budget. The tax paying public are demanding increased accountability for spending wisely and simply are not prepared to keep funding the cost of government without any clear evidence of a major and fundamental move to decrease costs.'
>
> (p 3)

The authors contend that the difference between the new approach and the former central services provided by staff functions is that the ethos of shared service is based around a more customer-centric mindset, than the attitude and arrogant ethos, which they argue would have previously been shown by central staff groups acting as a monopoly mandated supplier.

> 'Staff groups, like outside suppliers, must prove themselves competent at meeting or exceeding client expectations. In true shared services, business units retain the right to go outside and purchase services externally if the internal groups cannot meet expectations.'
>
> (p 14)

Quinn, Cooke and Kris also outline essential characteristics such as the existence of strong governance procedures and state that service activities should be separated out from the governance and strategic aspects – to avoid the dichotomy of being both corporate cop and friendly helpful service provider.

I propose to examine these conditions, which Quinn, Cooke and Kris set out as necessary for success and determine how far PR and communications shared service needs to go to meet them.

The shared services journey

Shared services, according to Quinn, Cooke and Kris, is often referred to as a journey or continuum.

The metaphor not only applies to the functions in scope, but also to the complexity of the processes themselves, moving from routine transactions through to complex advisory functions. Many shared service centres were originally set up to run what were described as *transactional* or '*back office*' processes, where clear rules and common technology platforms facilitated standardized approaches to business processes like billing, expense payments etc.

As early as 2003, the government of the day asked Sir Peter Gershon to review the scope of efficiencies in government service:

> 'This document sets out the conclusions of the Gershon review.
> In particular, it sets out the scope for further efficiencies that have
> been identified within the public sector's back office, procurement,
> transaction service and policy-making functions... and makes a series
> of cross-cutting recommendations to further embed efficiency across the
> public sector.'

Progress in the UK public sector has taken time with varying degrees of success at even the more basic transactional level. The following is taken from a National Audit Office (2007) review of a shared services project in the Department of Transport:

> 'The performance of shared services has improved since June 2007,
> but it still does not meet the majority of key performance targets...

It met only four of its 18 key performance indicators in January 2008. Performance in some areas, like prompt payment of suppliers, remains worse than before the agencies joined shared services... Some users remain sceptical about the benefits to them.'

So the concept of shared services is not universally popular or successful. Quinn, Cooke and Kris (2000) argue that shared services are divided into transactional and professional services. PR and communications will have elements of both, even if the bias is more towards the professional end. Certain processes like media monitoring, website hosting, print etc. would lend themselves to joining up spend rather than leaking buying power via individually negotiated smaller deals. They are also more readily specified as a generic activity, similar in most organizations or can be converged onto a common platform.

On the growth of shared services, Quinn, Cooke and Kris also point to the vested interests of consultancy firms and suggest that once the low-hanging fruit of transactional processes have been taken, they move up the tree to advocate shared services for the professions.

In the public sector, we have also seen shared service combinations built around either geography or type of organization. The drive to sharing professional service across contiguous geographic boundaries is one way in which local authorities in particular are sharing services to save money and sustain services.

Other innovative council communications departments are looking to organizations with analogous activities either to combine and share services or to offer fee for service consultancy. The trade publication *PR Week* reported:

'Nineteen public bodies have bought comms services from two councils in the past year... Essex County Council made more than £50,000 from selling comms services... The trend is expected to grow... Brighton and Hove City Council is proposing a more wide ranging model that would create a "comms hub" of local authority, primary care trust, NHS, council, police and fire services.'

– *Matt Cartmell*, PR Week, *29 October 2010*

Applying shared services principles to PR and communications

Quinn, Cooke and Kris (2000) set out a number of key principles without which they say a shared service approach cannot be readily adopted.

Key operating principles

- No duplication of a service in the business once it has been designated a shared service;
- Services charged at a rate to cover fully loaded costs;
- Governance-related activities paid for centrally by the business;
- Exclusive supplier status for the shared service operation for a two-year period of grace;
- Following a period of grace, outsourcing to be based on clear business case;
- Joint accountability from business units for success of shared service;
- Shared service to benchmark costs vs. external equivalent and gather internal client satisfaction;
- Annual reporting on costs and satisfaction levels;
- A shift in line management accountability.

What will make it successful?

- Visible executive endorsement;
- Trades union involvement;
- Simple service level agreements;
- A shared services advisory committee;
- Culture change and client education;
- Alignment of performance management systems.

PR and communications shared services

The **no duplication rule** is an important one in businesses and public sector organizations used to having their own bespoke communicators. Business unit leaders will naturally worry about losing specialist communicators, especially in sensitive areas for public sector bodies like children's services. In shared services for professions, it's important to retain knowledge, continuity and often, key staff, in order to provide reassurance about loss of expertise.

Fully loaded costs is self-explanatory and it is important to get the true picture of the in-house provision, not least because it is often cost effective when factoring PR and communications specifics like a 24-hour on call roster.

Governance-related matters would require a degree of judgement as to what's in and out and what is best left to the service level agreement.

On **exclusive supplier** status, the period of grace is a good idea, but PR and communications shared services will need to exercise care on the degree to which the business may subsequently procure outside services. Some of the business cases in PR and communications shared services efficiencies swing on comparatively small amounts of money. There is an inherent tension where the ultimate sanction is external procurement from outside the shared services group as it potentially detracts from the economies of scale in the shared service and crucially hinges upon intelligent clients in the business. The ideal state is for the shared services operation to be so good that outside procurement is unusual.

Buy-in to the success of shared service is crucial and, from experience, it is the softer cultural issues which can derail the operation. It is important to plan the introduction of shared service for communications using the same stakeholder engagement tools one would apply to any communications campaign!

Benchmarking is one of the most difficult areas for communications because departments are so diverse that it's hard to compare 'apples with apples'. However, there are established sources such as the

Corporate Executive Board, the European Communications Directors Association and Melcrum who provide survey data. In the public sector, excellent work has been done as part of a reputation project, led by LG Communications and grounded in researched priorities about what matters to the public (**www.lga.gov.uk/reputation**).

When it comes to reporting on **costs and satisfaction levels**, the latter is the lifeblood of a successful shared service business in terms of measuring performance and improving. One of the key issues for in-house PR and communications groups in costs and service level agreements is time recording. PR agencies and law firms know this discipline is key to profitability and client satisfaction; in-house communications have to take a leaf out of their book and commit to proper time recording.

In considering the key success factors advanced by Quinn, Cooke and Kris (2000), and referenced above, I propose to examine in detail the issues of service levels, culture change and educating the internal client. These success factors present significant challenges.

PR and communications service levels lead to the thorny issue of measurement and evaluation. In our work, a complex media enquiry or Freedom of Information request may take weeks to research accurately but ultimately result in an outcome which does not reflect the time taken. Skilled media relations professionals may count successes when damage is limited, which is hard to quantify. Web analytics give some more meaningful performance measures but for many communications teams, the proof of the pudding is in the changes to attitude and behaviour among target groups, especially in the public sector. Tench and Yeomans (2006, Chapter 30) give a useful explanation of marketing versus social marketing, emphasizing the commercial nature of the former and the behavioural change nature of the latter – usually in the context of the change being for the general social 'good'.

Many public sector communications departments have expanded to include customer insight, engagement and behaviour change. Tench and Yeomans say:

'Is public sector communication a type of public relations or is it social marketing? It all depends on how you look at it... including the role and purpose of the organization, the social issues it has to deal with, its resources and, of course, the experience, education and training of staff performing the (PR) co-ordinating role.'

In dealing with culture, it is important to understand the motivations and needs of different clients – a skill the consultant knows well, but the in-house practitioner may need to develop. Local public sector professionals will need to consider the needs of elected members and those serving government departments have to consider escalation of issues to national levels in fast-paced media environments and on reputation-critical matters. The external reputation challenges and stakeholder management aspects of the PR and communications job make those judgement matters harder to call – and even harder to write down as a process for a service centre.

From my experience and observations, there are four critical areas, which make PR and communications shared services less standardized and capable of fitting the model of other staff functions. The main challenges are:

- **Lack of business understanding** about what communications can or cannot do. The mismatch between the expectations of business customers, including leaders in public sector organizations, is still a significant issue. In Managing the Unmanageable (Watson Helsby, 2005), senior PR practitioners were interviewed in depth about the challenges of their roles. One said, under the heading of 'What makes the job so tough?': 'Managing the expectations of senior management teams who can be extremely sensitive to negative media coverage, particularly if they feel it is unjustified. The responsibility for educating senior management as to why things "turn out a certain way", or why the levels of influence one can have... can vary substantially, is a constant challenge.'

- **Mismatched expectations** can also take the form of internal clients approaching the shared service with a predetermined idea. I mentioned the concept of the intelligent client and this is where the problems can arise. Simply satisfying client demand is not enough for the intelligent shared service supplier of communications. Responding to calls for 'I want a website', means that the communicators are not properly consulting with the client. Too often, those outside of communications focus on tactics and outputs, not strategy and outcomes. It's our job to help the business get the best from strategic communications, aligned to the business plan and wean clients off tactics.

- Allied to the business not knowing what its PR and communications teams do, is the issue of having consistent processes, **a body of knowledge** and way of doing things which is best practice and replicable. We don't want to eliminate creativity, but PR and communications needs to standardize processes and evaluation where it would add value and help our customers to understand how we work. The recent Barcelona Accords on evaluation and measurement are examples.

- The public sector shared services initiatives offer a great test bed to see how evaluation and processes can be shared across different businesses from healthcare to fire services. Recent developments, for example, in communications planning software and media enquiry knowledge management databases like the Solcarra system used in a number of public sector news teams are examples of capturing, retaining and reporting on media enquiries, plus they can replace some of the corporate memory locked in the heads of talented people who may leave the organization.

- And the fourth challenge for applying shared services to PR and communications is the **skill levels and business acumen of practitioners**. The diversity of routes into the profession, patchy understanding of appropriate qualifications, variable consulting and project management skills are all still issues for our profession. In their wide ranging text *Public Relations – Critical debates and contemporary practice*, L'Etang and Pieczka (2006) examine the question of professionalism itself, observing:

'The use of professionalism is normally linked in our field with the expression of a need to improve occupational standing. The familiar troika – body of knowledge, ethics and certification is understood as the defining characteristics of a profession, and there has been a consistent effort expounded by public relations professional associations and educators to develop these characteristics.' (p 271)

The good news is that these are all things we can change, develop and grow. We can work on them and indeed we have already come a long way. Communications directors and heads of communications often report to chief executives. We are earning that place at the decision-making table and we are getting much better at directly linking communications to business and service outcomes that matter to people. We have more evidence and case study materials to demonstrate that communications works as a carefully targeted and cost-effective intervention, saving the public purse and acting in the public interest.

Shared services for PR and communications may offer a way of standardizing and harmonizing some of our transactional process and unlocking more investment for front-line communications activity to support our organizations' aims and the public good. But the journey for more integrated professional shared services at the more strategic levels is only just beginning.

A perspective for 2014–15: author's note

Whilst this Chartered Practitioner essay was assessed in 2011 and represents a snapshot in time of the journey towards shared services in the public sector, with a particular focus on the applicability of sharing services in PR and communications, it's interesting to note the progress made in 2014.

A radical overhaul of the communications support to government departments took place in 2011–12 and shared services became a greater part of the agenda to develop a more consistent offer to support the implementation of government policy, to respond to austerity pressures and to deliver efficiency and value for money. Government communicators now operate as a recognized profession within a Government Communications Service. The following extract, from the 2014–15 Government Communications Plan, perhaps serves to illustrate that shared services in public sector communications may indeed now – to return to the title of this essay – be more of an idea for which the time has come, than a 'passing phase':

> 'Of equal importance will be the creation of the first formal support function for government communications. Based in the Cabinet Office, the new team will support departments to deliver increased efficiency and effectiveness; strip out waste and duplication; ensure that insight and research is better shared; and encourage an atmosphere of innovation across government communications. It will also support departments to set up shared centres of excellence in areas such as behaviour change marketing, design and professional development – again as a way of reducing costs and duplication and raising standards and consistency.'

Further reading

Cartmell, M (2010) Councils to pool comms resources, *PR Week*, 29 October, p 3.

HM Government (2005) Releasing resources to the front Line: independent review of public sector efficiency, Sir Peter Gershon CBE, Crown Copyright 2004, published with the permission of HM Treasury on behalf of the Controller of Her Majesty's Stationery Office.

HM Government (2014) The Government Communications Plan 2014–15, published by the Cabinet Office under Open Government Licence [Online] https://gcn.civilservice.gov.uk/wp-content/uploads/2014/05/Government-Communications-Plan_201415_webSmll.pdf [accessed July 2014].

Lane-Fox, M (2010) Directgov 2010 and Beyond: Revolution not Evolution, Cabinet Office Report, November, Directgov Strategic Review by Transform Innovation Ltd, 29 September 2010.

L'Etang, J and Pieczka, M (2006) Public Relations – *Critical Debates and Contemporary Practice*, Stirling Media Research Institute/Lawrence Erlbaum Associates, Mahwah NJ.

Locke, C, Levine, R, Searls, D and Weinberger, D (2009) *The Cluetrain Manifesto*, 10th edn, Basic Books, New York.

Local Government Association (2010) Local Government Communications, New Reputation Project, December [Online] www.lga.gov.uk/reputation

National Audit Office (2007) Improving corporate functions using shared services, report by the Comptroller and Auditor General ordered by the House of Commons, 29 November 2007.

Quinn, B, Cooke, R and Kris, A (2000) *Shared Services – Mining for Corporate Gold*, Pearson Education, Harlow.

Tench, R and Yeomans, L (eds) (2006) *Exploring Public Relations*, Pearson Education, Harlow.

Watson Helsby (2005) Managing the unmanageable, Watson Helsby Report, May.

PART II
Developing areas of practice

– an exploration of the opportunity in developing areas of public relations

Passport to the win-win zone?

07

The role of psychology in public relations practice and education

BEN VERINDER CHART.PR, MCIPR

This paper was originally written in November 2013. Minor edits have been made to the original text for this book to reduce the length.

In 2009 the second edition of *Nudge*, Thaler and Sunstein's hymn to behavioural economics, was published in the UK, heralding the Behavioural Insights team of the new government (commonly called the Nudge Unit), intent on applying insights from academic research in behavioural economics and psychology to public policy, communications and services.

In the same year the Central Office of Information published its paper on 'Communications and Behaviour Change'. 'The starting point for effective communications should be a deep understanding of human behaviour and how to change it,' it declared (COI 2009, p 59).

So, arguing for an explicit role for psychology within public relations practice and education – at least in relation to behavioural economics (the study of psychology as it relates to economic decision-making processes) – is not without precedent.

Set out below, however, is a new case for the wider application of psychology within public relations practice and education, with a proposal that:

- limiting its application to behaviour change is under-ambitious;

- understanding the psychological mechanisms of attitude, belief and behaviour is so useful to the practitioner as to be indispensable;

- it can support (and be the generator of) practical, ethical, two-way symmetrical public relations.

Along the way we will consider counter-arguments related to required skills, excellent practice, over-simplistic behavioural models and ethics.

I will not be arguing that psychology deserves exclusivity or primacy over other social sciences in public relations practice but will instead be seeking to make a case for its utility.

Beyond behaviour

If psychology is 'the study of the human mind and its functions... and the mental characteristics or attitude of a person or group' (*Collins English Dictionary* 1988) it may be useful to the understanding of communications' effect on attitude as well as behaviour.

Take, for instance, the impact of online reviews on attitudes to companies or services. 'Asymmetrical affective perseverance' (ASP) describes the phenomenon whereby a positive attitude continues to influence our judgement when replaced by a negative attitude, but negative attitudes do not continue to influence judgement when replaced by a positive attitude under the same conditions. Coker's (2013) studies confirm that we remain impressed after reading early positive online reviews, even if negative reviews come later. It is easy to imagine how an understanding of ASP might prove very useful for a public relations practitioner with a social media portfolio.

The utility of applied psychology to public relations practice extends beyond the formation of attitudes online or government health campaigns. Difonzo and Toth's (2001) bibliography of psychological research of import to public relations practitioners covers attitude change, cognitive processing, consumer attitudes and behaviours, framing effects, inter-group relations, the internet, issues management, political attitudes, reputation management, risk communication, rumour and social identity. The heuristics (common mental rules of thumb) described by Thaler and Sunstein (2009, pp 21–23) can help us shift our planning from the theoretical to the real world of human fallibility. People often make educated guesses based on how easily they can recall or imagine something (applying the availability and simulation heuristics, respectively) and whether it has happened before. We also tend to exercise hyperbolic discounting, prioritizing short-term reward over long-term gain, are loss averse and have a natural preference for the status quo.

Beyond beliefs and behaviours, psychology is regularly applied to raise or affect awareness in communications design. Chapman (2013) and others describe how we employ the psychology of design (from using images to reinforce concept, colour psychology and an understanding of Z-shaped online reading patterns) in order to stimulate awareness of what we are trying to communicate through a website.

Models of excellence

Despite evidence that the application of psychology in public relations benefits practice, standard academic models of excellence generally pay it scant regard.

Cutlip and colleagues' (2000) categorization of public relations work includes 'counselling' activities (advising management on social, political and regulatory environments and crisis avoidance) but there is no explicit reference to understanding what drives awareness, attitudes and behaviours in those environments.

Grunig and Reper (1992) emphasize that PR must operate strategically in order to be respected and used effectively by senior management. They propose that public relations is:

- most likely to be excellent – to contribute to organizational effectiveness – when it is an integral part of the strategic management process;

- managed strategically when it identifies stakeholders, segments active publics from stakeholder categories, and resolves issues created by the interaction of organization and publics through symmetrical communications programmes.

Yet in their analysis of the concepts and techniques for identifying, segmenting and engaging with publics they barely tip their hat to either psychological or social characteristics. They briefly discuss the psychological characteristics of people in the context of a proprietary values and lifestyles measurement system (that combines Maslow's psychological hierarchy of needs with Riesman's concept of people who are inner and outer directed) before cataloguing various criticisms of that system. In a book of 666 pages about excellence in public relations, that's all.

Aside from the cursory glance at psychology here, these arguments hint at a common criticism – that the models using psychological profiling are over-simplistic.

When the COI announced its intention to employ a panel of psychologists and sociologists, Band & Brown Communications' Simon Francis said that 'the biggest challenge for this panel will be to overcome the limits of behavioural models – which are deliberately kept simple and theoretical' (Cartmell 2009).

Alps (2013) describes another problem: 'For most government campaigns, where behaviour change is going to be difficult and tedious, "nudging" can too easily become nagging, which all too easily becomes inaudible... To get people to the brink of wanting to undertake serious behavioural change requires highly emotional and motivating messaging.'

These may constitute legitimate critiques of over-simplified attempts to use psychology in order to predict or influence behaviour, but they are not an attack on the utility of psychology in public relations performance.

Also, more sophisticated models are available. The Dual Path Theory (Gibbons, Gerrard and Lane 2003) is an effective way of addressing risk issues where there is no direct correlation between attitude and behaviour, as evidenced by the success of the 'FRANK' drug campaign in which it was applied. This model reflects the fact that drug taking involves rational, irrational and social factors and informs four potential roles for intervention communications:

- boosting young people's resistance (behavioural willingness);
- encouraging young people to see drug use as marginal rather than mainstream (subjective norms peers' behaviour);
- emphasizing the risks involved in taking drugs (personal vulnerability);
- undermining the image of drug users (risk images).

Problem solver

In defining practitioner types, Dozier and Broom (1995) divide communications managers into three sub-sets:

- the expert prescriber, who researches and defines PR problems and then implements programmes to tackle them;
- the communication facilitator, who acts as a communication broker, maintaining two-way communication between an organization and its publics;
- the problem-solving process facilitator, who helps others solve their communication problems, and counsels on the planning and implementation of programmes.

Among the role items of the process facilitator they list 'diagnosing public relations problems and explaining them to others in the organization' and 'plan and recommend courses of action for solving public relations problems'.

The examples of the benefits of applying psychological principles to diagnostics and solutions set out in this paper (and in much greater detail in many of the referenced papers) suggest that they should be standard features in the process facilitator's problem-solving kit.

To put it another way: research is integral to planning, the functions of successful public relations are underpinned by intelligence gathering (L'Etang 1996) and effective practice is centred around reducing uncertainty for the organization (Lauzen 1992). Defining publics by virtue of their affiliations and actions, without reference to available and relevant information on the psychology underpinning those beliefs and behaviours, is tantamount to passing over useful intelligence and opportunities to diminish uncertainty. If knowledge of psychological theory is a professional proficiency, there are corresponding implications for the function, whose influence comes as a result, at least in part, of the expertise of the practitioner (L Grunig 1987). It need not be the role of the HR manager to advise a leader, for instance, to use the 'liking principle' in solving boardroom conflict. This is a communications issue.

> 'A skilful leader is able to bring the most likeable characteristics of each member to the attention of the group. Re-orientating the group to look for these likeable factors allows people to begin communicating. It allows warring boards to recognize that each person has a value.'
>
> *– Martin (2010)* The art of persuasion

What constitutes professional expertise in general practice? Let us imagine, as a communications manager in a large further education college, we are asked to help solve three problems. Firstly, we want to help students stop smoking. An understanding of social norms theory, whereby group 'rules' of 'acceptable' behaviour shape behaviours, would prove extremely useful; social norms have been successfully deployed in campaigns with such diverse aims as encouraging reluctant Minnesota citizens to pay their tax on time, Texan youths to stop littering highways (Thaler and Sunstein 2009), beach-goers to apply sunscreen (Mahler *et al* 2008), and hotel guests to re-use towels (Goldstein, Cialdini and Griskevicius 2008).

Communications campaigns that reflect a group's over-estimation of risk-taking activities (such as smoking or unprotected sex) back on itself, essentially correcting a mistaken view of the social norm, have proved particularly effective.[1]

Our second challenge is to help improve online student safety. In this context, being aware of the work of psychologist George Loewenstein (Leslie 2013) would prove extremely useful. Loewenstein found evidence for a 'control paradox' – just as many people mistakenly think that driving is safer than flying because they feel they have more control over it, so giving people more privacy settings makes them worry less about what they actually divulge. In the context of a campaign that might otherwise seek to solve the problem by suggesting young people adjust their social media privacy settings, this is very useful information.

For our third challenge, we are asked to contribute to a social media campaign aimed at supplying student advocates with course information and content in order to engage school students as part of a wider recruitment campaign. A working knowledge of Ernest Dichter's (1966) study on peer to peer communications would be valuable; it shows that over 60 per cent of sharing is about the sharer themselves (desiring to gain attention, show they have inside information, reach out, demonstrate friendship or humour) rather than the content being shared. The goal is to help advocates to feel powerful about themselves.

Conversely, failure to pay sufficient regard to psychology theory and practice can increase the risk of public relations failure.

In 2007 a team of psychologists reviewed 31 leaflets published in the UK to help persuade people to reduce their alcohol intake (Abraham *et al* 2007). The team found that none encouraged readers to believe that they have the ability to abstain or drink moderately and only 7 per cent gave instructions on how to set oneself drinking-related goals. Central to modern psychiatric practice and interventions such as cognitive behavioural therapy is the concept of efficacy – *believing* that you can modify your actions is a necessary condition for behavioural change. The researchers concluded that their findings had highlighted a gap 'between, on the one hand, psychologists who apply predictive models to alcohol use and make recommendations concerning potentially effective persuasive communication and, on the other hand, health promoters who write educational leaflets designed to reduce alcohol intake.'

Not the core discipline?

Aside from analysing theoretical models of professional excellence, it should be possible to understand more about the place of applied psychology in professional practice by taking a closer look at how it features in public relations qualifications. (Especially if, as L'Etang (2002) contests, education is the 'crucial plank in PR's quest for professional status'.)

Miller-Rogers (2013) writes about the Masters of Science in Communications Management at Syracuse University:

> '...each day brought on more and more of the realization that without an understanding of how people's minds work toward the "greatest possible cognitive result for the smallest processing effort", PR professionals cannot effectively meet the objectives of organizations and clients.'

While the syllabus of Mount St Vincent University's (2013) degree in public relations includes a core module in social psychology, Bournemouth University's (2013) PR degree's electives related to psychology are all optional. The London College of Communication's (2013) PR degree includes a third-year unit entitled 'Persuasive communications, campaigning and public opinion' but this is the extent of its ambition to embrace psychology in practice.

The CIPR's (2013) Diploma syllabus says learners will be able to locate public relations theory in wider academic and social contexts' by the end of Unit 2.1 (PR Theory and Practice), but there is no specific references to what those contexts are and, in practice, neither psychological theories nor their application in PR were prominent in the syllabus as I experienced it.

It appears that syllabi reflect academic prescriptions of best practice rather than new developments in professional activity. 'As other disciplines increasingly adopt public relations methodologies in order to further relationships in their organizational sphere, so practitioners have been developing new competencies' (Arrow 2009). Do 'academic' courses struggle to reflect these?

Ethical practice?

Critiques of the normative two-way symmetric communications model are now commonplace. It is idealistic (L'Etang 1996), based on unreliable research methods (Cheney and Christensen 2001) and contains contradictions between inclusion and the interests of the dominant coalition (Pieczka 1996). Grunig's (2001) response was to develop a model in which asymmetrical communications occurs at the fringes and symmetric mixed-motive communications is practised in what was called (using the language of game theory) the 'win-win' zone, where the organization and its publics enter into a dialogue of enlightened self-interest, negotiation, persuasion and compromise.

Notwithstanding relativist and other assaults on the normative model, we might then accept that public relations should be the planned and sustained effort to establish and maintain goodwill and mutual understanding between an organization and its publics (as defined by the CIPR) with two-way symmetrical communications at its core.

Applying psychology to practice in this regard, we might find ourselves haunted by the ghost of Edward Bernays, godfather of public relations, nephew of Sigmund Freud, and of the belief that social and individual psychology could be used to engineer public opinion for the good of society. As Childers (1989) explains:

> 'The ethical problem that arises with regard to this suggestion centres around the problem of who is to decide what is good for society. With the two-way asymmetrical model, organizations believe that they can decide and then sell this decision to their publics.'

The intention is to 'manipulate the behaviour of publics for the assumed, if not actual, benefit of the manipulated publics as well as the organization' (J Grunig 1987). In the long view, we know that Bernays' freedom torch campaign to promote smoking to women was not a social good.

Thaler and Sunstein (2009 p 5) are well aware of the challenge:

> 'The... misconception is that paternalism always involves coercion. We argue for self-conscious efforts, by institutions in the private sector and

also by government, to steer people's choices in directions that will improve their lives. In our understanding, a policy is "paternalistic" if it tries to influence choices in a way that will make choosers better off, as judged by themselves.'

The application of psychology – in common with other social sciences – to public relations practice is, in fact, amoral. Our intentions and behaviours in its application carry the weight of morality, and these are (at least nominally) policed by the various codes of conduct and ethics of our respective professional associations.

As with other areas of expertise, it can be the tool through which public relations professionals shift their organizations into the win-win zone of compromise, ethical practice and symmetry. Imagine, for example, that you are set a fourth challenge at the college – to manage internal communications following a major restructuring exercise which has resulted in a significant number of redundancies among support staff.

Understanding the psychological impact on remaining staff, in particular the likelihood of 'survivor syndrome' and its effect on behaviours, is paramount.[2]

According to occupational psychologist and business consultant Leona Deakin (2013): 'How committed people feel to the organization affects the level of discretionary effort which in turn impacts on productivity and ultimately the companies' success and survival.'

Communication plays a fundamental role in determining that level of commitment.

There are two key factors to consider in mediating survivors' commitment to an organization:

1 Perceived fairness – which relates to how survivors feel the victims were treated, how well the process of lay-offs was conducted.

2 Perceived control – how involved, consulted and clear people are about what is happening and specifically how it impacts on them personally.

To address factor #1, communicators must explain why the change is necessary in a clear, timely, considerate and truthful manner.

To address factor #2, communicators must remember that people first focus on what changes mean to them personally and that, accordingly, we should reduce uncertainty by communicating quickly, clearly and honestly about what is and will happen. This consultation and involvement will 'maintain confidence within the workforce that they have the skills and abilities needed to make the required changes' (Deakin 2013). Two way comms is therefore critical. Incorporating psychology in practice here not only helps determine what and how the organization communicates but how the organization behaves. It is a passport to the win-win zone.

Further reading

Abraham, C, Southby, L, Quandte, S, Krahe, B and Van Der Sluijs, W (2007) What's in a leaflet? Identifying research-based persuasive messages in European alcohol education leaflets, *Psychology and Health*, 22, pp 31–60.

Alps, T (2013) Most irritating things in media #8 Nudging, Thinkbox Blog, Brand Republic 9 August 2013 [Online] http://thinkboxblog.brandrepublic.com/2013/08/09/most-irritating-things-in-media-8-nudging/[accessed 1 August, 2013].

Arrow, C (2009) The Future Practitioner, CIPR Chartered Practitioner Application – Stage II Submission, CIPR, London, [Online] http://www.cipr.co.uk/content/careers-cpd/chartered-practitioner/stage-2-applications [accessed 5 July 2013].

Azjen, I (1991) The theory of planned behavior, *Organizational Behaviour and Human Decision Processes*, 50, pp 179–211.

Baruch, Y and Hind, P (1999) 'Survivor syndrome' – a management myth?, *Journal of Managerial Psychology*, 15 (1), pp 29–45.

Bournemouth University (2013) Public Relations BA Hons, [Online] http://courses.bournemouth.ac.uk/courses/undergraduate-degree/public-relations/ba-hons/41/course_content-course_content/ [accessed 16 August 2013].

Brockner, J (1988) The effects of work layoffs on survivors: research, theory, and practice, *Research in Organizational Behaviour*, 10, pp 213–55.

Brockner, J (1992) Managing the effects of layoffs on survivors, *California Management Review*, 34 (2), pp 9–28.

Central Office of Information (2009) Communications and behaviour change, COI Publications, London.

Chartered Institute of Public Relations (2013) Diploma in Public Relations syllabus [Online] http://www.cipr.co.uk/content/policy-resources/students/studyhub/diploma/syllabus [accessed 16 August 2013].

Chapman, C (2013) The psychology of web design [Online] http://www.webdesignerdepot.com/2010/05/the-psychology-of-web-design/ [accessed 10 August 2013].

Childers, L (1989) J Grunig's asymmetrical and symmetrical models of public relations: contrasting features and ethical dimensions, *86 IEEE Transactions on professional communication*, **32** (2), June.

Cheney, G and Christensen, L (2001) Public relations as contested terrain, a critical response, in *Handbook of Public Relations*, ed R Heath, Sage, Thousand Oaks CA.

Deakin, L (2013) Re: Dealing with survivor syndrome, August 14, email to Ben Verinder.

Dozier, D and Broom, G (1995) Evolution of the managerial role in public relations practice, *Journal of Public Relations Research*, **7** (2), p 17.

Cartmell, M (2009) COI to court experts in behaviour change, *PR Week*, 11 December.

Coker, B (2012) Seeking the opinions of others online: evidence of evaluation overshoot, *Journal of Economic Psychology*, **33** (6), pp 1033–42.

Collins (1998) *Collins English Dictionary*, 4th edn, Harper Collins, Glasgow.

Conte, H, Ratto, R and Karusa, T (1996) The psychological mindedness scale: factor structure and relationship to outcome of psychotherapy, *Journal of Psychotherapy Practice and Research*, **5** (3), pp 250–59.

Cutlip, S, Center, A and Broom, G (2000) *Effective Public Relations*, 8th edn, Pearson Education, Upper Saddle River.

Dichter, E (1966) How word of mouth advertising works, *Harvard Business Review*, **44** (6), pp 147–61.

DiFonzo, N and Toth, R (2001) Annotated bibliography of recent and significant psychological research of import to public relations practitioners, Institute for Public Relations, University of Florida.

Festinger, L (1957) *A Theory of Cognitive Dissonance*, Stanford University Press, Palo Alto.

Gibbons, F, Gerrard, M and Lane, D (2003) A Social Reaction Model of Adolescent Health Risk, in eds J Suls and K Wallston *Social Psychological Foundations of Health and Illness*, Blackwell, Oxford.

Goldstein, N, Cialdini, R and Griskevicius, V (2008) A room with a viewpoint: using social norms to motivate environmental conservation in hotels, *Journal of Consumer Research*, **35**, pp 472–82.

Grunig, J (1987) Symmetrical presuppositions as a framework for public relations theory, presented at the Conference on Communication Theory and Public Relations, Illinois State University, May, Normal IL.

Grunig, I. (1987) Power in the public relations department as function of values, professionalism and organisational structure, presented at the 16th Annual Communications Conference, February, Washington DC.

Grunig, J and Repper, F (1992) Strategic management, publics and issues, in *Excellence in Public Relations and Communications Management*, ed J E Grunig, Lawrence Erlbaum Associates, Hillsdale NJ.

Hall, J (1992) Psychological-mindedness: a conceptual model, *American Journal of Psychotherapy*, **46** (1), pp 131–40.

Jackson, Jackson and Wagner agency [Online] http://www.jjwpr.com/ [accessed 16 August 2013].

Kübler-Ross, E (1970) *On Death and Dying*, Tavistock Publications Limited, London.

Lastovicka, J (1982) On the validation of lifestyle traits: a review and illustration, *Journal of Marketing Research*, **19** (February), pp 126–38.

Lauzen, M (1992) Public relations roles, inter-organisational power and encroachment, *Journal of Public Relations Research*, **4** (2), pp 61–80.

Leslie, I (2013) Do we have an instinct for privacy?, *Aeon Magazine*, 7 August 2013 [Online] http://www.aeonmagazine.com/living-together/do-we-have-a-privacy-instinct-or-are-we-wired-to share/ [accessed 30 July 2013].

Lesser, J and Hughes, M (1986) The generalisability of psychographic market segments across geographic locations, *Journal of Marketing*, **50** (January), pp 18–27.

L'Etang, J (1996) Corporate responsibility and public relations ethics, in *Critical Perspectives in Public Relations*, eds J L'Etang and M Pieczka, International Thomson Business Press, London.

L'Etang, J (2002) Public relations education in Britain: a review at the outset of the millennium and thoughts for a different research agenda, *Journal of Communications Management*, **7** (1), pp 43–53.

L'Etang, J (2003) The myth of the 'ethical guardian': an examination of its origins, potency and illusions, *Journal of Communication Management*, **8** (1), pp 53–67.

London College of Communication (2013) BA (Hons) Public Relations [Online] http://www.lcc.arts.ac.uk/courses/courses-by-level/ba-public-relations/ [accessed 16 August 2013].

McAleny, J, Bewick, B and Hughes, C (2011) The international development of the 'social norms' approach to drug education and prevention, *Drugs: Education, Prevention and Policy 2011*, **18** (2), pp 81–89.

Macleod, S (2011) The ABC of reputation, *PR Week*, 14 September.

Mahler, H, Kulik, J, Butler, H, Gerrard, M and Gibbons, F (2008) Social norms information enhances the efficacy of an appearance-based sun protection intervention, *Social Science and Medicine*, **67**, pp 321–29.

Martin, S (2010) The art of persuasion, *Director Magazine*, Institute of Directors, December [Online] http://www.director.co.uk/MAGAZINE/2010/11_December/behavioural-psychology_64_04.html [accessed 1 August 2013].

Miller Rogers, M (2013) The psychology of PR, Aubia blog [Online] http://www.aubiacommunications.com/the-psychology-of-pr/ [accessed 2 August 2013].

Mount St Vincent University (2013) Bachelors Degree In Public Relations Program [Online] http://www.msvu.ca/en/home/programsdepartments/professionalstudies/Department_of_Communication_Studies/publicrelations/default.aspx [accessed 16 August 2013].

Pieczka, M (1996) Paradigms, systems theory and public relations, in *Public relations: Critical debate and Contemporary Practice* (2006) eds J L'Etang and M Pieczka, Lawrence Erlbaum Associates, Mahwah, NJ.

Sahdev, K (2004) Revisiting the survivor syndrome: the role of leadership in implementing downsizing, *European Journal of Work and Organizational Psychology*, **13** (2), pp 165–96.

Savva, G, Edlin, B, Knighton, T and Bewick, B (2012) What the flock? A social norms approach to correct student misperceptions of substance use, European Symposium on Substance Use among Students, June 2012, Bradford.

Thaler, R and Sunstein, C (2008) *Nudge: Improving decisions about health, wealth and happiness*, Yale University Press, New Haven CT.

Triandis, H (1977) *Interpersonal Behavior*, Brooks/Cole, Monterey CA.

Worrall, L, Campbell, F and Cooper, C (1999) Surviving redundancy: the perceptions of UK managers, *Journal of Managerial Psychology*, **15** (5), pp 460–76.

Notes

1   McAleny, Bewick, Hughes (2011): 'The social norms approach differs by recognizing that individuals, particularly young adults, tend to overestimate how heavily and frequently their peers consume alcohol, and that these perceptions lead them to drink more heavily themselves than they would otherwise do. Similar misperceptions have been found in a range of other health and non-health behaviours. The social norms approach aims to reduce these misperceptions, and thus personal consumption, through the use of media campaigns and personal feedback. Although the numbers of completed social norms projects outside the USA is small, the evidence from them is that the approach can be equally effective in both European and Australian contexts.'

2   Research into the impact of job losses and downsizing on the emotions of employees who remain finds that guilt, anger, anxiety, depression and loss of motivation are common (Sahdev 2004; Worrall, Campbell and Cooper 1999; Baruch and Hind 1999; Brockner 1988). There is a high likelihood that employees feel that the change was poorly managed – research by the Chartered Institute for Personnel and Development found that, in a study of 3,000 'survivors', 81 per cent mistrust management and only a quarter report any consultation.

An analysis of the role of quantification in public relations evaluation

08

PAUL NOBLE CHART.PR, FCIPR

This paper was originally written in September 2009. No changes have been made to the original text for this book.

For decades, public relations has struggled to prove its worth. But two important principles have begun to emerge. First, that it is important to evaluate both the process (outputs) and the impact (outcomes) of public relations activity. The former provides feedback to improve practice while the latter provides a wider justification of the PR effort – accountability. Second, evaluation is a research-based activity with all the rigour that this implies, as well as the threat of a loss of credibility if this rigour is absent.

In seeking simple solutions to complex problems, there has been a lot of interest in the quantification of public relations efforts. Quantifying the effect of PR has the advantage, particularly if a monetary value is involved, of 'translating' public relations outputs into language other members of the organization, or client personnel, can understand. But are these figures meaningful and credible?

Were public relations to be simply concerned with raising awareness, then there is an argument that exposure – easily quantified – has some relevance to judging its effectiveness. The argument is that widespread exposure to appropriate publics is likely to generate awareness among them.

However, as users of PR become more sophisticated, they increasingly look towards it influencing the qualitative concepts of attitude, opinion and motivation. For example, Smith (2005, p 74) describes an 'ordered hierarchy' of communications objectives which grow out of 'a logical progression through stages of persuasion: awareness, acceptance and action'. While awareness is often a necessary first step, increasingly public relations is being asked to go further.

AVE, OTS and ROI

Advertising value equivalency (AVE) is an approach to valuing editorial coverage that has been around for some time. The extent to which it is criticized by commentators and researchers in public relations is only matched by the extent that the concept is used in practice, particularly in a consultancy environment. Jeffries-Fox (2003) explains that AVEs are derived by recording the size of print coverage or the elapsed time of broadcast coverage. Relevant advertising rates can then be used to calculate how much an equivalent advertisement would have cost.

There are a host of problems associated with AVEs. First, they assume that PR and advertising are performing a similar role. They imply that, in some way, public relations is 'cheap advertising'. Then there is the problem that either a media outlet does not carry advertising at all, or does not accept advertising in certain sections. Also, no reputable media buying agency would pay rate card figures when buying space. There are also occasions when the role of the practitioner is to reduce or prevent coverage appearing. And finally, there are issues such as the treatment of negative stories, and an extensive story covering a range of topics, with only a passing mention of the organization in question, as well as coverage in an 'expensive' medium aimed at the wrong target audience.

There is a case for AVEs. They do translate the output of practitioner efforts into a language that the rest of the organization can understand. Also, there is some basis on which advertising rates are calculated such as circulation and credibility: 'Specifically, since AVEs are based on both circulation and media credibility, it is a reasonably good measure for the "prominence" of your media coverage' (Jeffries-Fox 2003, p 4).

Putting the agency practitioner perspective, Sharp (2009) implies that the use of AVEs may well be driven by clients, who in turn are seeking measures to justify the agency internally. 'As an agency, we are a little bit against AVEs because they seem like an oversimplification, so it is normally the client who drives it.' He adds that clients are often seeking a monetary value to present to their own senior management.

The waters are further muddied by taking AVEs one step further through multiplying the advertising value to arrive at a figure often referred to as 'PR value'. This multiplier is justified on the basis of the received wisdom that editorial coverage is more credible than advertising. In the UK, a figure of three seems to be the most common, but Weiner and Bartholomew (2006, p 2) report: 'Factors ranging from 2.5 to 8.0 have been reported anecdotally.'

While this credibility assumption is widespread it is, at best, questionable. Weiner and Bartholomew (2006, p 4) state quite baldly: 'The fact is there is no known objective research to support this claim.'

They review a number of research studies on the relative credibility of editorial and advertising and conclude that the results varied significantly and there was no clear conclusion.

Another concept that has been introduced to quantify editorial coverage is opportunities to see (OTS) – frequently referred to as impressions in North America. OTS/impressions are used to illustrate the reach of media coverage. Particularly when public relations operates in a marketing context, the concept can be seductive because all marketing communications channels (both print and poster sites, for example) have an OTS figure, although the methodologies behind their calculation vary.

Leinemann and Baikaltseva (2004) point out that the concept becomes more problematical for broadcast media as the reach varies, according to programme day and time. It becomes more of a guessing game with online media where 'readers' are frequently only an estimate. Hits is one measure but unique visitors are preferred – identified by the IP address of the computer from which they connected to the web page.

Another commonplace piece of management jargon that has been imported to at least imply that the effect of public relations efforts can be quantified in a monetary fashion is ROI (return on investment). Likely, Rockland and Weiner (2006) explain that ROI is an established means of calculating the value of an investment by dividing the return on that investment by the cost. So if £1,000 is invested for a return of £10,000 then the ROI is 10:1.

The authors then go on to outline a series of increasingly bizarre ROI models mostly based on the assumption that media coverage can directly influence behaviour/sales. Finally, they present their Return on Earned Media Model which combines the two (some would say flawed) concepts of ROI and AVE. Note that 'earned media' refers to editorial coverage to distinguish it from 'paid media' or advertising. They adjust the 'raw' AVE figure both by a multiplier, on the basis that earned media is more valuable than paid media, and a divisor. This divisor is used to account for the editorial placement not being perfect: 'Media relations publicity is often not able to deliver the full set of messages to the right people at the right time in the way that advertising can.' The authors declare that the multiplier is 'altogether subjective and arbitrary' and there is no evidence that the divisor (which they elevate to the status of an algorithm) is not in the same camp (Likely, Rockland and Weiner 2006, p 9).

A simpler use of AVEs to calculate ROI was illustrated by a recent feature in *PR Week*. The director of a public relations consultancy is quoted as saying: 'Our client... set us an objective of achieving £50,000 in terms of AVE. At the end of the period, we generated more than £13m worth of coverage, providing an ROI of more than 1,600 to one' (Wallace 2009, p 21).

The most obvious lesson to be learnt is probably that the client needs to be more demanding in their objective setting, given that the same feature reports Metrica's PR Benchmarking Report 2008/09 as stating that the AVE per article for an average UK organization in

2008 was £6,358, giving them a target of fewer than eight articles. It is tempting to envisage the financial director of the client asking: 'Where's the cheque [for £13 million]?'

An alternative approach is the combination of ROI and OTS which is exemplified by the Canadian Public Relations Society's MRP (Media Relations Rating Point). In addition to 'scoring' campaigns out of a maximum of 10, this approach also provides a claimed ROI figure by dividing campaign budget by the total number of impressions to give a cost per contact figure (**www.cprs.ca**).

Online media

Online there is potential to link behavioural outputs back to communications inputs. Sharp (2009) agrees that online is 'potentially easier to evaluate because you can often track back to the source of an enquiry'. For example as long ago as 2005, the US *Golden Ruler Award for Excellence in Public Relations Measurement* trumpeted: 'You Are Now Free to Link PR and Sales'. This was when commending Southwest Airlines for its efforts to combine search engine optimization and public relations. Unfortunately the methodology behind the claim lacks credibility. The case demonstrates that consumers searching for cheap flights bought Southwest Airlines tickets after following links embedded in press releases. This is claimed to 'prove' that public relations achieved the sale. But a key question is not addressed: if the press release had not been issued, might the search have still been successful and might the consumer still have bought the ticket through another route?

Also, the emphasis on process rather than impact remains: '... most efforts to assess the effectiveness of Internet communication campaigns focus on the tool rather than on the results' (Holtz 2002, p 349). For example, a hit simply records a request for a file and has no direct link to the number of visitors, let alone whether they were part of your target audience, and whether their visit influenced them in any way. To be fair, there is now increasing effort on identifying unique visitors and their behaviour.

In addition, particularly online, much of the terminology employed results in quantitative measures being veiled in qualitative clothing. Take, for example, the 'authority' rating allocated to blogs. The dictionary definition of the word is 'recognized knowledge or expertise'. However, leading blog search engine Technorati defines authority as 'the number of blogs linking to a website in the last six months. The higher the number, the more Technorati Authority the blog has' (**www.technorati.com**). The suggestion is that this quantitative measure is more an indicator of popularity than authority.

So, quantification plays a role in evaluating PR activity based on new media, as well as traditional media. Traditional indicators such as volume and reach, as well as an authority ranking for blogs and a raft of statistics for websites (see **www.alexa.com**), are used to justify the effectiveness of new media. Indeed this online quantification is becoming increasingly exotic with concepts such as conversation index, depth of coverage, net promoter's index and engagement metrics all taking a bow.

The conversation index was developed by Boyd (cited in Paine 2007) and simply calculates the average number of comments per posting; a 1:1 ratio is regarded as 'acceptable' (p 5). Sharp (2009) is ambivalent, suggesting that blogs get a lot of spam comments. He feels it is a potentially valuable measure if comments are moderated to ensure they are valuable.

Paine (2007) suggests the use of depth of coverage as one of the criteria to be employed when analysing a blog. It is defined as the 'number of times your brand or issue is mentioned within a posting' (p 7). This strikes a chord with Sharp (2009) who feels this has potential for quantifying relevance.

Rogers (cited in Paine 2007) has developed a 'net promoters index' based on establishing the number of bloggers who would recommend the brand, subtracted by the number who would not, to come up with an index number. There is a claim that there is a 'direct correlation between the index and sales' (p 8), although this claim is not substantiated. Sharp (2009) suggests that, in isolation, this could be dangerous as the positioning of the brand needs to be taken into consideration. Two other approaches reported by Paine (2007) are 'media signal' (p 8) and an 'engagement metric' (p 9). The former combines tone and links and connections to arrive at an index which claims to gauge the total impact of the blog. In contrast (although aimed at websites rather than blogs), engagement is purely quantitative being based on total visits, average minutes per visit, and average visits per usage per day. Sharp (2009) makes the point starkly: 'Just getting raw numbers is quite dangerous'.

Share of discussion

This concept of share of discussion (SoD) is of particular interest as it is declared to combine both quantitative and qualitative approaches. It was developed by Jeffrey, Michaelson and Stacks (2007) from 'share of coverage' defined as the proportion of coverage assigned to a particular product or organization. This is discussed in the context of the 'competitive landscape', so all competitive products or competitive organizations have to be monitored and their volume of coverage calculated, enabling the calculation of the proportion of 'your' product or organization's coverage.

The reasonable concern expressed with this concept (share of voice) is that it is limited to quantitative measurement only, with no qualitative element. So, for example, both negative and positive coverage would be counted and no differentiation made between them. Hence the introduction of this new term 'share of discussion' (SoD) which compares both the quantity and quality of an organization's media coverage with that of its competitors. Quantity relates to volume. Jeffrey, Michaelson and Stacks (2007) suggest either 'media value' (AVE), opportunities to see (also known as impressions) or clippings.

Quality relates to tone and other subjective factors. This qualitative element varies. Most commonly (and at its simplest), only tone – positive, negative and neutral – is used. Each quantitative element is assessed for tone: positive, negative and neutral leading to the measure 'tone qualified clip counts'. All positive and neutral elements are added together and the total of negative elements subtracted to arrive at a 'net favourable' figure. This figure is then divided by the total net favourable figure for all organizations (your organization and all competitors being monitored) to arrive at an SoD. Finally, share of discussion and a chosen outcome are tracked against time and any correlation noted. It is normally assumed that there is a time lag between any changes in SoD and any effect on the chosen outcome.

There are two main concerns with this concept: standardization and practicality. First, the use of different quantitative and qualitative measures makes comparison between different campaigns problematical. Also, the use of different outcomes is a concern. The cases used a mixture of attitudinal and behavioural outcomes: favourability, sales volumes, and sales closing ratio.

Second, these competitive analyses require monitoring of all competitors concerned, and then the quantitative and qualitative analysis of all organizations concerned. This is potentially resource-intensive although technology might help.

Content analysis

Content analysis is an established research method. For example, Denscombe (2003, p 212) includes content analysis when discussing documents as a 'source of *data in their own right* – in effect an alternative to questionnaires, interviews or observation.' There is a consensus (Denscombe 2003; Stacks 2002) that content analysis can be applied to a wide range of 'texts', including written, oral and video content.

Denscombe (2003, p 222) states clearly that 'The main strength of content analysis is that it provides a means for quantifying the contents of text,' and that it does so in a fashion that is clear and repeatable. From a public relations perspective, Stacks (2002, p 107) confirms that: 'Content analysis enables us to look at qualitative data in a quantitative manner'. Indeed, although the phrase is rarely used, content analysis is commonly applied in public relations as much media evaluation would be better referred to as content analysis. And Stacks (2002) confirms that public relations has long employed content analysis to examine media coverage. Similarly, Smith (2005, p 295) states that: '...content analysis has been used for years to study mass media.' From the practitioner perspective, Sharp (2009) confirms that content analysis is not a term he or his colleagues employ, but: 'It percolates through everything we do; it is something that is ingrained in our company culture.' This particularly applies to media evaluation where coverage is assessed on the basis of the presence – or otherwise – of client messaging. His concern, however, is that it can be time consuming. In contrast, Smith (2005, p 296) suggests that one of content analysis' advantages is 'a low investment of time and money'.

Denscombe (2003) argues that content analysis identifies the presence of relevant words or ideas (for example), frequency and whether views are positive or negative. And there is a broadly standard approach to how content analysis is undertaken (Denscombe 2003; Stacks 2002; Smith 2005). It involves identifying the content to be analysed (eg key messages), what is to be analysed (eg media coverage), the approach to categorization (eg positive, negative and neutral), and then the coding, counting and recording. In some circumstances, sampling may be employed so that not every artefact needs to be examined.

Public relations writers Cutlip, Center and Broom (2006, p 302) confirm the definition of content analysis, reinforce its role in analysing media coverage, and outline its limitations: 'Content analysis is the application of systematic procedures for objectively determining what is being reported in the media. Press clippings and broadcast monitor reports, all available from commercial services, have long been used as the bases for content analysis. They indicate only what is being printed or broadcast, not what is read or heard. And they do not measure whether or not the audiences learned or believed message content.'

Paine (2007) extends the role of content analysis to new media by arguing that blogs can employ content analysis to 'look for messages and themes to determine how your customers and constituencies perceive your organization or brand' (p 6). She suggests that, by quantifying recurring themes, decisions can be made on whether or not action is required. But she also suggests a 'well-crafted' survey would more effective in determining what publics have actually understood. So, in the online environment, content analysis is still more about process evaluation than impact.

Conclusion

The widespread use of AVEs – despite their equally widespread condemnation – demonstrates the superficial attraction of attempting to quantify the qualitative. The problem with quantification such as OTS, AVEs and the like, is that they may say something about the process of public relations but are not valid measures of the impact of PR. OTS, for example, needs to be taken literally: it represents an opportunity for a member of a public to attend to a message, absolutely no indication (let alone guarantee) that they did so. And when, either independently or in harness with them, impact terminology such as ROI is employed, then credibility is seriously threatened.

New media has the potential to harness technology to establish linkages between cause and effect. But, nonetheless, most of the evaluative effort of new media is focused on quantification. The difference seems to be that, rather than being overtly quantitative in the way that AVEs and impressions are, online terminology adds a qualitative feel: terms such as authority and engagement are used as a cloak to give quantitative measures additional weight.

Share of discussion was selected as a concept that might point the way forward. It was consciously developed from a pure quantitative measure (share of voice) by adding a qualitative element. There is a hint that this moves the measure to a more impact rather than purely process orientation. But to do so, rigour is abandoned as there is an assumption that, if there is a change in SoD followed by an outcome being achieved, the latter is necessarily the result of the former. And the practicalities of gathering the data to calculate the SoD appear challenging. Finally, is a concept such as a 'net favourable tone qualified clip count' likely to be readily understood and accepted by client and managers?

The way forward is not to continually seek simple solutions to complex problems. But there is a possible means of making some progress in the form of content analysis. This is a widely-accepted research method. But it is also an accepted part of public relations evaluation even if the precise term is not universally employed: media evaluation is a form of content analysis. And content analysis is all about quantifying qualitative data. Sharp (2009) reacts positively to the term content analysis: 'Not a term that we use, but it makes a lot of sense. It's not something we do overtly, but it does percolate through everything that we do.'

Content analysis is not the cure for the challenges that remain in evaluating public relations. Its main role lies in process evaluation which is important (to enhance effectiveness) but needs to be balanced by impact evaluation to provide accountability to clients and managers. But content analysis is a widely-recognized research methodology accepted well beyond the public relations community. So content analysis can both underpin more effective process evaluation and provide much needed enhancement to the credibility of public relations evaluation in general.

Content analysis is generally restricted to process evaluation because it addresses only what is present in communications, not what is understood and acted upon. But it is a reliable – and hence credible – means of undertaking that process evaluation.

It is possible to introduce elements of quantification into a professional approach to public relations evaluation that are helpful in terms of developing best practice, and have sufficient credibility to form part of an effort to justify PR effort to a wider audience. The broader application of the established research method of content analysis is a start. Content analysis is the respectable aspect of the desire to quantify the qualitative.

Further reading

Alexa, www.alexa.com

Boyd, S (www.stoweboyd.com) (2007) cited in *How to Measure Social Media Relations*, K D Paine, Institute for Public Relations [Online] http://www.instituteforpr.org

Canadian Public Relations Society (2009) New media relations rating points system [Online] http://www.cprs.ca [accessed 24 July 2009].

Cutlip, S, Center, A and Broom, G (2006) *Effective Public Relations*, 9th edn, Pearson Education, Upper Saddle River.

Denscombe, M (2003) *The Good Research Guide*, 2nd edn, Open University, Maidenhead.

Holtz, S (2002) *Public Relations on the Net*, 2nd edn, Amacom, New York.

Jeffrey, A, Michaelson, D and Stacks, D (2007) Exploring the link between share of media coverage and business outcomes, Institute for Public Relations [Online] http://www.instituteforpr.org

Jeffries-Fox, B (2003) Advertising Equivalency (AVE), Institute for Public Relations [Online] http://www.instituteforpr.org

Leinemann, R and Baikaltseva, E (2004) *Media Relations Measurement*, Gower, Aldershot.

Likely, F, Rockland, D and Weiner, W (2006) Perspectives on the ROI of media relations publicity efforts, Institute for Public Relations [Online] http://www.instituteforpr.org

Sharp, C (2009) Account manager, Spark Communications, interview undertaken and transcribed, 22 July, London.

Smith, R (2005) *Strategic Planning for Public Relations*, 2nd edn, Lawrence Erlbaum, London.

Stacks, D (2002) *Primer of Public Relations Research*, The Guildford Press, London.

Technorati, www.technorati.com

Wallace, C (2009) The AVE debate, *PR Week*, 8 May, p 21.

Weiner, M and Bartholomew, D (2006) Dispelling the myth of PR multipliers and other inflationary audience measures, Institute for Public Relations [Online] http://www.instituteforpr.org

Internal communications
Poor relation or powerhouse?

09

LINDA ROLF CHART.PR, MCIPR

More than 25 years ago, Corbett[1] said of internal communications that it is 'often something of a stepchild or poor relative, in the public relations spectrum'. As recently as 2010 Kevin Ruck,[2] launching *Exploring Internal Communication*, made a similar observation: 'For a long time internal communication has been something of a poor relation to the seemingly more glamorous and high profile media teams.'

Looking at the public relations world today, there appears to be some truth in the statement. In industry awards ceremonies the external PR categories tend to outnumber the internal PR ones by at least ten to one. There is a similar bias in the coverage of internal communications in PR publications and networks. The CIPR defines PR as 'the planned and sustained effort to maintain goodwill and mutual understanding between an organization and its publics', which can be taken to include internal as well as external publics. Yet up until 2011 the 'What is PR?' section of the CIPR's website – intended to explain to potential students and visitors what PR is all about – made no reference to the internal public of employees.

By contrast – and arguably stimulated by the PR world's neglect of internal communications – there are several thriving networks for people who work in internal communication, such as Melcrum and the Institute of Internal Communication. And in these networks it is rare for internal communications to be discussed within the context of public relations.

The 'disparate range of organizations' that represent internal communication means that it lacks 'a strong unified voice' says Ruck in his predictions for 2014.[3] One of the consequences of this, he argues, is that the number of people working in internal communication in the UK is almost certainly under-estimated as is the contribution they make to the success of organizations and the economy.

I will declare a personal interest in the question of whether internal communications is a poor relation of PR, having moved five years ago from the role of Director of International PR for Specsavers, reporting to the Director of International Marketing, to that of Director of Internal Communications and Employee Engagement, reporting to the Group HR Director.

In making the move, I felt confident that the skills and experience I had developed through studying and working in PR would be relevant in my new role. I was surprised however at the extent to which colleagues and agency contacts felt I was 'walking away from PR', and going to work in a much less 'sexy' area. They predicted I would miss the adrenalin hit of getting national news coverage for a story or organizing a high-profile event or campaign. I was reassured however when I asked the Managing Director for his view of my potential move: 'Gone are the days in which a few of us could take a decision in a room, or in a corridor, and go out there and make it happen,' he said. 'If we are going to succeed, we need to invest in proper internal communications.' As he saw it, internal communication had the potential to help power the success of the business.

So to what extent can internal communications be said to be a powerhouse? What are the drivers of business success, whether in the public or private sector?

If you had asked that question in the 1980s, the answer would have been that success comes from the four marketing Ps of price, product, place and promotion, with PR playing its part through promotion.

And 1980s management literature, inspired by Peters and Waterman's *In Search of Excellence*, would also tell you success came from having a strong 'transforming' leader, someone who articulated a vision for the organization and communicated it by his or her passion and charisma – as Beverly Alimo-Metcalfe[4] terms it, the myth of the 'heroic' usually male, white leader.

One of the most significant shifts in thinking about what drives business success can be traced to groundbreaking research published in the *Harvard Business Review*[5] about the employee–customer –profit chain at Sears. It told the story of the dramatic turnaround of US retailer Sears in the 1990s as the result of a thorough self-examination that focused on the links between how employees felt about working at Sears; how their behaviour affected customers' shopping experience; and how customers' experience affected profits.

The company found that a 5 per cent increase in employee attitude resulted in a 1.3 unit increase in customer positivity which resulted in a revenue growth of 0.5 per cent. It demonstrated that there was a clear and measurable link between employee attitudes and business success.

To begin with, however, Sears found that employees misunderstood what was expected of them; creating a real barrier to effective change and trust. Internal communications played a key role in setting up town hall meetings, which included learning maps, dialogue, and action plans. In particular Rucci reports, 'We discovered that an employee's ability to see the connection between his or her work and the company's strategic objectives was a driver of positive behaviour.'

The insight from the Sears research was reinforced by a number of other researchers who also made the link between employee attitudes – or, as it was starting to be known, employee engagement – and business success.

The Corporate Leadership Council[6] surveyed over 19,000 employees from 34 companies, seven industry groups and 29 countries and found that the top five drivers of engagement – and the extent to which they contribute to high performance expressed in percentage terms – are:

1 Fairness and accuracy of informal feedback +39 per cent

2 Risk-taking culture +39 per cent

3 Emphasis in formal review on strengths +36 per cent

4 Employee understanding of performance standards +36 per cent

5 Internal communication +34 per cent

(Note that internal communication appears in the top five.)

In 'First break all the rules',[7] based on performance data from 2,500 businesses and opinion data from 105,000 employees, Gallup proved the link between employee opinions and productivity, profit, customer satisfaction and the rate of turnover. They found that the front-line manager is the key to attracting and retaining talented employees, and identified the 12 simple questions (the Gallup 12) that distinguish the strongest departments of a company from all the rest.

Gallup added the 5th P – People – to the marketing mix.[8] 'Research into the fast food industry has shown that it's not the taste of the food (Product), or the restaurant (Place) or advertising (Promotion) that lures customers to come back... It's by far the people who serve them.'

Researching the airline industry, they found that customers who rated United Airlines' employees highly, were 18 times more likely to choose United again than those who did not, whereas customers who rated the airline's advertising as outstanding were only six times more likely to fly with it again.

Alimo-Metcalfe's research involved the largest investigation yet of the nature of day-to-day leadership.[9] She found that the quality that has the most positive impact on success is not that of a heroic and distant leader but is that of a leader who demonstrates, 'Genuine concern for others – showing a genuine interest in staff as individuals, valuing their contributions, developing their strengths through coaching and mentoring; having positive expectations of what staff can achieve'.

The other qualities in the top five were (in order of importance):

- Communicator, networker and achiever – able to communicate the goals enthusiastically, work in partnership with others, celebrate accomplishments;
- Trust others to lead;
- Honest and consistent;
- Accessible, approachable, flexible.

Alimo-Metcalfe's key finding is backed up by research by Towers Perrin ISR[10] which showed that of 75 possible drivers of engagement the one that was rated the most important was the extent to which employees believed that their senior management had a sincere interest in their well-being.

In the UK, this new research and new way of thinking culminated in the publication of the MacLeod and Clarke report[11] to government in 2009. In a major review of research and submissions, they set out a clear case for employee engagement as a vital differentiator in today's competitive world. The four critical broad enablers of engagement identified were:

- Leadership – providing a strong strategic narrative which has widespread ownership and commitment from managers and employees at all levels. Employees have a clear line of sight between their job and the narrative, and understand where their work fits in.

- Engaging managers – at the heart of the organizational culture. They facilitate and empower rather than control and restrict their staff.

- Voice – an effective and empowered employee voice... enabled by effective communication.

- Integrity – behaviour throughout the organization is consistent with stated values, leading to trust and a sense of integrity.

Recent research in the NHS[12] has shown that engagement is not just a differentiator in business; it can also be a matter of life or death. Higher levels of employee engagement in hospitals have been shown to be linked to both lower levels of mortality and lower hospital-acquired infection.

The McLeod report refers to the 'lightbulb moment'[13] when company leaders realize the full potential of employee engagement to boost business success. But what is the particular role of internal communications in this?

As Alexander, Lindsay-Smith and Joerin (2009) observe:[14]

'Many of us have felt uncomfortable about drawing too hard a line between the communication we do and the engagement indices devised by our companies. "It's about line management", we say. Or "Engagement is really an HR topic".'

In fact the evidence for a 'hard line' between communication and engagement was already there. In 2004 Watson Wyatt[15] published the definitive study linking organizational communication to financial performance. Their study found that a significant improvement in communication levels is associated with an increase in market value of up to 29.5 per cent, whereas companies which communicated least effectively saw their value fall.

In 2010, as Towers Watson,[16] a key finding was:

'Effective employee communication is a leading indicator of financial performance and a driver of employee engagement. Companies that are highly effective communicators had 47 per cent higher total returns to shareholders over the last five years compared with firms that are the least effective communicators.'

In 2014[17] they found a continued strong relationship between superior financial performance and effective communication, and in particular that companies with high effectiveness in communication and change management are three and a half times more likely to significantly outperform their industry peers.

The results of the NHS staff survey for 2013, reported by Dromey,[18] show a very strong relationship between engagement in the NHS and perceptions of effective communication between senior managers and staff.

Gay, Mahoney and Graves (2005) have also argued that internal communication is 'the most fundamental driver of business performance'.[19]

In their report MacLeod and Clarke expand on the role of internal communication in driving engagement. Examples of good practice are highlighted such as the John Lewis Partnership where partners (employees) are 'informed about strategic business decisions through a wide range of communications'[20] and Microsoft who use a wide variety of communication tools, with a strong emphasis on face-to-face. In the case study of how the Co-operative Group reinvented itself as a business relevant to 21st century customers, he highlights how the group communications function, 'using a deep understanding of the drivers of engagement, began to create messages that helped people re-appreciate what the Group was about and find the evidence they need to begin to feel more committed.'[21]

The understanding that internal communication drives engagement has helped us to develop a clear objective for our internal communications plan at Specsavers: the development of an engaged and motivated workforce through the delivery of communications that are:

- Supporting the key objectives of the business;
- In line with our vision and values;
- Of a consistently high standard;
- Globally consistent, locally relevant.

In other words, we help to create and sustain employee engagement by planning and delivering excellent internal communication.

Perhaps the issue is not whether internal communication is a poor relation of PR or a major powerhouse of business success, but whether it sits within the profession of PR or has evolved to become an independent profession in its own right?

In terms of organizational structures, it is increasingly rare to find internal communications sitting within a PR department. In 2005 Bill Quirke[22] reported that in a survey of 100 leading international blue-chip companies, the majority (38 per cent) of internal communication heads reported to HR. Research in 2008[23] among more than 1,000 communicators showed that the idea that HR professionals can manage internal communication is getting stronger all the time, with 33 per cent of those who said it was managed by HR felt it was given high enough priority compared with 18 per cent who said it was managed by PR and was given high enough priority.

A study of global best practice in internal communication, instigated by HSBC,[24] observed that the position of internal communications affected its focus. 'When linked to HR, internal communication focuses on employee engagement. When working with marketing it's on customer service. And when working with external communication, it's geared towards the internal management of the news agenda, and corporate social responsibility.'

Nevertheless from my own study and experience, I would argue that the practice of internal communications owes much to the PR body of evidence and practice and should be seen as part of the profession of PR.

Academics in PR were early adopters of systems theory – the concept that an organization should be viewed and treated as an entity like a living organism – and applied it to our understanding of communications within organizations to the extent that systems theory became the 'dominant paradigm' in public relations.[25]

Systems theory was an influence on the development of Grunig's model of symmetrical PR. Long before the MacLeod report, the IABC's excellence project[26] – said to be the largest research project in the history of PR – identified that excellent organizations practise symmetrical communication that is 'employee-centred and based on the concepts of trust, credibility, openness, reciprocity, relationships, feedback, adequacy of information and tolerance of disagreement'.

PR theory also gives us better insight into how to take into account the formal and informal side of organizations when we communicate. As Bettinghaus and Cody[27] point out:

'Most organizations include both formal and informal networks. Which can be used with the most effectiveness is a decision the communicator makes after careful analysis of the situation.'

An organization's formal networks and channels of communication are defined by its structure. The informal side can be understood by identifying communications groups: sets of individuals who routinely communicate with each other. Certain individuals act as 'bridges' between one group and another. Bettinghaus and Cody (1994) point out that knowledge of which individuals act as liaisons or bridges is extremely important in influencing others. If the liaisons can be persuaded early in the process, they will help spread the word, persuade and influence others and reduce resistance.[28]

Developed long before online communication was alive in most companies, their theories have significant implications for the way that social networking can be used to power internal and external communications in the 21st century.

Moving on from the body of evidence, there are many ways in which a skilled PR practitioner can help to power employee engagement through the practice of excellent internal communication.

Enabling employee voice – the Grunig model of symmetrical communication is all about dialogue, and dialogue is at the heart of the

CIPR definition of PR as the discipline that 'establishes and maintains goodwill and mutual understanding between an organization and its publics'. PR practitioners are very well placed to create the channels and the environment in which employee voice can flourish. We recognize that, as Patrick Lencioni[29] demonstrated, people will not buy into something when their opinions and thoughts on the matter were not included and discussed: 'If they don't weigh in, then they won't buy in.'

Message formulation and delivery – as we have seen 'line of sight' is a key factor in engagement: people need to understand the overall goals of the organization, and how they fit in; how what they do contributes to the success of the business. An experienced PR and communications professional can work with the leaders of the business to ensure objectives are simple, clear and consistent, and easy to understand, and that they are communicated – visually and verbally – across the organization. In general the ability to take a corporate message, and strip it of its jargon and its circumlocutions to ensure it is communicated clearly is a key skill, much in use in internal communications.

Bringing messages to life through storytelling – in working with the news media, PR practitioners have long known how to bring a corporate message alive by turning it into a story.

Issue management – the practice of scanning the horizon for issues that might affect your public, and taking action to maximize opportunities for positive issues and to minimize the risk that negative issues turn into crises.

Coaching skills – often in PR we coach executives to understand the importance of the news media and to improve the way they communicate when they 'face the media'. This approach is even more important when coaching leaders and managers to understand what drives engagement and to improve their face-to-face communications with their teams. As we know from Alimo-Metcalfe's research, 'Genuine concern for others' is the most important driver of employee engagement and, while not for a moment suggesting that executives can be coached to fake concern, we can certainly help them to understand that it is a good thing to demonstrate the concern they undoubtedly feel inside.

Brand alignment – PR practitioners have a very good understanding of brand management, often developed through working closely with marketing colleagues. They are well-placed to define and communicate the internal brand – the employee value proposition – and to ensure it is closely aligned with an organization's external brand.

Understanding of the news media – PR practitioners can anticipate whether and how the media are likely to cover a story and align the timing and messaging of internal communications accordingly.

Event management – as important in internal communication as it is in external PR. Not just booking the venue and organizing the schedule, but ensuring that an event such as a staff communications meeting has clear objectives and that these objectives are delivered through the format, style and tone of the event.

A passion for developments in communication – which increasingly means understanding the potential of social media to improve internal communications, and familiarity with the technology needed to deliver communications.

Expertise in research and evaluation – understanding when and how to use qualitative or quantitative research, and how to interpret and act on the findings. Carrying out research to understand better employee attitudes and opinions is a vital first step in improving employee engagement.

And finally, great internal communications can develop not just engagement but also something that Hay Group call 'enablement'.[30] In their model it is 'employee effectiveness' that drives business success, as measured by financial return and customer satisfaction. Effectiveness is a combination of engagement (hearts and minds) and enablement (the tools to do the job). On their enablement/engagement matrix, they highlight the risk of 'frustrated' employees: people who are highly engaged and passionate about the business but have low enablement so that they struggle to achieve anything. Here, the skills of a good communicator are also important as we can help to improve enablement by highlighting where the problem areas are and by developing and communicating the solutions.

This paper started with the question: is internal communication the poor relation of PR or is it a powerhouse of business success? To understand this further we looked at the drivers of business success and concluded that the most important was employee engagement. Then we looked at the hard links between excellent internal communication and employee engagement. Having thus established that internal communication is a powerhouse of employee engagement and business success, we looked at whether it should sit within the profession of PR or be considered as a profession in its own right, one which is perhaps more closely allied to HR than to PR. We identified many ways in which the practice of internal communications is indebted to PR evidence and experience.

If in doubt, it is always worth consulting the doyen of PR research, James Grunig. His view is that:

'Employees are a strategic public for nearly all organizations and programmes to communicate with them should be part of an integrated and managed communication programme – that is, public relations.'[31]

In my own experience, internal communication is definitely not a poor relation. It is an incredibly interesting and challenging area to work in. It is informed by PR theory and experience, while also drawing on research and best practice in management and HR. And the fact that I wrote this paper as part of my application to become a chartered member of the CIPR indicates that overall I view what I do as an intrinsic part of the broad church of PR.

Notes

1 Corbett, W (1988) Internal communications: Where it all starts, *International Public Relations Review*, **12** (2), pp 15–24.

2 Ruck K, www.cipr.co.uk/content/news-opinion/bookshelf/4966/book-review-exploring-internal-communication

3 Ruck K, http://www.exploringinternalcommunication.com/another-year-of-stagnation-ahead-unless-we-create-a-stronger-voice/

4 Alimo-Metcalfe, B and Alban-Metcalfe, J (2009) Engaging leadership: creating organisations that maximise the potential of their people,

CIPD Research Insight, CIPD London [Online] http://www.cipd.co.uk/binaries/engaging-leadership_2008-updated-01-2010.pdf [accessed November 2014].

5 Rucci, A, Kirn, P and Quinn, R (1988) The employee-customer-profit chain at Sears, *Harvard Business Review*, **6** (1), pp 83–97.

6 Corporate Leadership Council (2004) Driving performance and retention through employee engagement: a quantitative analysis of effective engagement strategies, Corporate Executive Board, Washington DC.

7 Buckingham, M and Coffman, C (1999) *First break all the rules*, Simon & Schuster, New York.

8 Cited in Barning, T and Rothweiler, H (2010) Employer branding – 2010: marketing and HR; HR and marketing, CRF Institute [Online] www.britainstopemployers.co.uk

9 Alimo-Metcalfe, B (2008) Building leadership capacity through engaging leadership, selected reports from the 12th World HR Congress, London.

10 Dubaldehorde, Y (2009) ISR Review of employee engagement, June 2009, prepared for MacLeod review.

11 MacLeod, D and Clarke, N (2009) Engaging for success: enhancing performance through employee engagement, report to government, Department for Business, Innovation and Skills, www.bis.gov.uk

12 Reported in Dromey, J (2014) Meeting the challenge: successful employee engagement in the NHS, IPA.

13 MacLeod, p 4. (As in Note 11 above.)

14 Alexander, J, Lindsay-Smith, S and Joerin, C (2009) On the quest for world-class internal communication, *Strategic Communication Management*, **13** (4), pp 33–35.

15 Watson Wyatt Worldwide (2004) Connecting organisational communication to financial performance – 2003/2004, communication ROI study [Online] www.watsonwyatt.com

16 Towers Watson (2010) Capitalizing on effective communication: how courage, innovation and discipline drive business results in challenging times [Online] www.towerswatson.com

17 Towers Watson (2014) 2013–2014 Change and Communication ROI, report [Online] www.towerswatson.com

18 Dromey (2014), p 14.

19 Gay, C, Mahoney, M and Graves, J (2005) Best practices in employee communication: a study of global challenges and approaches, IABC Research Foundation, San Francisco.

20 MacLeod, p 94. (See Note 11 above.)

21 MacLeod, p 45. (See Note 11 above.)

22 Quirke, W (2005) in *How to Structure Internal Communication*, Melcrum Publishing, London.

23 Crush, P (2008) Internal communications. Whose job is it? Who shouts the loudest? hrmagazine.co.uk, July [Online] http://www.hrmagazine.co.uk

24 Alexander, Lindsay-Smith and Joerin (2009).

25 L'Etang, J and Pieczka, M (1996) *Critical Perspectives in Public Relations*, International Thomson Business Press, London.

26 Grunig, J (ed) (1992) *Excellence in Public Relations and Communications Management*, Lawrence Erlbaum Associates, Hillsdale NJ.

27 Bettinghaus, E and Cody, M (1994) *Persuasive Communication*, 5th edn, Harcourt Brace, Orlando FL, p 359.

28 Bettinghaus and Cody (1994), p 357.

29 Lencioni, P (2002) *The Five Dysfunctions of a Team: A leadership fable*, Jossey-Bass, San Francisco.

30 Hay Group (2008) Hay Group Insight's employee effectiveness framework, in *The Enemy of Engagement* (2012) M Royal and T Agnew, Hay Group Inc, Amacon, New York.

31 Grunig (ed) (1992), p 534.

Communicable viruses

10

The adaptation of the public relations profession to the changing anatomy of the web

MATT MCKAY CHART.PR, FCIPR

This paper was originally written in August 2009. Minor revisions have been made to the original text for this book to reflect developments in media, technology and practice.

> 'We are all susceptible to the pull of viral ideas. Like mass hysteria. Or a tune that gets into your head that you keep on humming all day until you spread it to someone else. Jokes. Urban legends. Crackpot religions. Marxism. No matter how smart we get, there is always this deep irrational part that makes us potential hosts for self-replicating information.'
>
> – *Neal Stephenson*, Snow Crash

The anatomy of the web

Assessing the current size of the web is next to impossible. No index does, or could ever exist, which would catalogue the vast collection of information stored on the countless servers located around the world. The web is now immeasurably large and its growth continues unabated.

Assessing the overall structure of the web is an equally hard task. What was once just a tool for linking military computers together into a network has through immense growth and widespread adoption brought about a revolutionary transformation in the way that people find, access and communicate information. A new anatomy of the web has developed, built upon a growing expectation from users that information is logically organized, relevant and universally accessible. It is an organic anatomy, ever changing, evolving and mutating. Citizens can now become journalists; stories can spread in mere seconds. Blogs, mashups, podcasts, RSS feeds, social networks, widgets and wikis have all become part of our daily lives without many of us even noticing it.

The web has fundamentally changed the realities of distributing information and therefore with this, the landscape of public relations practice has also been transformed.

Information viruses

PR practitioners are fundamentally concerned with managing the flow of information between organizations and publics (Grunig, Hunt and Todd 1984). The method of communication employed is often just as important as the contents of the message itself and the development of the web has had a profound impact on the tools available to practitioners to disseminate their messages. There is now a multitude of channels and electronic mediums that can be used to spread messages, raise awareness and manage expectations and reputations. These new tools are becoming increasingly important for practitioners. They are sophisticated, synchronized and viral.

The term 'viral' derives from viral marketing, which describes a strategy where individuals are encouraged to spread messages to others, creating the potential for exponential growth in a message's exposure and influence (MetaBlocks 2009). Like biological viruses, viral marketing takes advantage of rapid multiplication and replication to transmit a message to thousands or possibly even to millions of people.

Viral marketing has developed greatly since Tim Draper's original suggestion of using email to geometrically spread product information to target audiences (Crunchbase 2008). The global explosion of internet access now means that the likelihood of any message 'going viral' has increased exponentially. Tools such as micro-blogs and other social networks facilitate the spread of information without prompt or pre-determined action from practitioners. Now, every morsel of knowledge, or smallest fact, can become viral in a matter of seconds, and online social content influences the news agenda of the traditional media.

The web allows messages to be propagated at a speed which 10 years ago would have been inconceivable. It can be argued that practitioners have never had full control over all the information flows into and out of organizations. However, the viral nature of the web means that they certainly could not today. Positive and negative information about organizations' products, practices and perceived reputations are flooding the web.

Viral hosts

We have all become unwitting hosts to information viruses. We are carriers of vast amounts of information transmitted from colleagues, commentators, communities and companies and we are passing this information onto others. It is in our inquisitive nature to consume information and we are no longer getting our daily fix of knowledge from papers, radio and TV alone.

Our audiences are now clamouring not only for up-to-date online content, but also for places, spaces and mechanisms to help them analyse and disseminate information for themselves. Our citizens have become journalists in their own right, discussing, evaluating and disseminating news for themselves and the reach and authority of online sources is growing progressively.

Information is being spread from one host individual to the next, presenting PR practitioners with a conundrum. Do they look to vaccinate against information viruses – countering the negatives in the hope that their audiences build a resistance to bad news? Or do they themselves look to proliferate positive viruses, infecting their publics with constructive and affirmative knowledge with an expectation that this will improve the reputation of their organizations? Regardless of the treatment method selected, it is clear that online communication and social engagement can no longer be ignored as passing fads.

Whereas traditional newsprint fades over time, web content can be permanently accessible. Users' digital comments and discussions on products, people and practices leaves an indelible mark for all to see and thus can have huge bearing on the perceived image and reputations of an organization.

Monitoring and diagnoses

The web has forced organizations to put a more human face to their operations. Therefore PR practitioners have to deal with online communications more proactively than prescribing the use of simple one-way channels such as news releases and media statements. The new landscape of PR practice necessitates all of us getting actively involved online, engaging in real-time dialogues, monitoring and measuring sentiment and opinions and becoming dynamic cogs of an ever-changing machine.

To maximize the potential of digital communications and to limit the damage of negative opinion spreading virally, the PR profession is looking to utilize increasingly intricate tools to help them understand and engage with audiences online. In order to optimize outreach and engagement on web platforms practitioners need to track and analyse hundreds of blogs, video sharing sites, micro-blogs like Twitter, social networks such as Facebook, groups and forums. This is no small task. Practitioners are now employing a wide range of paid-for and free applications that allow them to monitor, identify, treat and even initiate their own viral outbreaks.

Diagnosing the source of a viral occurrence is a crucial endeavour for practitioners. Without knowing the context of the original message and the authority of its writer, it is next to impossible, indeed foolhardy, for us to try to gauge an appropriate response. This is a fundamental task that practitioners need to commence in an extremely timely fashion. If messages are allowed to proliferate for too long, identifying the original source becomes a much more complicated and involved task and it is also highly likely that the message in question would have already by then mutated through its journey from host to host.

Many organizations and agencies are now employing online 'mining' and 'aggregating' applications that use the power of search engines to highlight and group conversations, themes and sentiments, as they are posted in real-time. These tools not only allow practitioners to rapidly consider where and how messages are being spread, but they also assist us with the monitoring of vast swathes of the online environment. This in turn lessens the risk of the messages we are interested in being lost in a sea of background noise.

Mining tools and aggregators are helping practitioners assess how messages and opinions are changing and evolving as information spreads virally across the web. This knowledge is essential for us as it helps us judge the potential magnitude of impacts, the speed of outbreaks and their likelihood of penetrating deep into our audience bases. By compiling and analysing this data, practitioners can decide rationally how to respond to any given situation. PROs who are not actively monitoring their online environments will only be taking stabs in the dark with their responses. Their knowledge of their online audiences will be incomplete and as such their recommended treatments and inoculations will be unlikely to be effective.

Bedside manner

Engagement online gives PROs entirely different ways to communicate with their audiences. Online content is publishable, findable, social, syndicable, linkable and viral (Scoble and Israel 2006, p 28). It is also invariably conversational.

The 2014 Edelman Trust Barometer, which is an annual worldwide survey of the level of trust which the public has for different professions, ranks media spokespersons as the least trusted influencers within organizations (**http://www.edelman.com/insights/intellectual-property/ 2014-edelman-trust-barometer/about-trust/global-results/** – Slide 36). There is a widespread perception that PROs are information gatekeepers or worse, spin doctors. Online users, particularly bloggers, enjoy the opposite reputation (Scoble and Israel 2006, p 100).

Organizations, and particularly PR practitioners, need to join online conversations because through them, trust can be built over time. Engaging online allows us to humanize the image of organizations, demonstrating a willingness of both the PR profession and companies to share a part of our souls with the outside world. PROs can and should be using blogs and other online networking platforms not to transmit information in a one-way fashion, but to hold two-way asymmetrical conversations (Grunig, Hunt and Todd 1984), which build mutual trust and understanding between organizations and their publics.

There are now two distinct groups amongst the PR profession. Those who maintain that practitioners should continue communicating in the same method to the same audiences and with the same set of rules, and those who are embracing a new communications agenda where listening and participating have become fundamentally essential to their daily duties.

It is apparent that in the space of a few years, the web has proved to be a highly disruptive technology. Audiences themselves are now able to influence the news agenda directly. Trust and transparency have been driven to the fore as publics now have the power to communicate together on a massive scale about the activities and moralities of organizations and their staff members.

In order to maximize our success using online channels and to protect and enhance the reputation of our profession we have to adapt our bedside manner towards online users. Digital channels have truly challenged the status quo of public relations. Whilst the fundamental rules of media relations still apply to communicating online, the methods practitioners employ and the announcements they make should never be the same as their approaches to traditional journalists.

Superbugs

Many practitioners have embraced the new anatomy of the web and have changed their communication strategies to reflect the markedly different PR environment that now exists. These individuals and organizations are trailblazers for our profession, demonstrating the massive impact that viral messages can have and the huge benefits that can be wrought from successful online engagement.

The 'Best Job in the World' campaign produced by CumminsNitro on behalf of Tourism Queensland asked people to apply for the position of caretaker of an Australian 'paradise island'. Applicants were asked to submit a promotional video to the campaign website and then to undertake their own publicity in order to generate votes for their submission. The response to the campaign was massive. Tourism Queensland claimed that the campaign generated more than $80 million (£49 million) of equivalent media advertising space (*The Guardian* 2009).

However, the campaign did not only encourage raw publicity for Tourist Queensland through one initial clever idea. Following a 'first round' of applications, CumminsNitro provided shortlisted competitors from each country with PR advice. This included encouraging them to call up radio and TV stations in an effort to campaign for votes. This created a massive viral and word-of-mouth effect with applicants themselves undertaking the task of promoting their videos and thus the campaign itself.

CumminsNitro had a very small budget for this campaign, yet managed to create huge worldwide coverage using the viral nature of both the web and people themselves. The campaign won the Cannes Lions PR Grand Prix, which was the first time that public relations has been included in the 56-year history of the event (*PR Week* 2009). The publicity for the campaign is still highly visible across the web – both a blog and a Twitter feed are available and both of these link directly back to Tourism Queensland's web presence showing a truly joined up approach to managing online communications.

To promote the launch of the sixth film in the Harry Potter series, Warner Bros used Twitter in an innovative campaign designed to raise interest in the film prior to its launch (*Revolution* Magazine 2009). A custom website called **www.harrypottertweet.com** was built enabling

Twitter users to send wizard-themed messages and gifts to their followers on the platform.

FIGURE 10.1   Harry Potter (number of matching Twitter posts per day)

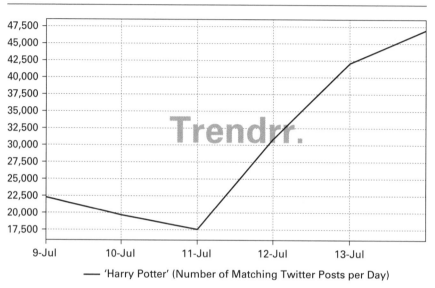

— 'Harry Potter' (Number of Matching Twitter Posts per Day)

The graph above shows the massive viral velocity which erupted prior to the launch of the film (on 15 July 2009), driven in part by the development of the custom Twitter website which allowed users to virally spread the launch announcement of the film within their Tweets. Subtler than the use of pop-up advertising for a feature film, this campaign demonstrated that micro-blogs can be highly effective tools to build on existing levels of excitement in anticipation for the launch of a new product or service.

In March 2009 well-known confectionery brand Skittles launched a new website which immediately raised eyebrows across the PR and marketing professions. The new site opens directly onto the Skittles Facebook page, immediately putting users in potential contact with over 1 million 'fans' of the brand. The site has a small floating navigational function box in the top left-hand corner of the page, which too fully embraces social media. The products tab, showing the wider range of confectionery available links through to entries on Wikipedia, product videos that are drawn from YouTube and pictures that are fed from the image sharing site Flickr. A chat function is provided which is based on Twitter. The entire web presence for the new Skittles website has been built around social media.

Charleen Lin, influential blogger commenting on the decision to tie the Skittles website into social media said at the time:

> '...they're getting people to talk about and engage with the brand.
> It's hard to get people to engage with a candy, but this is generating incredible buzz and PR. This is a big brand pushing the envelope toward what a brand will be in the future.'
>
> – *Marketing Pilgrim (2009)*

This approach demonstrates a true desire for the brand to engage directly with customers. Whilst some of the links offer a level of 'PR control' (deciding what videos and images to show for instance), the decision to inherently link up all aspects of Skittles' social web presence into one single space is both bold and innovative.

Whilst it can be argued that Skittles is perhaps missing a trick by not entering into any direct conversations held on the website itself (Search Marketing Gurus 2009), the decision to inherently link social media into the very fabric of the brand shows a recognition from parent company Mars that a brand's strength is directly related to the volume of conversation there is about it. Highlighting the growing significance of viral messaging, the new site also acknowledges that what the customer has to say about a brand is just as important as what a brand has to say about itself (Marketing Profs 2009).

Recent campaigns have likewise folded the consumer experience into the digital space. Tipp Ex's Hunter Shoots Bear Campaign (**https://www.youtube.com/user/tippexperience**) not only invites the consumer to actively engage with interactive content hosted online, but also promotes users to share and talk about their experiences with others, thus spreading both messages and brand awareness widely. Other campaigns have sought to produce inherently viral concepts which by their very nature encourage users to propagate the content through their own networks. The Liquid Mountaineering campaign from Adidas is an excellent example of this: **https://www.youtube.com/watch?v=Oe3St1GgoHQ** with some 13 million views and counting.

Self-infection

My first job in public relations involved pens and paper and fax machines. It was a far cry from our new digital age. So how have I responded to the new anatomy of the web working within scientific publishing?

Public relations is a key function for working with organizations at the forefront of science. The key findings reported in the research published in journals need to be communicated in a timely, newsworthy and cutting-edge way.

The percentage of news coverage devoted to science has never been particularly high, hovering around 4–6 per cent from the mid-1970s till 2001. But, according to the Pew Research Center's State of the News Media (Pew Research Center Publications 2008), science news has now been squeezed to around 2 per cent of the total. This drop does not reflect a falling public interest in science, as much as an increasingly diverse and competitive media world. The internet has now overtaken television and newspapers as the public's main source for scientific news.

To give some workplace examples, BioMed Central where I headed up their communications function now has a blog that is highly visible on the company homepage. The blog is updated regularly by a wide variety of employees, demonstrating a wide, customer-facing approach to communications. The blog is syndicable via RSS feeds and also streamed directly into BioMed Central's Facebook and Twitter pages, linking up these audiences across platforms.

They have ensured that the organization's approach to social media is now all-encompassing. Twitter, Facebook and YouTube have all been employed not only to disseminate key corporate messages, but also to gather feedback and converse with our publics in order to better understand their opinions, needs and perception of the business. Adoption of webcasting technologies has allowed my team to offer messages in new formats. Continuing medical education (CME) programmes have been produced, which encourage interaction with our organization, whilst fulfilling a fundamental need for lifelong learning.

Their web channels are all linked ensuring that strategically important messages are exposed to the highest number of users, thus maximizing their inherent viral effect. Whilst media relations will always be a crucial element of the work of a PRO, I believe that public relations departments within organizations should always strive to be more than just a mechanism for obtaining publicity.

Immunology

There is undoubtedly a massive amount of online innovation and knowledge within our industry. However, not all practitioners are armed with the diverse set of skills required to successfully manage both online and traditional PR in conjunction.

For as much as the web presents our profession with great opportunities to demonstrate our creativity, it also represents a space where badly planned and implemented communications can have serious repercussions. One only needs to look at furniture store Habitat's disastrous use of Twitter (Sky News 2009) to recognize that successful online engagement requires not only ingenuity, but also a strong grounding in communications fundamentals.

Two distinct groups have now emerged at the peripheries of our profession: traditional practitioners who do not/cannot understand the new language of online engagement and social engagers who fully understand the nature of the web, but have not been armed with the basic principles of public relations theory and practice.

Controlling and initiating viral outbreaks is a skill requiring both practitioner knowledge and innovation in engagement. It is all too easy for traditional practitioners to ignore the benefits of new platforms and for social engagers to ignore the potential for poor communications to damage reputation. There is a danger that if we as a profession do not rectify the immunity of these two groups to acknowledge and learn from one another, that we will not as an industry be able to match the high levels of success demonstrated by our trailblazers.

Vaccination

It is an essential part of senior PR practitioners' roles to ensure that their staff, their colleagues and indeed their profession are armed with the greatest amount of knowledge and experience to succeed. A clear disparity between the level of knowledge and practice which practitioners possess and the level of knowledge and practice which practitioners require to successfully engage online exists. However, the industry has not rested on its laurels in seeking to close this gap.

Extensive training on web engagement, social media, tools and techniques is available in a variety of formats for practitioners. Likewise, broad, relevant training on public relations fundamentals is available for those whose background is more focused on social engagement. The web has allowed a proliferation of electronic advice, webinars, guides and case studies all suitable to aid the development of our fellow practitioners.

So if this is the case, then why are some practitioners still immune and perhaps even frightened to link public relations with social engagement on a fundamental level?

Part of the answer to this question lies with us – the profession's senior practitioners. It is essential that we as leaders of the industry ensure that our PROs understand why further skills and knowledge are essential and why having only a passing interest and basic knowledge is not good enough. We must lead the PR profession to celebrate its trailblazers and best practice; we must ensure the suitability and uptake of essential training and development. But above all, we ourselves must not become vaccinated and therefore immune to new trends, technologies and tools.

Mutation

Whilst viral messages mutate as they pass through hosts, the web itself is also constantly evolving and transforming. Our use of the web and social engagement must always reflect the strategic requirements of business and not simply be employed because the tools exist.

Whilst ensuring that our profession has the skills and knowledge it requires to effectively utilize the web in a strategic manner, we must recognize that it is changing rapidly. As the leaders of the public relations industry we must ensure that we are aware of the potential impacts of developing trends, technologies and tools, and that we are using them strategically for the benefit of our organizations and clients, and that we are imparting our knowledge back to our profession, ensuring a steady cycle of improvement and development.

The anatomy of the web is constantly changing and mutating. We must ensure that the anatomy of the PR profession is therefore one of constant adaptation.

'Life moves pretty fast. If you don't stop and look around once in a while, you could miss it.'

– Ferris Bueller, Ferris Bueller's Day Off

Further reading

Crunchbase (2009) Timothy Draper [Online] http://www.crunchbase.com/person/timothy-draper [accessed 4 August 2009]

Edelman (2005) Sixth Annual Edelman Trust Barometer [Online] www.edelman.co.uk/trustbarometer [accessed 12 August 2009].

Grunig, J and Hunt, T (1984) *Managing Public Relations,* Thompson Learning, New York.

Hughes, J (director) (1986) *Ferris Bueller's Day Off,* motion picture, Paramount Pictures, United States.

Marketing Pilgrim (2009) Skittles social media campaign: FTW or epic fail? [Online] http://www.marketingpilgrim.com/2009/03/skittles-social-media-campaign-ftw-or-epic-fail.html [accessed 12 August 2009].

Marketing Profs (2009) Skittles social media experiment, fad or trend? [Online] http://www.mpdailyfix.com/2009/03/skittles_social_media_experime.html [accessed 12 August 2009].

Mashable (2009) *Harry Potter and the Half-Blood Prince*: a social media blockbuster? [Online] http://mashable.com/2009/07/14/harry-potter-and-the-half-blood-prince/ [accessed 12 August 2009].

MetaBlocks (2009) Viral marketing 101: understanding viral marketing [Online] http://www.metablocks.com/blog/category/viral-marketing/ [accessed 11 July 2009].

Pew Research Center Publications (2008) State of the News Media 2008 [Online] http://pewresearch.org/pubs/767/state-of-the-news-media-2008 [accessed 15 August 2009].

PR Week (2009) Best job in the world campaign wins top PR award at Cannes [Online] http://www.prweek.com/news/914983/Best-job-world-campaign-wins-top-PR-award-Cannes/ [accessed 29 July 2009].

Revolution Magazine (2009) Harry Potter spreads love potion on Twitter [Online] http://www.revolutionmagazine.com/news/921813/Harry-Potter-spreads-love-potion-Twitter/ [accessed 30 July 2009].

Search Marketing Gurus (2009) Skittles and social media – obviously a company that doesn't get it [Online] http://www.searchmarketinggurus.com/search_marketing_gurus/2009/03/skittles-social-media-obviously-a-company-that-doesnt-get-it.html [accessed 12 August 2009].

Scoble, R and Israel, S (2006) *Naked Conversations*, John Wiley & Sons Inc, New Jersey.

Sky News (2009) Habitat blames intern for PR disaster [Online] http://news.sky.com/skynews/Home/Business/Habitat-Twitter-Row-UK-Furniture-Chain-Blame-Intern-For-Using-Iran-To-Promote-Spring-Sale/Article/200906415319105 [accessed 23 July 2009].

Stephenson, N (1992) *Snow Crash*, Bantam Books, New York.

The Guardian (2009) Best job in the world campaign storms Cannes Lions advertising awards [Online] http://www.guardian.co.uk/media/2009/jun/23/best-job-advertising-awards [accessed 29 July 2009].

Communications micro-strategies

11

MARTIN TURNER CHART.PR, MCIPR

This paper was originally written in August 2009. Minor revisions have been made to the original text for this book to reflect developments in media, technology and practice.

Public relations is initially attractive to many organizations because of its offer of communication via unpaid, credible third-parties, and as a defence against negative press. But public relations has more to offer, and a strategic framework developed for PR can provide leadership for integrated campaigns covering areas more traditionally associated with marketing, branding, advertising and internal communications.

This paper outlines an integrative and scalable campaign model, tested over 18 years in the arts, automotive, the NHS and charities, which is well suited for winning board and senior decision-maker support. In our experience, gaining internal support is at least as difficult as other public relations activities, and so it is essential that the model is easily comprehensible and lends itself to an internal and external consultation process.

Characteristics of a micro-strategy model

In developing and subsequently testing the model, we set ourselves a number of criteria. These were:

Intuitive but systematic: we wanted a model which other practitioners could recognize as describing their own thought processes, even if they had never conceived of it in such terms before.

Agile but scalable: from the beginning, we had ambitions of extending our media relations remit to cover the full spectrum of communications activities. Therefore, we looked for a model which could be scaled up without redesign, but which could also be used quickly for very small problems.

Inclusive rather than prescriptive: we looked for a model which could be filled out with new learning and research as it became available, rather than prescribing a single kind of campaign.

Simple but complete: we looked for the simplest possible model which would generate all the information and decisions necessary to run a successful campaign.

Actionable but evaluable: while communications programmes are often plagued by a lack of evaluability, business strategy units and public health departments have often faced the opposite problem, of research without actionable conclusions.

Directive but persuasive: we looked for a model which would win over project and senior managers, giving them confidence to take the model to their peers as part of their larger strategy proposals, and which could easily be explained to non-specialists by a non-specialist.

A model for micro-strategies

Our approach begins with a physical form – a tetrahedron. In an initial consultation, we generally sketch out this shape as shown in Figure 11.1:

Outcomes – the goals of campaign, set out in the format 'this will have happened by...'

Audiences – the people who we have to persuade in order for the outcome to happen, along with their influencers, and any gatekeepers, who can impair the campaign, even if they cannot further it.

FIGURE 11.1   A model for communication micro-strategies

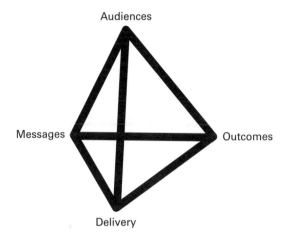

Messages – what we need to tell the audience which, if they understand it, believe it and think it relevant, will persuade them to fulfil the outcome.

Delivery – the means by which the messages will reach the audiences credibly, relevantly and clearly, so that the outcome happens.

The model in depth

Outcomes are goals expressed in a format which specifies their mode of evaluation, or 'how we will know when it's done'. Most project managers expect conversations around communications campaigns to be either woolly and non-specific, or entirely focused on the means, not the result. We are typically presented with goals such as 'raise awareness of palliative care' or 'create a website on...'. The first type is insufficient because it does not identify a measurable or quantifiable result, and the second because the output has no direct value to the organization's or project's true priorities. Although we prefer the term outcome, occasionally we meet people who find it confusing. In these cases, we sometimes talk about 'the endgame', and sometimes say 'a year from now, we are going to look back at this, and say it was the most brilliant campaign ever – now, what are the results going to be that make us say that?' Although we are generally confronted with goals which are too unambitious, occasionally we are set problems which cannot be solved by a communications means, in which case we explain that our campaigns can only influence people's behaviour by influencing their thinking.

In this directive model, we are only interested in the **audiences** which have a bearing on the outcome, either because they themselves control it (smokers, in a quit smoking campaign, or teenage girls and their sexual partners in a teenage pregnancy campaign), or because they are the key influencers for those people, or because they are the gatekeepers who possess the power to reduce the effectiveness of the campaign, or to stop it happening. We prefer the term audiences over 'stakeholders' because many of our audiences are not aware that they have a stake in things before our campaign begins. We prefer it over 'publics' because, although we will initially segment the audiences based on all available knowledge, our final segmentation will be based on what kinds of delivery are available – in other words, what the natural groups are in which people can hear our message. Finally, we prefer it over the term 'market segments', with its associated sub-terms such as 'cherry pickers', 'silver surfers', and so on, because we find the marketing metaphor inappropriate for many of our campaigns.

We define our **messages** as 'what will persuade the audience – if they believe it and remember it – to fulfil the outcome'. Although we will eventually look for messages which are robust and transmissible, we find that non-communications specialists too quickly jump to slogans. We are much more interested in understanding from them – based on their knowledge of the outcomes and the audiences they want us to reach – what things have resonated in the past, and what particular information the audience needs to know. Once we have understood the underlying content of the messages, we work, either with the commissioning manager or in a separate meeting, on a sub-framework which we call 'ICE COLD'.

The first part is based on research published by the Advertising Standards Authority in 2002 on the kinds of messages which work in the UK.[1] These are:

- **Informative** – people like to hear and act on things which make them more informed.

- **Clever** – people like and act on messages which are clever, in an entertaining sense.
- **Enter popular culture** – messages which enter daily use multiply their effectiveness.

To this research, we have added our own observations:

- **Crisp**: The eye takes in an average of 18 letters in one go, and the ear is attuned to phrases which are rhythmic.
- **Obviously true**: The message should not need explanation or defence.
- **Linger in the mind**: Memorable.
- **Decisive**: They lead the audience to complete the outcome.

It is important to note that, in a mixed-media campaign we would expect the messages (generally three, but possibly as many as seven) to be literally embedded in press releases, but we would not necessarily use them as the attention-slogan in an advertisement. The actual text of advertisements we would consider to be properly part of the delivery section.

Delivery is the means by which the messages get inside the minds of the audiences. The term is chosen carefully over other terms including 'media', 'channels', 'tools' or 'resources'. To our minds, all of these fall short of the imperative to actually complete the delivery process. Our delivery section might include the text of the press release, the copy and artwork of an advertisement, the means by which a word-of-mouth item is propagated, and so on. The selected delivery means is dependent on the choice of audiences, but they themselves influence how we segment these audiences. When running a multi-media campaign across a region of 5.6 million people, there are realistically only a limited number of affordable options. Any segmentation must be done with an understanding of the demographics of consumers of purchased and generated media, and further segmentation must be done by stimulating the interest of particular groups, such as by use of particular language, sounds or artwork.

In selecting our delivery means, we look for channels which are **relevant, clear,** and **credible** in reaching the required audience. Anonymous direct mailing can result in the delivery of an entirely clear leaflet to every household, but it is generally understood that most householders will consider 'junk mail' to be irrelevant, and possibly unreliable. By contrast, an addressed, personal letter signed by a GP, provided that it is clear, will generally be considered to be relevant and highly credible. Word-of-mouth has enormous relevance and high credibility, but messages must be carefully constructed if they are to survive the process with clarity.

As a rule of thumb, we suggest that the delivery must reach audiences an average of 3.5 times or more through different media *before the audience notices it.* When considering specific media, however, we use consumption data provided by the media outlet so that, for example, with public transport advertising, we aim to reach 77 per cent of a target audience 12 times each, whereas a radio campaign might have a target reach of five times per listener.

The model in action

A typical initial one-hour internal consultation between ourselves and a project manager follows these lines:

FIGURE 11.2   The anatomy of a typical one-hour initial conversation

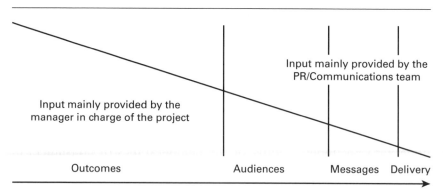

Input mainly provided by the PR/Communications team

Input mainly provided by the manager in charge of the project

Outcomes   Audiences   Messages   Delivery

In minutes 1–30, we explore outcomes. At this point, we expect the manager to have almost all of the knowledge. However, they may not be able to express outcomes in terms that can be delivered by a communications campaign, they may have too large or too small a scale in mind, and they may not have identified how valuable these outcomes are, and hence the available budget. Our most successful outcomes have been expressed tightly: increase the uptake of cervical screening across the West Midlands region by 12 per cent over three years in the 25–29 age group, decrease the misuse of Accident and Emergency services by 10 per cent over the two week period around Christmas, gain popular support for the closure of a hospital. Managers are often unwilling to commit in the first meeting to the level of specificity we are looking for, and so further follow-up is needed.

In minutes 31–45, we examine which audiences control the agreed outcomes. For example, in a Quit Smoking campaign, only the person who smokes controls their individual outcome, and we must persuade each smoker individually, and continue to persuade them. Our audience section is not merely about naming the audiences, but also logging as much intelligence on their values and behaviours as possible. At this point, we expect the manager to have the majority of the knowledge, though we will expect to have some information ourselves, to be supplemented later with desk research, focus groups and polling, as appropriate.

In minutes 46–55, we set down the content of the messages. Frequently, when dealing with front line clinicians who are very skilled at working one to one with a patient, but inexperienced in mass-media, we ask them to tell us what they would say if they were on the bus with a member of their target audience, and had just 30 seconds to get across their key points.

At this stage, we are not looking for the wording of the message, only its content. Generally speaking, we are looking for about three messages for the key decision-making audience, though, in a complex situation, there may be a number of mutually exclusive key audiences, and differing messages will be developed for each. Quite frequently, fully formed messages will already have occurred during the conversation. At this stage in the consultation, we are expecting to lead the conversation. If the messages produced are incomplete, unpolished, or seem to fail one of our tests, we book a further one-hour session to brainstorm, which will largely be made up of communications team members.

TABLE 11.1 Notional scores for typical delivery means in use by NHS Walsall

Delivery means	Clarity	Credibility	Relevance	Reach	Cost/OTE
Face to face	1	1	1	1	£100s
Word of mouth (friend)	0.1	0.7	0.7	100s, 1000s	–
Personal letter	0.5–0.7	0.9	0.8	10s 100s	£50s
Radio presenter	0.5–0.7	0.8	0.7	100,000s	–
Local news article	0.2–0.8	0.6	0.5	10,000s	–
National news article	0.2–0.8	0.3–0.5	0.6	millions	–
Personalized letter	0.5–0.7	0.6	0.6	1,000s	50p
Local radio ad	0.2–0.4	0.4–0.6	0.7	100,000s	3p
Outdoor advertising	0.2–0.4	0.1–0.4	0.6	millions	3p
Newspaper ad	0.5–0.9	0.1–0.4	0.4	10,000s	3p
Phone campaign	0.1–1.0	0.1–0.7	0.1–0.8	1,000s	£10s
Anonymous mailing	0.5–0.8	0.1–0.2	0.1–0.2	10,000s	8p

NOTE: These rule-of-thumb scores were based on evaluation of over 200 campaigns over 8 years. They relate to the intrinsic clarity (ie ability to deliver the intended message and necessary information), credibility and relevance (ie how relevant the recipient expects the communication to be, based on format) of the medium. Cost/OTE is the cost per single 'Opportunity to Experience'.

In the final five minutes, we suggest, based on the level of spend identified in the Outcomes section, and the size and particular characteristics of the audience, a suite of delivery means which will reach the each member of the audience an average of 3.5 times or better with the message. Frequently, we find that project managers want the highest-status delivery means that their budget will support, however, we remind them that 'high gloss = low touch', in other words, that it is the most personal and apparently 'home made' delivery which is the most effective. Where it is possible to reach the full audience, we favour personal meetings, phone calls, personal letters and stories in favourite newspapers or favoured radio shows, over mass-media advertising. Notwithstanding this, we have successfully applied this model to very large scale campaigns with a substantial advertising spend.

Observations on the model

It should be noted that this is a self-evaluating model: the expression of goals in terms of outcomes insists that we have something to measure, or, at least, to answer the question 'how do we know when it's done'. Equally, at each stage it requires us to conform the audience, message or delivery to the outcome, and, when we discuss the delivery phase, to assess the proportionality of the resource expended to the outcome which is being achieved.

Equally, this is an iterative model – once we have established which audiences we must reach in order to achieve a particular outcome, the internal customer often returns to the outcomes and suggests a more ambitious or more refined target.

Finally, in accordance with our own dictum, this is a model which is 'obviously true', once explained: managers swiftly recognize the inevitable validity of matching the delivery to the message and the audience, and matching the message and the audience to the outcome, and assuring that the outcome and delivery are proportionate. This is important, because we want to focus time spent not on defending the model, but on populating it with the knowledge needed to generate a successful campaign.

Practical examples

I have asserted that this micro-strategy model is suitable for campaigns at many scales. Two examples illustrate the use of the model at both the micro and macro level.

CASE STUDY Recruitment problem

In 2001, a department of Walsall Community Health Trust contacted the communications team to discuss a problem in recruiting a particular specialist clinician. The senior manager explained that the job had been advertised in all the usual places, but that there had been no interest. Rather than invest a further £3,000 in advertising costs, she had been advised to contact us. Having briefly explained the model, we looked at the outcome – the recruitment of the specialist, and then the audience. On probing, we asked 'how many people are there in this country capable of doing the job?' The answer was just 12 – and the senior manager already had their names and contact details. We then worked out what offer would interest these particular people, and the senior manager sent out 12 personal letters inviting the specialists to consider applying, which resulted in a subsequent appointment.

In this particular case, any PR professional could have given the relevant advice. However, crucially, the senior manager was introduced to the model and, the next time she faced a communications problem, specifically requested that we use our 'pyramid thing' to solve the problem with her, rather than for her.

CASE STUDY Cervical screening

By 2006 cervical screening across the UK was facing a year on year decline of 2 per cent. In the West Midlands, this meant that the programme had already dropped below its target threshold. Other regions had tried a variety of advertising and promotional approaches, but no region had been able to demonstrate a measurable upswing linked to any campaign.

In the initial meeting, we explored the model, and agreed the following:

Outcome: 12 per cent increase in cervical screening uptake over 3 years for the West Midlands Region (5.6 million population).

Audiences: the key audience was the gateway group of 25s–29s, since data showed that those who took up cervical screening at that age generally continued, whereas those that did not never started. Survey research had shown that women learned from each other that the process was likely to be unpleasant, and that women were particularly unlikely to be interested in the views of their mothers or of their male partners on the subject. We were also aware of a number of gatekeeper groups, which included religious communities which opposed overt sexual health advertising, the particular rules of some media providers, and the Advertising Standards Authority. The most important gatekeepers, however, were the cervical screening leads at the local level, who held an effective veto over the campaign.

Messages: the actual wording of the message was left undefined at this stage, but research showed that i) most women were keenly aware that the procedure was uncomfortable, inconvenient and embarrassing and ii) that few women were aware what the actual benefit was. It was agreed that the message should strongly support PR coverage and word-of-mouth.

Delivery: based on the size of the audience, and the inability to segment them further, we proposed a region-wide campaign combining media relations, radio advertising, bus advertising and Adshel, along with the inclusion of a mailer in the existing calling letters, and the distribution of collateral through the Body Shop, Virgin Vie, and other outlets. We agreed that the artwork should be attractive to the key age group, and should be designed in such a way that it would neither offend minorities, nor provoke comment from male partners.

In defining the message, we conducted an informal focus group which brought the immediate response from one participant: 'I don't go, because it's pants!' Further research suggested that the disparaging term 'pants' was resonant for the target age-group, but almost incomprehensible for the majority of over 50s.

In a second meeting, we reviewed the model, and proposed: 'What's pants, but can save your life?', supplemented with information derived from public health data, eventually condensed to 'Cervical Screening saves the life of one woman in our region every day'. We agreed to bring a mock-up of the advertisement to a regional meeting of all screening leads.

At the subsequent meeting we explored the model with the wider group, gaining agreement on the outcomes and the audiences, and on the wording of the message. At that point we described the possible campaign, before revealing the artwork, mocked up in Photoshop. Of the 30 people present, 28 agreed that the message and the artwork – once refined and executed properly – entirely satisfied the brief as described by exploring the model. One person insisted that it be tested on Asian women of the relevant age-group, and one person stated that Asian women would not accept the campaign in her area, and it should not be run. We were able to accommodate the focus group testing, but we were subsequently unable to win over the last dissenter.

In developing the campaign, we identified an unexpected gatekeeper: the NHS Information Authority initially refused our request for the URL **www.pants.nhs.uk**, because they thought it was irreverent. We were able to use the strategy documentation to persuade them that we were serious.

Results: 'What's pants but can save your life?' doubled the uptake of cervical screening at two labs during the initial campaign month, and an overall 16 per cent increase in uptake across all labs after six months. It resulted in two lives directly saved. It has since been adopted by the National Social Marketing Centre (NSMC) as one of the NHS key case studies in Social Marketing, and was published in the Chief Medical Officer's Report, as well as in the George Washington University School of Public Health journal.[2] It was a finalist in the Health Service Journal awards 2008, and is now widely regarded as the most successful screening campaign ever run at the regional level in the UK, despite a modest budget of £55,000 in year one. A subsequent survey of 2,000 target audience indicated that 30 per cent of women of all ages recognized the iconic five pairs of contrasting pants, and 18 per cent said that this made them more likely to undertake cervical screening.

Conclusions

It is my passionate belief that PR needs to present itself as the strategic leader in the communications disciplines. Branding, advertising, marketing, PR, internal communications, customer relations and propaganda are overlapping disciplines. In general, marketing as a profession has been better at selling its wares than PR: most business people are aware of the need for a 'marketing plan', and anyone coming out of an MBA course can be expected to know what the 4Ps are, as well as be able to talk about USPs.

Part of the reason that PR has had less prominence as a strategic discipline is that PR agencies treat their strategy frameworks as proprietary, while in-house practitioners often see the requirement to produce strategies as an unwelcome distraction. Published studies, of which Grunig's is the best known, tend to focus on describing different kinds of PR. Unlike marketing's 4Ps, however, Grunig's and others' frameworks provide analysis, not a recipe.

Another reason is that Public Relations deals with a much wider set of potential outcomes, encompassing not only selling, but reputation, policy formation, cultural change and almost all other forms of persuasion.

When introducing senior colleagues to this model for the first time, and explaining what can and cannot be achieved by a communications approach, I often share my levers of Influence analogy as shown in Figure 11.3. The application of direct power to a problem is analogous to attempting to twist a simple cylinder between the thumb and forefinger. If the cylinder is small, light, and there is little resistance, this can be accomplished easily. However, where it is larger, heavier, or in some way fixed, direct power is insufficient. Taking hold of a lever enables the application of the principle of moments – going further from the cylinder means that a reasonable amount of force still turns it. This mirrors the way in which an organization's direct power through its paid staff, assets and contracts is often insufficient. In this case, three possible levers are available, which are enforcement, incentive, and persuasion. Enforcement ranges from the creation of new legislation (banning of smoking in pubs, for example) to forcible eviction or even military action. Incentive can be as simple as offering a wage in return for a job, or more subtle, as in the structuring of taxation to reward particular behaviour. Our communications micro-strategies address the third form of influence – persuasion. Persuasion is easily combined with one of the other two, although attempts to persuade, enforce and incentivize frequently meet with less success.

FIGURE 11.3 Levers of influence

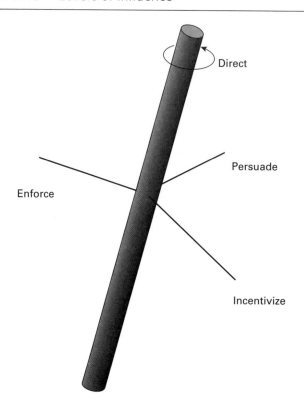

The model I have put forward in this paper aims to do for PR what the 4Ps have done for marketing: provide a simple, directive and memorable framework which can be applied again and again to problems great and small – and can then give the leadership of the entire campaign to the PR strategist, so that any specialists who are subsequently commissioned are brought in for their special expertise in fulfilling a part of the brief, not in taking control of all of it. But, because it applies to much wider issues of persuasion, I see it, and the PR profession, as encompassing, rather than competing with, existing marketing and marketing communications approaches.

Notes

1   Ford-Hutchinson, S and Rothwell, A (2002) The public's perception of advertising in today's society, Advertising Standards Authority, p 25 [Online] http://www.asa.org.uk/NR/rdonlyres/A351FFA3-22D2-4A03-942E-F653A700B6EC/0/ASA_Public_Perception_of_Advertising_Feb_2002.pdf

2   Andrews, S and Turner, M (2009) What's pants, but could save your life? Increasing cervical cancer screening utilization in England, *Cases in Public Health Communication & Marketing*, **3**, pp 186–203.

Is public relations evolving into reputation management?

12

JULIE MCCABE CHART.PR, MCIPR

This paper was originally written in December 2011. Minor revisions have been made to the original text for this book to reflect developments in media, technology and practice.

> 'Character is like a tree and reputation like its shadow. The shadow is what we think of it, the tree is the real thing.' – *Abraham Lincoln*

'Reputation Management' is a term being increasingly used to describe online PR, crisis management, corporate PR and as a rationale for the practice of PR itself. Campbell, Herman and Noble (2006) also suggest that the term may have been introduced to counter negative associations and gain status for the practice of PR. This report will examine what reputation management is, the link between PR and reputation management and consider if the PR industry is evolving into a complete reputation management function.

What is reputation?

'Public relations is about reputation – the result of what you do, what you say and what others say about you. Public relations is the discipline which looks after reputation, with the aim of earning understanding and support and influencing opinion and behaviour. It is the planned and sustained effort to establish and maintain goodwill and mutual understanding between an organization and its publics.'

– The Chartered Institute of Public Relations

Reputation is a vital asset to any organization and can determine its success or failure. Dalton and Croft (2003, p 8) describe reputation as 'the sum of the values that stakeholders attribute to a company, based on their perception and interpretation of the image the company communicates and its behaviour over time,' whereas Doorley and Garcia (2011, p 4) give a more simplistic definition by stating that reputation is a combination of an organization's 'performance, behaviour and communication'.

These are only two of the many definitions of reputation available and although they vary slightly, the common underpinning factors are that stakeholders control reputation and how an organization communicates and conducts itself determines stakeholders' opinions. Therefore in order to effectively promote and help to shape an organization's reputation, the attitudes of stakeholders need to be influenced over a period of time.

To do this successfully organizations must live up to their core values, the most important of which are honesty, integrity and trustworthiness, and ensure they deliver on their promises. This is because stakeholders form their opinions based on expectations, experiences, the messages they are exposed to and the conversations they participate in or observe (CIPR 2011).

What is the link between PR and reputation?

From the CIPR definition, we can see the focus put on the term 'reputation'; however Campbell (2006) argues that this definition assumes that PR practitioners produce reputation, even though engineers and accountants could have more of an influence. She also believes that reputations develop with or without the intervention of PR practitioners. Whilst this is a valid sentiment, it does not encompass the full scope of PR in looking after reputation, which is done in good and bad times for an organization by promoting and protecting it.

Dalton (2003, 2005) believes that PR is one of the most effective tools to help manage the factors affecting reputation through brand and brand experience. However, he differentiates PR and reputation by outlining that PR involves more specific issues including media relations, public affairs, crisis management, event management and branding, whereas reputation management is more holistic in its approach and involves all employees. We must also not forget that other marketing disciplines including advertising play a contributory role in helping to manage an organization's reputation, but they focus on the image and controlled viewpoint or visual look of the organization, whereas PR focuses on reputation, trust and credibility (Davies, 2003).

Another definition of PR is 'the management function that establishes and maintains mutually beneficial relationships between an organization and the publics on who its success or failure depends' (Cutlip, Center and Broom 2006). This also complements the definition given by the CIPR and helps to demonstrate the broad range of activities carried out by PR professionals, whilst further emphasizing the importance of PR as a strategic function in organizations.

This definition by Cutlip also complements the two-way symmetrical model of PR put forward by Grunig and Hunt (1984) as the ideal model for practitioners to work from because a two-way channel of communication is needed between a company and its stakeholders. This is particularly significant now with the increased use of social media and consumer generated content which gives stakeholders the chance to openly discuss and criticize organizations. It also emphasizes the importance of PR in building mutually beneficial relationships with stakeholders and communicating the reputation of an organization if it wants to be successful.

Based on this, I believe that reputation management can be explained as being a result of PR activities implemented as part of a strategy to build, manage and interpret the relationships between an organization and its stakeholders. This is done by encouraging listening and engaging in conversation in order to protect and maintain reputations (Murray and White 2004, 2005).

What are the advantages of having a good corporate reputation?

Building a good reputation has both tangible and intangible benefits (Doorley and Garcia 2011) and can drive business success in the long term (Lord Browne 2010). A good reputation also raises expectations about the kind of product(s) or service a company provides and enhances its reputation (Dalton 2003).

The concept of managing and developing a reputation is of course not new, but what is new is the recognition by organizations of their need to adopt a more inclusive approach to a much wider range of stakeholders and to commit more resources to this activity (Dalton 2003).

Can reputation be managed?

'The number one role of a leader is to communicate. And the number one role of a CEO is to be the chief communicator, to make sure that the people inside the organization know what is important, as well as our partner community and our customers and our shareholders.'

– *Jonathan Schwartz, CEO, Sun Microsystems*

To try to manage reputation, the behaviour of the organization must be examined as it is the strongest driver of reputation. This includes the behaviour of the CEO, who is ultimately in charge of an organization's reputation and the management team, because their support to PR and reputation strategies is essential for success. Members of staff also play a vital role as company ambassadors, as they affect the experience stakeholders have when they engage with the organization.

I have identified five main factors which I feel contribute to effective and successful PR initiatives and help to manage the reputation of an organization. These will now be discussed in turn:

Strategy and planning

Planning and implementing a competitive strategy is vitally important to ensure that an organization's key messages are delivered and its brand is effectively communicated to stakeholders. This takes into account organizational needs, objectives, target audiences and factors which affect reputation. It also identifies ways in which to promote and protect reputation as well as initiatives to influence stakeholder perceptions, support behaviours and drive business results, which together help build advantage in the marketplace.

In my experience PR strategies are driven by consistent information about what is relevant and important to specific stakeholders and to be effective they need to be implemented as a planned and sustained programme of activity. This is because infrequent PR exercises can and will only generate short-term and short-lived publicity. It is also important when setting aims and objectives to include evaluation methods for key indicators so that the plan can be analysed and amended as required.

Internal and external communications

Murray and White (2005, p 26) describe internal communications as the 'sleeping giant' of reputation management and they believe that employee engagement is crucial in effective brand and reputation engagement.

The importance of internal communications was also reinforced at The CIPR Conference on Reputation (June 2011) along with the powerful potential of employees currently being underutilized as an advocate base by many organizations.

At the conference Claire Cater of Bell Pottinger suggested that the balance of spend for the internal/external communications should be 60/40 in favour of internal. She also recommended that staff be profiled in the same way consumers are by organizations to better assess how to engage them because employees carry the reputation of the organization both in and out of work. I feel that this is an important point and is something which many organizations have not considered before, but moving forward is very relevant and will prove beneficial.

When looking at external communications Murray and White (2005, p 26) highlight that PR professionals need to be more targeted in their approach and integrated on their delivery because 'dealing with reputation management in PR requires an integrated, holistic communications approach'. This is echoed by Dalton and Croft (2003) who believe that consistent communication to internal and external audiences coupled with integrated marketing communications are both essential to effectively manage reputation.

The increased need for integrated communications is certainly something which I have noticed in recent years and there is rarely a campaign that doesn't need it now to ensure key messages reach and engage our stakeholders and ultimately help to influence them.

Crisis/issues and risk management

'Our reputation is more important than the last hundred million dollars.'

– *Rupert Murdoch*

It is a harsh reality that reputation takes years to build up, but can be destroyed very quickly. We only need to look at the closure of the News of the World to see the consequences that a crisis can have on a company's reputation. Despite being the biggest selling English language newspaper in the world at one time, the reputation of this newspaper could not survive the phone hacking scandal. It is therefore fair to emphasize the importance of reputation in an organization's general strategic thinking and in its ongoing PR activities and not just as something to think about in times of crisis.

Although reputation is linked to risk/issues and crisis management, the main aim for companies now is to anticipate, understand and plan for perceived threats to their reputation both internally and externally, before they become crises to help protect the company from reputational harm (Doorley and Garcia 2011).

More recently, if an issue or crisis does unfold the positive aspect of social media is that it provides a speedy platform which the organization can use to issue the relevant information out into the public domain with the urgency required.

When asked how a company should seek to recover from a difficult high-profile issue, Andrew Griffin, CEO, Regester Larkin (2010) said:

'The best way to restore reputation is to build trust by doing the basics right. People are rightly sceptical about PR campaigns designed to restore image. They want to see that lessons have been learnt but they also want to be reassured that there is absolute commitment to the product or services that helped build up the organization's reputation in the first place'.

Corporate social responsibility (CSR) and corporate ethics

'Social obligation is much bigger than supporting worthy causes. It includes anything that impacts people and the quality of their lives.'
– *William Ford Jnr., Chairman, Ford Motor Co*

Increasing levels of interest in reputation by businesses and media in recent years means that it is more important than ever for organizations to behave in a socially and environmentally responsible way if they want to succeed. Corporate Social Responsibility (CSR) can enhance an organization's reputation if used properly and can also bring economic benefits (Werther and Chandler 2006). The so-called triple bottom-line of economic, social and environmental concerns is described by Dalton (2003) as being at the centre of reputation management. CSR is however not just about 'doing good' or being seen to do good, it is about recognizing a company's responsibility to all stakeholders and always acting in their best interests. A holistic approach is imperative because to be successful an organization needs to be perceived by multiple stakeholder audiences as being capable, trustworthy, credible, responsible, consistent and having integrity. Management support is also essential to ensure all CSR activities are specifically linked to business objectives; otherwise customers will not believe that the organization is being genuine.

CSR is often linked to business ethics which refers to morally appropriate behaviours and decisions by an organization; however CSR activities are no guarantee of ethical behaviour. A company that does not pay attention to ethics is risking considerable harm to its reputation as well as other important intangible corporate assets – including employee morale and productivity, demand for a company's products, confidence in a company's executives and stock performance (Doorley and Garcia 2011).

To be ethical in business Sinclair (1993) advises that organizations need strong leadership to ensure ethical standards and an ethical corporate culture. Doorley and Garcia (2011, p 73) add that 'codes of ethics are valuable because they establish normative standards of behaviour that become habitual through repetition.' Murphy (1988) and Tsalikis and Fritzsche (1989) expand on this with their belief that codes of conduct represent the most effective way of implementing an ethical policy and reducing ethical conflict.

In the case of the CIPR I believe that the code of conduct is useful in outlining an ideal total quality approach by PR professionals and anyone working in the industry should be bound by integrity, competence and confidentiality in their practice. However, my worry is that these principles may be too broad and processes that support their enforcement may be needed as well as measures introduced to monitor the behaviour of practitioners.

The CIPR's Continuing Professional Development (CPD) scheme is a strong base for the integration of education and professional standards of PR professionalism and I believe should be compulsory for all members.

Online public relations

'Reputation is holistic – it is not possible to sustain one image created through conventional media alongside a completely different one created through social media. Old and new media interact.'

– CIPR

In today's business climate reputation management is easier in one way but more difficult in another for organizations. This is due to the popularity of social networking sites, user generated content and the internet. PR practitioners now have the opportunity to provide greater access to content including optimization of corporate websites, press releases, blogs and other digital communications. Keywords and phrases relevant to the organization can also be used to increase ranking on search engines, which also helps to create a better image of the organization and their brand because the message is consistent in both traditional and social media.

Doorley and Garcia (2011, p 115) believe that social media engagement is crucial to a company's reputation management activities because 'deep social media engagement is indeed correlated to financial performance', however social media is by no means there to replace other forms of communication but instead complement, expand and enrich them.

I agree with this and think it is also important to point out that how an organization participates in social media depends on its audience and its general business goals. The growth of social media channels has also enabled the reach of each member of staff to grow considerably, which can be used to an organization's advantage. It also reinforces the importance of internal communication because if employees are kept advised of important information and key brand messages then they can help protect the reputation of the organization online through sensing any discontent and helping address an issue or crisis before it develops.

Whilst using online media to communicate good news about the organization to internal and external stakeholders it is equally important for an organization to listen to what their stakeholders are saying about them in the online world. In doing this the organization has the opportunity to engage with them, address any queries or concerns and respond appropriately and with the urgency required. This is an invaluable benefit of using online PR for reputation management purposes and justifies the emergence of dedicated specialist online reputation management companies in recent years, which primarily focus on the removal of negative posts about an organization from the internet.

Monitoring and measuring PR and reputation

'Everything that can be counted does not necessarily count; everything that counts cannot necessarily be counted.'

– *Albert Einstein*

Due to the complex nature of reputation it is difficult to define a clear cut way of measuring it. Doorley and Garcia (2011) believe that the most common approach to measuring reputation is to take comparative measures against similar organizations; however they also highlight the need for a new approach that will help companies and other organizations measure, monitor and manage their reputations and the factors that contribute to reputation, organization wide, over the long term.

Fombrun and Foss (2001) on the other hand put forward a set of six criteria that an organization can use to gauge its reputation and benchmark its competition. This includes: emotional appeal, products and services, social responsibility, workplace environment, vision and leadership, and financial performance.

Elliot Schreiber (2008) also put forward the reputation 'pillars' approach to measure reputation. The six pillars include: differentiation, relevance, esteem, expectations, knowledge and experience. Companies are advised to measure how they are perceived by stakeholders on each pillar, and then assess and close the gaps between current and desired perceptions.

All of these methods are useful and worth considering, however monitoring and measurement tools should also be selected based on the strategic requirements of the organization and what methods of communication are being used to target stakeholders.

Both quantitative and qualitative methods of evaluating PR and communication activities are needed to demonstrate their effectiveness and reinforce the important role of PR practitioners in performing a reputation management function. This includes evaluating both the output of PR activities through media evaluation techniques; statistics from social networking sites; online analytics and market research activities including surveys with stakeholders and the impact which the activities have on stakeholders including influencing their attitude, opinion and motivating them.

Thankfully the Barcelona Principles are available to provide an industry wide framework for PR practitioners to follow to help them gain credibility and respect for their work by demonstrating the effectiveness of PR as a reputation management function.

Conclusion

'The future of PR is bright because of the growing importance of "reputation management".'

– Matthew Freud

The PR industry has faced many challenges in recent years which have subsequently opened new doors for practitioners who are being forced to become more generalist in their activities. Social media in particular has reinvigorated the role of PR, forcing practitioners to expand their knowledge in this area and opening up organizations to many more stakeholder engagement opportunities, which at the same time has heightened their reputational risk.

At the same time the tough economic climate has also increased the focus on the power of reputation in driving organizational success. This has been a positive move for PR practitioners because although reputation is a 'complex phenomenon' (Davies and Miles 1997), it has to be carefully cultivated and its management undertaken with professionalism and integrity (Dalton 2003). As PR practitioners we are facilitating reputation management because PR helps to shape (Wartick 1992) and enhance an organization's reputation.

As a discipline reputation management is still emerging, but its main principle is that strong reputations result from initiatives and messages that are in tune with the characteristic values and personality of an organization, and which are meaningful to all stakeholders (Fombrun and Foss 2001).

I believe that reputation management is based on PR as a foundation but at the same time I think that the PR industry is slowly but steadily evolving into more of a strategic and holistic discipline of reputation management. This is mainly due to the potential of reputation management to be more readily accepted and respected as a business function.

Looking forward, organizations need to actively listen to their stakeholders as well as creating a two-way channel of communication with them. They also need to operate as if everything they say is in the public domain, because we are most certainly in an era where brand behaviour is as equally if not more important than brand messages and reputation is gained by consistently delivering on brand promises.

Further reading

Beal, A and Strauss, J (2008) *Radically Transparent: Monitoring and managing reputations Online*, Wiley, Hoboken NJ.

Benedixen, M and Abratt, R (2007) Corporate identity, ethics and reputation in supplier-buyer relationships, *Journal of Business Ethics*, **76**, pp 69–82.

Campbell, F E, Herman, R S and Noble, D (2006) Contradictions in 'reputation management', *Journal of Communication Management*, **10** (1): ABI/INFORM Global, pp 191–96.

Chartered Institute of Public Relations (CIPR) Code of Conduct [Online] www.cipr.co.uk/content/membership-networking/code-conduct; Social media guidelines (2009); Social media measurement guidance (2011); Reputation and the board – guidance for PR consultants and board directors (2011).

Cutlip, S M, Center, A H and Broom, G M (2006) *Effective Public Relations*, 9th edn, Pearson/Prentice Hall.

Da-Costa-Greaves, Carl (2010) Corporate reputation [Online] www.studiowide.co.uk/blog/corporate-reputation

Dalton, J and Croft, S (2003) Managing corporate reputation, a specially commissioned report, Thorogood, London.

Dalton, J (2005) 'Reputation Management' – a holistic business tool [Online] www.pr-school-london.com/index.php?page=reputation-management

Davies, G and Miles, L (1997) Reputation management: theory versus practice, *Corporate Reputation Review*, **2** (1), pp 16–27.

Davies, G, Chun, R, da Silva, R and Roper, S (2003) *Corporate Reputation and Competitiveness*, Routledge, London.

Doorley, J and Garcia, H F (2011) *Reputation Management – The key to successful public relations and corporate communication*, 2nd edn, Routledge, London.

Fombrun, C and Foss, C (2001) The Gauge, *Delahaye Medialinks Newsletter of Worldwide Communications Research*, **14** (3), p 11.

Gitomer, J (2011) *Social BOOM!: How to master business social media to brand yourself, sell yourself, sell your product, dominate your industry market, save your butt ... and grind your competition into the dirt*, Pearson, New Jersey.

Griffin, A (2008) *New Strategies for Reputation Management. Gaining Control of Issues, Crises and Corporate Social Responsibility*, Kogan Page, London.

Griffin, A (2010) – The long-term value of reputation to business, following an evening 'In Conversation with Lord Browne', 29 July [Online] http://www.regesterlarkin.com/uploads/the_longterm_value_ ofreputation_to_business.pdf [accessed November 2014].

Griffin, A and Archer, P (2010) Surviving scandal and healing the wounds, Raconteur supplement on Business Ethics, distributed with *The Times*, 23 November, p 11 [Online] http://www.regesterlarkin.com/uploads/the_times_2010.11.23_surviving_scandal_and_healing_the_wounds.pdf [accessed November 2014].

Grunig, L A, Grunig, J E and Dozier, D M (2002) *Excellent Public Relations and Effective Organisations: A study of communication management in three countries*, Routledge, New York.

Grunig, J E and Hunt, T (1984) *Managing Public Relations*, 1st edn, Holt, Rinehart & Winston, US.

Heath, R I and Ni, I (2008) Corporate social responsibility, University of Houston [Online] http://www.instituteforpr.org/corporate-social-responsibility [accessed November 2014].

Huey, A (2009) Reputation management – the newest in public relations [Online] www.media-relations.com/?p=589

Hutton, G, Alexander and Genest (2001) Reputation Management: the new face of corporate public relations, *Public Relations Review, A Global Journal of Research and Comment*, 27 (3), pp 247–61.

Institute for Public Relations, www.instituteforpr.com

Jordan, H (2011) CIPR conference reveals internal comms as essential to external reputation, CIPR Conference – Reputational Influencers, 22 June 2011, CIPR, London.

London School of Public Relations (nd) PR and reputation management [Online] http://www.lspr-education.com/index.php?page=lspr-pr-and-reputation-management [accessed November 2014].

Murray, K and White, J (2005) CEO views on reputation management: a report on the value of public relations, as perceived by organisational leaders, Chime Communications, London [Online] http://chimeplc.com/downloads/reputationkm.pdf [accessed November 2014]

PR Conversations, www.prconversations.com

Regester, M and Larkin, J (2005) *Risk Issues and Crisis Management, A casebook of best practice*, 3rd edn, in *PR in Practice* series, ed Anne Gregory (series editor), Kogan Page/Chartered Institute of Public Relations, London.

Reputation Institute, www.reputationinstitute.com

Reputation Online, www.reputationonline.co.uk

Schreiber, E S (2007) www.brandsandreputation, 31 January [Online] blogspot.com/2007/01/measuring-reputation.html

Schreiber, E S (2008) Reputation, 2 December [Online] http://www.instituteforpr.org/topics/reputation/

Sinclair, A (1993) Approaches to organisational culture and ethics, *Journal of Business Ethics*, 12 (1), pp 63–73.

Tsalikis, J and Fritzsche, D J (1989) Business ethics: a literature review with a focus on marketing ethics, *Journal of Business Ethics*, 8, pp 695–743.

Wartick, S (1992) The relationship between intense media exposure and change in corporate reputation, *Business and Society*, 31 (1), pp 33–49.

PART III
The application of best practice in markets

– an analysis of the application of public relations in different markets

Engineering the future?

13

Using influence to benefit society

ANNE MOIR CHART.PR, MCIPR

This paper was originally written in September 2009. Minor revisions have been made to the original text for this book to reflect developments in media, technology and practice.

Civil engineers are proud of their profession's legacy in the development of human civilization. Until relatively recently, civil engineers were held in high regard. Civil engineers are at the heart of the delivery of the essential infrastructure of energy, water, waste, communications, transport and flood protection, but their perception is that they are not recognized for the contribution they make.

As Peter Head, Fellow of the Institution and a hero of the environment in *Time*[1] magazine, said in his Brunel lecture[2] in June 2008:

> '...that engineers have [the] global experience... which will be essential for success and can design and deliver these... infrastructure systems.'

When engineers can influence the key opinion formers, then the right actions can be taken for a sustainable planet.

This paper argues that civil engineers can achieve their ambition and focuses on how a partnership between engineers and communications professionals can achieve these objectives.

The Institution of Civil Engineers (ICE) exists to serve society. This raison d'être is enshrined in its Royal Charter of 3 June 1828[3] (and subsequently amended):

'To foster and promote the art and science of Civil Engineering' where civil engineering is defined as 'being the art of directing the great sources of power in Nature for the use and convenience of man'.

In 2007 the institution also agreed a new vision[4] to put 'Civil engineers at the heart of society, delivering sustainable development through knowledge, skills and professional expertise'.

The purpose of the institution is to qualify professionals engaged in civil engineering, exchange knowledge and best practice, and promote their contribution to society.

So how can the institution achieve these objectives through its public affairs strategy?

Setting a benchmark

In 2002 a more rigorous approach to analysing and managing member requirements was introduced. Focus groups benchmarked a member satisfaction survey.[5] They identified the activities that were important to members and how satisfied they were with them. Five areas relating to reputation and public affairs were identified out of the top 14 areas of importance.

These stated importance scores are shown below where 1 is not important and 10 is very important:

- the reputation of ICE – 8.85;
- raising the profile of a civil engineer – 8.60;
- raising the importance of civil engineering to society – 8.53;
- encouraging young people into the profession – 8.52;
- influence on politicians and decision-makers – 7.57.

Members see the institution having a role in promoting their skills and expertise for the benefit of society.

They also indicated that they were not satisfied with the institution's performance. The satisfaction scores are shown below with the same rating methodology:

- the reputation of ICE – 7.46;
- raising the profile of a civil engineer – 5.81;
- raising the importance of civil engineering to society – 5.71;
- encouraging young people into the profession – 6.05;
- influence on politicians and decision-makers – 5.24.

This data confirmed that public affairs was important and showed that improvement in overall satisfaction could also support the need to attract and retain members.

Anecdotal evidence also showed that the institution, a leading professional body, had a very low level of recognition amongst its key external stakeholders – government, decision-makers, media, the public and the industry itself.

What public affairs were in place?

Since 2000, the institution had been partnering with Emap[6] to produce a bi-annual 'report card' for UK infrastructure under the title 'The State of the Nation's Infrastructure'.[7] The concept was sound; however the report was based on the opinions of a small panel of members. It gave a short commentary on various sectors[8] of infrastructure, awarded a score[9] for each and identified actions for government. The report had little impact on any of our audiences, received little media coverage and more importantly no follow-through programme was carried out.

The approach needed to change. ICE took full control of the development of the report and the NCE journalists became a media target.

Developing a new strategic approach to public affairs

Several factors were identified for review:

- a lack of a coherent strategy;
- a poorly functioning learned society unable to deliver policy;
- poor level of ongoing interaction with key stakeholders;
- lack of understanding of the needs of the media, lack of spokespeople and low media impact;
- lack of public awareness of the value of civil engineers and their contribution to society.

These issues were all combining to make the institution ineffective when it wanted to move into a strategic leadership role.

For the first time, the external strategy was driven by a communications professional, not an engineer. That presented some issues to be resolved:

- what did communications professionals know about civil engineering?
- what were the profession's views?
- how could communications present the profession's views?
- how could the function of communications gain the trust of the members?
- and how could the strategy balance the needs of society with the needs of the profession?

These questions all had to be addressed. The objectives were to provide a platform to build impact for the profession, to ensure that society was well served and to improve reputation, member satisfaction and trust.

The communications strategy was to create a programme that demonstrated policy thinking from the institution; provided clearer recommendations for action; and was targeted at the key stakeholders and the media, in tone and content. The programme was intended to demonstrate how the profession was acting in the interest of society, through delivering key recommendations for government action by attracting the interest of the public.

Building the State of the Nation's credibility

The first issue to be addressed was how to harness the enthusiasm and expertise of civil engineers, but deliver outputs in the most suitable and effective format?

Balancing these two objectives required a sustained education programme for the active members involved in the programme as they change on a regular basis. Members needed to be aware of the stakeholders' needs as well as understanding the role they play from developing a report to sustained activity after publication.

A new State of the Nation report was developed, written in plain English for a non-engineering audience, with consistent tone of voice and presented in an easy to absorb format, with design to support the content. The panel approach was continued with a more rigorous peer review. A policy position on each sector was then agreed and the score awarded as in the previous format.

The 2003 report[10] was much more robust, although there was still no detailed supporting research. There was a risk of challenge from the membership and a similar risk of challenge from the target audiences. But it was a risk worth taking.

The first report in the new format delivered huge impact:

- the launch event attracted many parliamentarians;
- media impact[11] was significant, including our energy lead story on the front page of *The Guardian*,[12] and TV coverage was obtained for the first time;
- it started the process of public recognition of civil engineers;
- it attracted wide acclaim from members;
- and it was a finalist in the 2004 IPR Excellence Awards.

What made it successful?

The lead media story addressed the issue of diversity of energy supply – one that needs to be understood by the public. It provoked wide debate on future energy sources. At the time of the report launch, in 2003, the public were predominantly anti-nuclear but the mood of the public has now changed[13] as a sense of reality has dawned. In 2009, the government approach to energy included diversity of supply, with nuclear energy as part of the mix and it remains concerned over the security of that supply. These were both strong messages from our 2003 report and ones that have endured over the intervening years. By 2013 nuclear energy topped a YouGov public opinion poll[14] for UK energy's future needs.

The institution believes that its report and its commentary on subsequent energy related infrastructure events[15] were a key factor in stimulating broad debate and widening general understanding of the issues faced in providing enough energy for the future.

Although the institution can rightly claim it had impact on the government policies in this area, that conclusion is difficult to prove. How can its key messages be linked to a change of government policy that takes many years to evolve, even with sustained effort to keep the issue in the public eye through the media and interaction with government?

This lack of evidence of cause and effect highlights the issue that any organization has in measuring its success[16] in public relations[17] and public affairs.[18] It is particularly difficult when the organization wants to change public sector investment in areas that are not particularly vote catching, or that extend beyond the duration of the average parliament.

Whilst the supply of energy is almost in the 'easy to attract attention' category, improving sewerage or maintaining roads do not exactly appeal to the public. So these issues present a constant challenge for the communications professionals to make the engineering messages interesting.

Continuing success?

However, the new programme was the catalyst for change. Over the following years[19] a report was produced annually using the same methodology, but learning and evolving from the previous year,[20] and adding regional activities alongside London centric activity. Each year a media lead story on a different sector was identified – waste, transport and water – with varying impact. The programme was extended to include region specific reports targeted at the former Regional Development Agencies in England and devolved administrations in London, Scotland, Wales and Northern Ireland to widen the sphere of influence. But there was still no formal research to back up the conclusions.

However over the years there were major benefits of the approach:

- more members are now engaged with the institution as regional topic experts;
- a gradual understanding of public affairs and the media emerged;
- UK members participated in email campaigns to their parliamentarians to lobby them to attend the reception and sign an early day motion (703);[21]
- the institution's reputation grew with its key stakeholders, particularly the media and government;
- the institution has become a respected source of independent expertise;
- and satisfaction levels in the member satisfaction survey of 2006 improved (see page 176).

It would have been easy to continue with that approach but the risks were growing.

It was difficult to see significant change to the infrastructure every year, the media story was becoming more difficult to find and the membership was beginning to challenge the need for 'spin' or raising controversy[22] to obtain media coverage. We still did not have research based policies on the topics being covered. Members and stakeholders needed to see tangible evidence to support the institution's views.

It was an annual gamble to put major effort into one project. Too many things could jeopardize success and the return on investment could be highly variable.

In addition managing the logistics of coordinated and simultaneous reports, as the number of regional reports grew, became a logistical challenge and limited the capacity of the organization to cover other areas of public affairs. A new approach was required.

Revitalizing the learned society function

A reform of the learned society function had been taking place in parallel to the public affairs efforts. This was designed to harness the expertise of the members and to ensure that their enthusiasm was channelled into productive outputs to improve the performance of the institution's objectives (see page 174).

One of the most important outputs was policy for the institution. This meant that for the first time clear policy positions were being developed that could be used to underpin public affairs programmes and the objectives of the Royal Charter.

So these new policies and the energy of the members could be used to revise the State of the Nation programme.

The dilemma

The experts that underpin the public affairs agenda are civil engineers, not lobbyists, not communications professionals and many are not experienced in delivering influence. The State of the Nation was now perceived by the active members as essential to that influence and increasing profile. Changing a much-loved format, that had placed the institution on the influence map and was perceived as **the** public affairs agenda, presented a significant challenge.

Attracting the attention of the institution's key stakeholders is a delicate balance between taking a controversial angle and being respected and factual (and potentially dull). Civil engineers are often altruistic and their focus can sometimes be on recognition of their expertise, rather than achieving the change they really want. They expect audiences to be interested, as they believe they have something important to say.

So there was a conflict between what would work in terms of the charitable objectives and what members thought was the right approach. Is it necessary to attract the media's attention? What happens when some of the members do not agree with the experts' views? Do the means justify the end?

All of these questions were addressed in developing a revised strategy.

Getting agreement to a new approach

If the institution's profile was to grow, it could not be dependent on one high cost annual report. The proposed approach was designed to be more rigorous using detailed research provided through members and the industry, as well as outsourced from independent organizations. The scope and final policy would still need to be agreed by the panels of experts. The policy 'bank' could then be used as the core content for topic based reports and influencing activity that would be timely and refined for the target audiences.

Not surprisingly, there was significant resistance to the proposed change. Across the UK some local committees were particularly resistant, as they had formed panels of specialists and had engaged with some members for the first time. Their regional member satisfaction[23] levels had increased and they were reluctant to change a perceived success.

In their view, the State of the Nation was giving them a platform for public affairs. And for those regions that had limited experience and were still building their local reputation, they believed passionately that the State of the Nation would give them what they wanted. They perceived a risk that new strategy might take away the opportunity for the region to have a share of the public voice success that others already enjoyed.

A lengthy process of consultation with the institution's Council,[24] committees and employees was undertaken to show members that their visibility and contribution could be increased through the new approach.

With some reluctance it was agreed to change the format.

Implementing change

In 2008 the new programme was launched with The State of the Nation – Transport.[25] Further publications[26] (see ICE website[27] for later reports) have been developed and used to promote the institution's views. Many regional briefing sheets[28] have also been created to support the topic specific reports. These have all had a longer 'shelf life' in the influencing agenda at national and regional level.

In 2008 a report[29] was published on flooding timed to coincide with the first anniversary of the 2007 floods and the publication of the Pitt review.[30] Discussion with Sir Michael Pitt, a Fellow of ICE, enabled his review to be launched at the institution and allowed the team to take full advantage of media interest[31] in both reports. It demonstrated how influence can be achieved outside the State of the Nation brand.

Using experts supported by independent research and evidence gathering[32] to develop the institution's policy and reports means that the public affairs strategy can deliver more impact, more often. It has more tools[33] at its disposal for regular and behind the scenes public affairs activity. It has more material for briefings, consultation responses and select committee inquiries and more material to support PR statements. It also has robust data to support its conclusions. And it has also allowed more expert members to be involved on specific reports on their field of expertise for a short period.

As a result of this refinement of strategy, the public affairs agenda has also been boosted through more focus across the organization and a dedicated spokesperson, the Director General (a civil engineer), who responds between major reports.

Use of members as key spokespersons can be difficult as members may not be readily available when required and there can be conflict in what the profession is saying versus how their organization might feel, especially when they work for a government body.

Measuring success

As identified earlier this is a major challenge for the institution. However the member satisfaction has given clear data for the members' perceptions. Over the seven surveys[34] to date, the importance factors have been consistent (although this is not measured in later surveys):

- the reputation of ICE;
- raising the profile of a civil engineer;
- raising the importance of civil engineering to society;
- encouraging young people into the profession;
- influence on politicians and decision-makers.

In the early surveys influencing politicians and decision-makers grew in importance more than all the rest. More activity in this area raised expectations; more disasters (natural and failure related) occurred that the public and members saw in the media, and the issue of climate change was highlighted widely.

Looking at satisfaction levels there has been an improvement over the years:

- the reputation of ICE (7.46 now 7.6);
- raising the profile of a civil engineer (5.81 now 6.7);
- raising the importance of civil engineering to society (5.71 rose to 6.61 then not scored);
- encouraging young people into the profession (6.05 now 7.1);
- influence on politicians and decision-makers (5.24 now 6.4).

The influence on politicians and decision-makers has seen a significant increase in perception over the period and that can also be linked to the resulting improvement in encouraging young people into the profession. Also overall satisfaction rates[35] have improved. This improvement is significant for a membership organization with demanding constituents.

A quarterly public opinion survey[36] measures the public's views on infrastructure. Relationships with the media have improved considerably and the response is no longer 'ICE – who?' Major reports regularly receive coverage and AVE was measured even if it is not a favoured option.[37] Ad hoc feedback from stakeholders indicates the institution's activity has improved its reputation.

The final challenge

In order for the members to feel positive about their institution they need to see and hear of the success that the institution is having. Many members are unaware of what is being achieved. A more vigorous approach through print and online member communications was implemented after the 2008 member satisfaction survey and a member communications[38] audit in 2009 confirmed a significant impact as outlined below.

Conclusions

Raising the influence of civil engineers is important for the benefit of society and for engineers themselves. The evolution of the public affairs strategy has addressed the critical requirement for the institution to be respected and sought after as a source of independent engineering expertise. It has enabled engineers to be more involved in the critical decision-making on issues such as flooding, energy and waste.

That is one of the institution's key objectives. Major progress has been made. My involvement in that success was significant.

Leadership of all those involved

Success required leadership to establish the State of the Nation brand and build its credibility with its target audiences and then to evolve a wider public affairs strategy to ensure the programme remained effective. The institution is a leader in its field and its public affairs experience has been sought out by professional bodies from other disciplines and other countries.

Strategy

Throughout the programme the right strategy was critical to ensure impact, growth of reputation and effective use of all the resources involved. I led the development and revisions to that strategy over seven years.

Learning

The public affairs agenda was a process of learning from experience and learning how to influence others to actively support the evolving strategy. By implementing a rigorous learning process, I was able to facilitate the members' trust of professional non-engineering advice.

Innovation

As the perceived success of the programme was growing there was a danger that it could actually fail. Thinking innovatively about how to build on that success and to obtain acceptance to that innovation was an essential part of the leadership of the programme.

Communication

Maintaining a strong focus on communicating what was being done was a key focus of the programme – communicating the value of public affairs and a sustained programme of member communications across a dispersed membership.

Overall I am proud of the difference I made to the institution, now a credible body of expertise that is respected and consulted by a range of stakeholders, and to the improved perception of civil engineering. Members have indicated that they value the improvement in their requirements.

Notes

1 Smith, A (2008) Heroes of the environment, *Time* magazine special report, 24 September [Online] http://www.time.com/time/specials/packages/article/0,28804,1841778_1841780_1841788,00.html

2 Head, P (2008) Brunel lecture, Institution of Civil Engineers Brunel lecture series [Online] http://www.ice.org.uk/getattachment/a32ccc12-a19d-4512-84a5-cf763b923c3b/Entering-the-ecological-age--the-engineer-s-ro-(1).aspx [accessed 3 December 2014].

3 Royal Charter, By-laws, Regulations and Rules of the Institution of Civil Engineers. Rev 2014 [Online] http://www.ice.org.uk/getattachment/94d6954a-d615-4fd9-b64c-1166a0e41d16/ICE-Royal-Charter,-By-laws,-Regulations-and-Rules.aspx [accessed 3 December 2014].

4 Vision, Institution of Civil Engineers, approved by Council, October 2007.

5 ICE Member Satisfaction Survey, 2003, prepared by The Leadership Factor. High performing organizations have ratings of over 8. Overall satisfaction level 66.6 per cent.

6 Emap/Institution of Civil Engineers (ICE) [Online] http://www.emap.com/ [accessed 12 August 2009]. Publishes NCE and NCEI magazines, distributed to members as part of their subscription.

7 Institution of Civil Engineers (2002) State of the Nation, Measuring the quality of the UK's infrastructure [Online] http://www.ice.org.uk/news_events/government_sotn2002.asp [accessed 6 June 2009].

8 Trunk roads and motorways, rail, local roads and transport, water, flood management, energy, urban regeneration and waste.

9 A=Good, B=Fair, C=Average, D=Poor, E=Bad.

10 Institution of Civil Engineers (2003) State of the Nation, report [Online] http://www.ice.org.uk/downloads/statenation_colour_full_03.pdf [accessed 4 July 2009].

11 Media references are included for illustration purposes only and are a small selection of the coverage obtained over the seven-year period.

12 Brown, P (2003) A vision of Britain in 2020: power cuts and the 3-day week, *The Guardian*, 1 July [Online] http://www.guardian.co.uk/science/2003/jul/01/sciencenews.greenpolitics [accessed 4 July 2009].

13 The Nuclear Industry Association (2008) Press release on the results of an Ipsos MORI public opinion poll carried out for the NIA, 4 December [Online] http://www.niauk.org/news/nia-press-releases/pollong-shows-public-support-for-nuclear-is-soaring-1541-125.html [accessed 2 August 2009].

14 RenewableUK (2013) [Online] http://www.renewableuk.com/en/news/press-releases.cfm/2013-02-10-yougov-poll-proves-renewables-still-the popular-choice-after-epic-week-for-wind [accessed 15 December 2014].

15 BBC (2009) news coverage on energy: Tube power failure [Online] http://news.bbc.co.uk/1/hi/england/london/3189755.stm; Security of gas supplies [Online] http://news.bbc.co.uk/1/hi/world/europe/ 4572712.stm; If the lights go out [Online] http://news.bbc.co.uk/ 1/hi/programmes/if/3487048.stm [all accessed 5 July 2009].

16 Lindenmann, W K (1997) Guidelines for measuring the effectiveness of PR programmes and activities, Institute for Public Relations [Online] www.instituteforpr.org17; Wallace, C (2009) The AVE debate: measuring the value of PR, *PR Week*, 6 May.

17 Gray, R (2003) PR examining the evidence, *Campaign*, 7 February [Online] http://www.campaignlive.co.uk/news/170100/PR-EXAMINING-EVIDENCE-measure-effectiveness-PR/?DCMP=ILC-SEARCH [accessed 2 August 2009].

18 ECPA (2004) The State of Public Affairs, 3rd ECPA Annual Conference, 19 February, Brussels.

19 Institution of Civil Engineers (2004) State of the Nation report [Online] http://www.ice.org.uk/downloads//SoN_2004.pdf; BBC (2004) News, 15 June [Online] http://news.bbc.co.uk/1/hi/uk/3808489.stm [accessed 11 July 2009]; Institution of Civil Engineers (2005) State of the Nation report [Online] http://www.ice.org.uk/downloads/state_of_ the_nation_2005.pdf; Institution of Civil Engineers (2006) State of the Nation report [Online] http://www.ice.org.uk/downloads/State%20 of%20the%20Nation%20report%202006.pdf; BBC (2006) News 17 October [Online] http://news.bbc.co.uk/1/hi/uk/6056206.stm [accessed 11 July 2009]; Jha, A (2006) First water ban in decade as drought fears escalate, *The Guardian*, 16 May, p 11 [Online] www.theguardian.com/environment/2006/may/.../water.ethicalliving [accessed 11 July 2009].

20 Introduction of assessment from the Plain English Campaign [Online] http://www.plainenglish.co.uk/

21 HC EDM 703 (2005–6) Letwin, O. Attracted 151 signatures supporting the report and recognizing the work of the profession.

22 Sky (2006) News, 17 October [Online] http://news.sky.com/skynews/ Home/Sky-News-Archive/Article/200806413547367 [accessed 18 July 2009].

23 Institution of Civil Engineers (2006) Member satisfaction survey, prepared by The Leadership Factor, available to CIPR members [Online] http://www.ice.org.uk/

24 Moir, A (2007) Institution of Civil Engineers, Council Paper C25-2007, 6 March.

25 Institution of Civil Engineers (2008) State of the Nation – Transport, October [Online] http://www.ice.org.uk/Information-resources/Document-Library/State-of-the-Nation-2008–Transport [accessed November 2014].

26 Institution of Civil Engineers (2008) Skills and capacities report, January [Online] http://www.ice.org.uk/Information-resources/Document-Library/State-of-the-Nation-2008-Report-Capacity-and-Skil [accessed November 2014]; (2009) Defending critical infrastructure, June [Online] http://www.ice.org.uk/Information-resources/Document-Library/State-of-the-Nation-Defending-Critical-Infrastruc [accessed November 2014].

27 http://www.ice.org.uk/

28 A4 sheets highlighting regional examples of the key messages developed by regional experts [Online] http://www.ice.org.uk/State-of-the-Nation/State-of-the-Nation-archive (see links to right of archive list).

29 Institution of Civil Engineers (2008) Flooding, engineering resilience report, 25 June [Online] http://www.ice.org.uk/Information-resources/Document-Library/Flooding–Engineering-resilience [accessed November 2014].

30 The Pitt Review (2008) Learning lessons from the 2007 floods report, http://webarchive.nationalarchives.gov.uk/20100807034701/http:/archive.cabinetoffice.gov.uk/pittreview/thepittreview/final_report.html [accessed 3 December 2014].

31 UKCIP (2008) Enews, July [Online] http://www.ukcip.org.uk/index.php?id=560&option=com_content&task=view [accessed 12 August 2009]; Eccleston, P (2008) UK too vulnerable to flooding, *Daily Telegraph,* 24 June.

32 BBC (2009) News, June [Online] http://news.bbc.co.uk/1/hi/uk/8116013.stm [accessed 12 August 2009].

33 http://www.ice.org.uk/Information-resources/Infrastructure-policy-and-reports [accessed 25 July 2014].

34 ICE Member satisfaction surveys, 2003, 2006, 2008, 2010, 2011, 2012, 2014, prepared by The Leadership Factor.

35 Overall satisfaction scores 66.6 per cent, 69.8 per cent, 72.9 per cent now 74.1 per cent.

36 Quarterly telephone survey of over 1,000 members of the public carried out by ComRes. Data demographically representative of all British adults.

37 Harrison, K (2009) Why AVEs are a fatally flawed measure of PR effectiveness, http://www.cuttingedgepr.com/ [accessed 12 August 2009].

38 Institution of Civil Engineers (2009) Communications audit, carried out in-house (3,053 respondents), February.

Defining the defence communicator

14

CLARE L PARKER CHART.PR, MCIPR

This paper was originally written in August 2013. Minor revisions have been made to the original text for this book to reflect developments in media, technology and practice.

> 'Positive media relations are not about propaganda... Rather, they are concerned with the enduring requirements of maintaining support for military action carried out on the public's behalf and about sustaining morale of the individuals involved.'
>
> – *Angus Taverner (2005)*[1]

There is much academic literature on the relationship between the British military and traditional mass media of print, radio and television. Often chronological, it critiques the managed relationships with journalists (dedicated war correspondents at that) and production staff representing mass media organizations. More recently, this literature has explored the fragmented demands of direct-to-audience communication through social media platforms, and the dichotomy of the historically slow-moving military mechanisms of releasing public information at odds with responding to the instant gratification of the new media and information environment.

The authors take their cue from conflict for evidence of the health of military public information yet the reality is more diverse. The military performs duties such as humanitarian relief, international engagement, search and rescue operations, recruitment, ceremonial events and public shows – all of which demand public engagement – but gain little exposure to communications research.

There is an enduring public information message in maintaining the relevance of defence in society and the skills required for effective media and communications engagement span wider than message management and relationships with journalists during conflict. Whilst the skills learned and knowledge gained on operations are important and need retaining, so peacetime duties require exposure in the modern and diverse media environment.

Specific challenges are involved in training professional media and communications (M&C) skills to military personnel.[2] There is no career stream for M&C in the British military, unlike their US and Canadian allies for example that have a 'Public Affairs' branch.[3] UK military personnel are posted into M&C roles often without any prior experience, complete the job for between six months and three years, and then may never return to the profession.[4] Many media jobs are 'secondary duties' carried out alongside a primary military task. Furthermore, the Royal Navy, British Army and Royal Air Force all have media specialist reserve forces that have wide experience but are relatively small in number.

A skills gap can exist between civilian M&C staff working in defence – who generally have a professional background in one or more communications disciplines – and military staff who do not, although both are engaged in M&C roles often at high levels of exposure and potential risk. Change had to occur to bring the military skills up to a professional level, with training over a short period of time to make the most of their compressed M&C careers.

This paper will explain how I led and championed the development and implementation of the Defence Media and Communications Competence Framework (the 'Framework') and concludes with wider implications of the Framework, such as building a managed cadre of trained people.

Defence communications organization: background

The governance of M&C engagement in the Ministry of Defence, its agencies[5] and the three services – the Royal Navy, the British Army and the Royal Air Force – is the responsibility of the Director of Defence Communications, who is a senior civil servant. The Directorate of Defence Communications (DDC) sets the direction for all communications activity but the single services and individual departmental organizations are responsible for many aspects of delivery.[6] Media and public engagement is also governed by defence doctrine in the form of Media Operations Joint Doctrine Publication 3-45.1, which instructs military personnel in how to engage with the media and plan for engagement as part of overall military strategy.

DDC operates the departmental 'Press Office' in Whitehall and orchestrates major information campaigns, such as Armed Forces Day, Remembrance Day, and cross-department announcements and maintaining the strategies for operations overseas in conjunction with the Permanent Joint Headquarters (PJHQ). The director is also the Head of Profession for M&C in defence, although it is worth noting that the majority of defence communicators do not work directly to the director in their management structure.

The single services and defence budgetary areas and agencies deliver their particular elements of the overarching Defence communications strategies and take responsibility for devising their own engagement activities, including public relations, internal communication, news management and recruitment. The public engagement activities of ships, units, squadrons and individual establishments are co-ordinated by the single services headquarters but delivered in part by those smaller units.

Responsibility for training military personnel in M&C lies with the Joint Media Operations Centre (JMOC).[7] Formed in 2004, it is a tri-service organization delivering media engagement capability primarily but not exclusively to support operations. It trains and educates military and some civilian staff in M&C engagement both as an individual and collectively by taking part in training exercises.

JMOC staff can also be deployed at short notice to support UK media engagement overseas.

Competence framework concept

In 2008 the government launched The Skills Strategy for Government 2008–2011 which proved the catalyst to a long-held aspiration to enhance and bring alignment to the professional skills of civilian and military staff in M&C.[8] Agreed by permanent secretaries and, for the armed forces the Chief of Defence Staff, the Heads of Profession were tasked with 'setting the standards on professional skills for their staff, helping to shape career and workplace planning and to support professional development'.[9] A pan-defence team was established to devise a set of competence frameworks for each profession (such as finance, analysis, and media) and compose staff development strategies to take into account the needs of both civil service and military staff in those professions.

My work began by analysing an existing competence framework for civil service communications staff across government and assessing its applicability to the military. The 2009 Government Communications Network (GCN)[10] Competency Framework was a prescriptive document covering the skills, knowledge and behaviours expected for all communications roles in government (press office, marketing, strategic communication, planning and measurement, for example).

A skills audit of military personnel in M&C roles raised several issues that would have restricted the precise application of the GCN Framework in its entirety:

- Expertise in M&C generally comes from longevity in the industry. Building on skills and experience would work for the specialist reservists, but regular military personnel having longevity in M&C would be impossible in the current constraints.

- The GCN Framework had a level of skill and knowledge aligned to the grade of the official. Whilst the military has a rank structure and read-across into equivalent ranks of the civil service, research showed that relatively low ranks could be involved in high-level stakeholder engagement and complex media strategy planning and delivery.

- There were separate disciplines (press and media relations, internal, digital and marketing) in addition to the skills of a professional communicator. The skills audit suggested that a unit press officer – based at an Army unit, on a RN ship or RAF station – could be a press officer, event manager, digital specialist and strategist rolled into one.

In consultation with the GCN's Development Adviser's Network and with senior communicators in other government departments that work closest with defence, I amended the GCN Framework into one for defence, ensuring that the main elements were not lost in translation. Indeed, the six headings as described in Table 14.1 remained almost identical and only the detail beneath each heading was subjected to change.

A major adaptation for the Framework was for it to be constructed with the lack of a military career stream and devised so that the most could be made out of a single posting into a M&C role. The aspiration was that the competences would be logged onto an individual's record of service and there was the potential to use these as a suggestion for future postings back into the profession. It was also envisaged to be the basis for a complete overhaul of M&C training in defence, starting at the JMOC (which would become the custodians of the standard), and deliver training robust enough to stand up to the highest standards of pan-defence training documentation and governance.

In hindsight, despite the wide consultation of the concept and my persistence in drafting, adopting the GCN Framework for military personnel and creating the defence Framework was the easiest part of the entire process. The professional recognition of the standards had already been achieved through the GCN, and the senior leadership of defence were aware of the Framework's potential to begin to professionalize military M&C skills; general acceptance across the wider defence communications community would be more challenging.

TABLE 14.1   The six competences of the Defence Media and
Communications Competence Framework

1: Communications – Drafting, layout and design	Produces clear, persuasive and accessible communications products.
2: Channels and Technologies	Uses the most appropriate channels and technologies to deliver communications.
3: Business Knowledge and Communications Environment	Understands defence business and how communication supports it; is aware of the wider communication context and GCN; is fully aware of and applies propriety guidelines.
4: Relationship and Account Management	Understands, responds to and satisfies the communications needs of diverse audiences – clients, government and stakeholder groups, partners, media and employees; builds and maintains constructive relationships and balances different channels.
5: Strategic Marketing and Strategic Communications	Plans, builds and manages delivery of strategies, campaigns and day-to-day marketing and communications services which are based in audience insight and are effective in getting across defence messages, delivered to the highest professional standards; promotes coherent and consistent defence brandings.
6: Evaluation, Research, Evidence	Gathers and interprets data on the effectiveness of communications strategies, campaigns and services and their impact on audience behaviour and business outcomes; identifies improvement opportunities.

Process of development and implementation

In November 2009, the Defence Media and Communications Competence Framework was published and jointly signed by the then
Director of Media and Communications and the Deputy Chief of

Defence Staff (Personnel). By accepting the Framework, defence was on the threshold of attitudinal change regarding communications training and the potential for professionalizing M&C skills into standards recognized outside of the department. As with any business change programme there was a requirement for wide consultation, engagement, defining customer requirements and establishing the governance for its implementation.

Training delivery

The JMOC was already delivering media training courses based upon customer (DDC and the single services) requirements to train personnel to be unit press officers and to conduct media operations[11] overseas. However with the professionalization agenda and the results of the skills audit suggesting a more multi-disciplined approach was needed, the JMOC used the Framework as the authority document to completely overhaul its training content.

The training development team was made up of three career military trainers and myself as the author of the Framework and M&C professional adviser. A catalyst for the design process was a stakeholder engagement day – hosted by a Raytheon Six Sigma facilitator – in order to gain both wider appreciation of the Framework and to gain expert opinion on its validity in developing new training regimes. The event was attended by military and civilian representatives from the single services communications teams, media specialist reservists, PJHQ to represent operational interests, DDC, JMOC staff and members of the media. There were voices supportive of the Framework, but some were sceptical of the benefits it would bring.

The attendees deconstructed the Framework and prioritized the details as to what should be trained in a new course. This led to further work to define what content could be trained in a reasonable length of time, and what parts of the Framework would be developed back in the workplace.

By April 2011, the Defence Communicators' Course (DCC) had been ratified by the Customer Executive Board[12] with content following the narrative of strategic communications engagement.[13] The

Framework suggested – and the customers accepted – the fundamentals of professional M&C practice: a clear vision set at the top of the organization; know the audience one is wishing to reach; craft clear and concise messages tailored to the audience; choose the right (and often multiple) channels to reach and engage with them; and conduct meaningful evaluation. It also embraced clear activity planning, as well as engaging with current media professionals through an evening networking event.

The content was drawn from instructors attending external media and PR training courses and experienced military and civilian staff who had been on operations or were in M&C roles across defence or wider UK government. The Framework had switched military terminology from mass media *management* to a full spectrum of public, media and new media *engagement*. Following wide consultation and recognition of the constraints of time and resource, the DCC awarded students Practitioner level in Competence 1 as a result of in-course assessment and Awareness level in Competences 2–6.

Job profiles and professional development

Part of the development of the Framework through 2009 was to map the desired competence level for every military M&C role – a complex task and perhaps impossible to achieve an end state, constrained by the current process of assigning personnel into roles and the lack of a specific career stream. The concept had been generally accepted in developing training courses but it had yet to be formally ratified across the community.

However, it was set into policy by the MOD Communications Capability Review (December 2011/January 2012), which stated:

'DMC and the Armed Services will review all communication roles against revised core competencies for government communication as part of the new workforce plan to ensure that the right skills mix is available to deliver the Defence Communication Strategy and the requirements of the single services and other key departmental stakeholders.'

In Spring 2012, backed by the Capability Review, that mapping exercise was completed, matching the competence framework with every M&C job across the single services, be they in the headquarters or at unit level, full time or 'double-hatted' roles. This was based upon conversations with a cross section of staff in those roles, asking them to scrutinize the Framework and suggest what level of competence would be required in their job. This document went out for further consultation with the senior managers of communicators in the single services and DDC. Full agreement from the Customer Executive Board was achieved by the Summer. By engaging with the stakeholders and customers, the acceptance of a new approach to developing M&C skills was much easier to achieve.

The Framework was setting the standard for devising training material and establishing an aspirational standard for incumbents into jobs. This aspiration would only be achieved by managing the right people with the right skills into their posting. In other words, the beginning of a cadre of trained, experienced military personnel.

The CIPR was approached to add the DCC to its Continuing Professional Development (CPD) scheme. Students who were CIPR members would be awarded 60 points for successful completion of the DCC. This was a large step in the Framework's development as a tri-Service military course in M&C was receiving recognition from the communications and public relations industry.

Illustration

A challenge for training in M&C is adapting language to suit the audience. Military personnel have terminology exclusive to their own service, let alone the tri-service defence environment. One of the key lessons throughout the DCC is clarity of the message, which is why the students are tested on writing communications material and awarded a practitioner level of Competence 1. There is particular emphasis on two components of the competence:

- 1.p.1 Demonstrates ability to adapt style and language to meet audience needs.

- 1.p.3 Advises policy officials about best practice in media layout and the need to translate complex issues into plain English.

Thus, a ship can be described as both:

'The Type 45 Destroyer, with long-range weapons systems to intercept air threats including super-agile manoeuvring missile with re-attack modes.'

– Naval Technology.com

And as:

'The new Type 45 warship [that] can track and destroy a target the size of a cricket ball travelling at three times the speed of sound.'

– BBC News

Use and engagement

'No matter what the issue – veterans or the budget, personnel or weapons systems – we must engage the public through all channels ... not only with the press, but also with community leaders and stakeholders, to deliver our message as many ways as possible.'

– George Little, Assistant to the United States Secretary of Defense for Public Affairs (2013)[14]

A key function of the Framework is the ability for individuals to use workplace evidence to upgrade their expertise and competence. This means that the initiative is very much on the individual to keep their competences fresh and relevant.

In order to upgrade, the language of the Framework (see Appendix) was changed so that the elements within the competences could be observed and measured. The three levels – Awareness, Practitioner and Expert – were replaced with Describe, Practice and Subject Matter Expert. Version 2.0 was released in November 2012 and upgrading began in January 2013.

The future of the framework and the professionalization agenda

The Competence Framework remains under constant review and the professionalization agenda continues. But the Framework has been forward looking in recognizing the multiple skills of the professional communicator required in today's congested, multi-channel information environment.

The DCC is also kept under review to remain relevant, drawing on the latest developments in the communications industry, best practice and case studies on operations. Civilian students have attended, who are either new to the department (requiring a package that frames M&C in the defence environment) or from other government departments that work closely with the Armed Forces.

As the requirements of the single services change so the Framework has been used to design future training courses and encourage more formal workplace learning. So far the Framework has been addressing the needs of regular personnel and established, full time job roles. Work is required to capture and register the skills and knowledge of the specialist media reservist cadre within the competence structure.

Conclusion

The process of developing and implementing the Defence Media and Communications Competence Framework was a large undertaking, which required business, cultural and attitudinal change. The implementation of the Framework was a series of smaller challenges that endured enthusiastic advocacy and vocal scepticism, which took management, persuasion and conversation to achieve acceptance.

For the first time, the language of the professional M&C industry was being applied to military training bringing some alignment with civilian colleagues. The Framework moved away from traditional media management and public relations opportunity into the engagement strategies required in the modern environment, and training people to be multi-skilled in the M&C disciplines. It has encouraged

M&C staff to professionalize their own skills and broaden their knowledge, including membership of professional institutions.

In 2013, the competence framework model was developing across other military roles. The credibility of the M&C Framework was bolstered by being held as an exemplar in its development and implementation, particularly in defining a programme of training and personal development – with a strong governance structure – matched to an expected set of skills, knowledge and behaviours.

The British military remains some way from creating a professional career stream dedicated to M&C, however the Framework established the practicalities of a cadre of trained and experienced personnel that could be managed into M&C roles. By bringing a more professional approach to M&C, it is also enhancing the reputation of M&C skills and effective planning of information activities within military strategies. These changes can only benefit the quality and professional delivery of the defence message to its audiences.

Appendix

The Defence Media and Communications Competence Framework (Version 2.0)

Section 1 – Introduction

Media and Communications Competence Framework – Version 2.0 20 Dec 12

There have been a number of formal drivers which have acted as a catalyst for the development of the Media and Communications functional competences which are contained in this document. These include:

- The Skills Strategy for Central Government. Signed by the Head of the Civil Service and the Chief of the Defence Staff in 2008, the agenda works to underpin all roles with reference to external standards and/or professional qualifications to make skills portable across Government and in the wider labour marketplace.

- The Defence Skills Framework. A major project to bring skills used by MOD civilians and military personnel together in a single cohesive format to allow the consistent application and recording of skills across defence.

- Changes in the media industry and associated technologies, and academic research into media and communications disciplines.

- Particular challenges in supporting media and communications activities on operations.

The functional competences – which underpin cross-government professional standards in this area – complement and run alongside other competence frameworks, including generic core competences used by MoD civilians and existing military HR practices. They are fundamental in underpinning training and development programmes, career planning and filling posts in media and communications. They will also ensure consistency in media and communications training across defence, whether for short-term postings to operational theatres or a career in this profession, enabling skills to be both relevant and transferable.

Section 2 – Using the Media and Communications Competence Framework

The Media and Communications Competence Framework has been designed to help individuals, line managers and career managers to identify those skills already possessed by individuals, and where they need to be developed to meet the demands of a position and to help the individual progress. It will help the department ensure that it has the right mix of skills to enable it to meet its objectives.

How to use the competence framework effectively

This functional competence framework has primarily been developed to enable effective appointing and skills planning for jobs that fall within the media and communications environment (although it is recognized that these skills may be used or developed in jobs that fall outside this narrow band of jobs). The scope of the media and com-munications 'job family' is identified in Section 3.

Against each of these competences there are three levels of assessment:

TABLE 14.2   Levels of assessment

Level I – Describe	Displays an understanding of what effective performance looks like. Demonstrates some practical application at work. Demonstrated by capability of explaining subject matter.
Level II – Practice	Displays detailed knowledge and understanding and is capable of providing evidence and guidance to others. Demonstrates practical application in a range of work situations.
Level III – Subject Matter Expert	Displays leadership, extensive knowledge and understanding, and is seen as a subject matter expert and a role model for others. Demonstrates consistent practical application in a wide range of work situations.

Individuals, in consultation with line managers and career managers, can use these competences (and levels of assessment) for developing their personal skills profile. In addition, post or position profiles, which outline the skill requirements of a job will identify what the required level of each competence will be to fulfil the responsibilities of a particular post. By mapping the requirements of the job against the abilities of the individual, better informed appointing decisions can be made and as appropriate, development programmes can be devised for individuals to help bridge any skills gap.

Note: For Government Communications Network (GCN) posts and members in defence, Levels I, II and III fall broadly in line with Assistant Information Officer (AIO), Information and Senior Information Officer (IO/SIO) and Grade 7. It is assumed that as you progress through the grades, so you progress through the levels.

Section 3 – The Media and Communications Competence Framework

The Competence Framework comprises the following competences:

- **Competence 1: Communications – drafting, layout and design**
  - This covers the ability to produce clear, persuasive and accessible communications products (oral and written communication content, use of plain English, correct defence design principles, etc).

- **Competence 2: Channels and Technologies**
  - The competence covers the ability to identify and use the most effective and appropriate channels and technologies to reach the right audiences.

- **Competence 3: Business Knowledge and Communications Environment**

  The competence shows an understanding of defence business and how communications supports it; awareness of the wider communication context across government and the GCN; awareness and application of propriety guidance.

- **Competence 4: Relationship and Account Management**
  - This covers the understanding of and responses to the communications requirements of diverse audiences; the ability to build and maintain constructive relationships, and balancing competing demands.

- **Competence 5: Strategic Marketing and Strategic Communications**
  - The competence covers planning, building and delivering strategies, campaigns and day-to-day marketing and communications services, based upon audience insights and are effective in getting across defence messages. Delivering to the highest professional standards and promoting coherent and consistent defence brandings.

- **Competence 6: Evaluation, Research, Evidence**
  - This covers gathering and interpreting data on the effectiveness of communications strategies, campaigns and services and their impact on audience behaviour and business decisions. Ability to identify improvement opportunities.

TABLE 14.3   Competence 1: Communications – Drafting, layout and design

Produces clear, persuasive and accessible communications products.		
Describe	Practice	Subject matter expertise
1.a.1 Describes internal and external audience needs with regard to language and style of message.	1.p.1 Demonstrates ability to adapt style and language to meet audience needs.	1.e.1 Evidence repeated influencing of ministers, senior officers and officials on communication and presentational issues.
1.a.2 Describes the principles of research and need for clear briefings.	1.p.2 Researches and drafts concise and accurate briefings for routine tasks.	1.e.2 Evidence the ability to anticipate the emerging news agenda and where appropriate react to emerging media needs resulting in changed presentational outcomes.
1.a.3 Writes clearly, concisely and accurately in plain English for all formats and describes how to source appropriate imagery.	1.p.3 Advises policy officials about best practice in media layout and the need to translate complex issues into plain English.	1.e.3 Displays authoritative, clear and sensitive spokesmanship with national and international audiences.
1.a.4 Describes the components of a robust communications/media plan.	1.p.4 Confident and able to present in formal, informal and public settings.	1.e.4 Coordinates and delivers a robust communications/ media plan.
1.a.5 Describes the principles of design and their application.	1.p.5 Can draft a logical and considered communications/ media plan.	1.e.5 Evidence the overseeing and scrutinizing of media and communications briefs for the most complex of tasks.
1.a.6 Describes what constitutes an effective design brief and how creative ideas increase the impact of communication products.	1.p.6 Challenges any communications product not up to standard.	
1.a.7 Describes the Defence and Armed Forces corporate visual identity and branding principles.	1.p.7 Prepares and presents effective design briefs and media strategies to a variety of clients and stakeholders.	
	1.p.8 Applies appropriate Defence and Armed Forces corporate identity and branding to communications products.	
	1.p.9 Identifies and anticipates Defence issues that will be of media/public interest and can plan accordingly.	

TABLE 14.4 Competence 2: Channels and technologies

Uses the most effective and appropriate channels and technologies to deliver communications.		
Describe	**Practice**	**Subject matter expertise**
2.a.1 Describes how different channels interact and work best together to achieve objectives.	2.p.1 Demonstrates how blending channel interactions logically enables the achievement of objectives.	2.e.1 Evidence composition of channel strategies to meet the overall defence communications objectives.
2.a.2 Describes the importance of audience access to various channels.	2.p.2 Applies knowledge and research into the rapid changes taking place in the media and communications environment, identifying key trends and their impact on defence communications.	2.e.2 Evidence how advice on the rapid changes taking place in the media and communications environment influenced stakeholders in the defence communications process.
2.a.3 Describes the rapid changes taking place in the media and communications environment, identifying key trends and their impact on defence communications.		
2.a.4 Describes the strengths and weaknesses of new technology in communicating with various audiences.	2.p.3 Assesses and advises on the strengths and weaknesses of new technology in communicating with various audiences.	2.e.3 Monitors and evaluates the strengths and weaknesses of new technology in communicating with various audiences.
2.a.5 Describes the key costs and benefits of using different media channels and describes objective ways to measure their effectiveness.	2.p.4 Evidences managing the key costs and benefits of using different media channels and applies objective ways to measure their effectiveness.	2.e.4 Evidence how the key costs and benefits of using different media channels were articulated to a communications team, along with objective ways to measure their effectiveness.
2.a.6 Describes the channels available to reach specific audiences.	2.p.5 Documents considered analysis of the channels available to reach specific audiences.	
2.a.7 Describes the breadth of print and electronic defence and single service communications channels available to reach target audiences.	2.p.6 Routinely identifies opportunities to promote MOD and Armed Forces messages in a wide range of media channels.	2.e.5 Evidence the building of team capability and knowledge of channels available to reach specific audiences.
2.a.8 Describes how defence uses interactive communications technology to reach and engage with audiences.	2.p.7 Routinely segments audiences to deliver communications through appropriate channels.	2.e.6 Encourages others to identify opportunities to promote MoD and Armed Forces messages in a wide range of media channels.

TABLE 14.4 *continued*

Uses the most effective and appropriate channels and technologies to deliver communications.		
Describe	**Practice**	**Subject matter expertise**
	2.p.8 Routinely uses and advises on the breadth of print and electronic defence and single service communications channels available to reach target audiences. 2.p.9 Applies interactive communications technology and relevant software where appropriate. 2.p.10 Evidences best practice in writing for and engaging with audiences through digital channels.	2.e.7 Advises on the breadth of print and electronic Defence and Single Service communications channels available to reach target audiences. 2.e.8 Evidences management of the application of interactive communications technology and relevant software. 2.e.9 Demonstrates best practice, accessibility and writing for digital channels and is able to provide e-communications advice to colleagues.

TABLE 14.5 Competence 3: Business knowledge and communications environment

Understands defence business and how communication supports it; is aware of the wider communication context and GCN; is fully aware of and applies propriety guidelines.		
Describe	**Practice**	**Subject matter expertise**
3.a.1 Describes the areas of defence relevant to daily work, and has awareness of the basic structure of wider defence, single services and agencies engaged in communications.	3.p.1 Evidence consultation with areas of defence relevant to daily work, and demonstrate working knowledge of other areas of defence, single services and agencies.	3.e.1 Evidence wide consultation with other areas of defence, single services and Agencies with regards to co-ordinating communications activities.
3.a.2 Describes the importance of keeping up to date with communications and media industry developments.	3.p.2 Researches current and evolving communications and media industry developments that may affect defence communications.	3.e.2 Consistently applies key defence, single service and ministerial policy priorities and can evidence advising communications teams on the issues driving these priorities.
3.a.3 Describes the key defence, single service and ministerial policy priorities and the issues driving these.	3.p.3 Demonstrates the application of key defence, single service and ministerial policy priorities and the issues driving these.	3.e.3 Evidence personal involvement with devising the Defence Communications Strategy and/or the strategies of the single services.
3.a.4 Describes the Defence Communications Strategy and the strategies of the singles services.	3.p.4 Demonstrates incorporation of the Defence Communications Strategy and the Strategies of the Singles Services in communications activities planning.	3.e.4 Evidence influencing communications policy and engagement based upon keeping abreast of current affairs and the implications of the broader political/government context, pertaining to how defence is covered by the media.
3.a.5 Describes the role and function of the Directorate of Media and Communications (DMC).	3.p.5 Demonstrates liaison with DMC on pertinent matters.	3.e.5 Evidence the provision of management-level advice on what information can and cannot be released and is coherent in OPSEC, PERSEC and the D Notices.
3.a.6 Describes how to keep up to date with current affairs and is aware of the broader political/government context, and in particular on how defence is covered by the media.	3.p.6 Documents keeping up to date with current affairs and maintaining awareness of the broader political/government context pertaining to how defence is covered by the media.	
3.a.7 Describes what information can and cannot be released and is coherent in OPSEC, PERSEC and the D Notices.		

TABLE 14.5 *continued*

Understands defence business and how communication supports it; is aware of the wider communication context and GCN; is fully aware of and applies propriety guidelines.		
Describe	**Practice**	**Subject matter expertise**
3.a.8 Describes the pressures from and demands of ministers/ senior officers/chief executives and officials and the effect this can have on defence communications.	3.p.7 Advises on what information can and cannot be released and is coherent in OPSEC, PERSEC and the D Notices.	3.e.6 Evidence clear articulation – to a communications team – of the relevant communication audiences and their requirements.
3.a.9 Describes the relevant communication audiences and their requirements.	3.p.8 Applies knowledge of the relevant communication audiences and their requirements during communications planning.	3.e.7 Evidence how advice given to communicators of how other communications disciplines operate was used to inform communication activities.
3.a.10 Describes how identifying the publicity or news values of policy or operational developments impacts on communications activities.	3.p.9 Routinely identifies the publicity or news values of policy or operational developments.	3.e.8 Routinely makes persuasive and objective case to support communications advice.
3.a.11 Describes how other communications disciplines operate.	3.p.10 Applies knowledge of how other communications disciplines operate.	3.e.9 Evidence providing sound strategic/operational-level advice on propriety guidance.
3.a.12 Describes how propriety guidance informs communications activities.	3.p.11 Routinely applies knowledge of propriety guidance.	

TABLE 14.6   Competence 4: Relationship and account management

Understands, responds to and satisfies the communications needs of diverse audiences – clients, government stakeholder groups, partners, media and employees; builds and maintains constructive relationships and balances different demands.		
Describe	**Practice**	**Subject matter expertise**
4.a.1 Describes the key relationships and importance of networks for defence communications.	4.p.1 Demonstrates active engagement with a broad range of internal stakeholders from the single services, policy, finance and other areas in shaping communications.	4.e.1 Evidence coordination of good relationships with a broad range of internal stakeholders from the single services, policy, finance and other areas in shaping communications.
4.a.2 Describes the necessity of engaging with a broad range of internal stakeholders from the single services, policy, finance and other areas in shaping communications.	4.p.2 Demonstrates established and sustained stakeholder relationships using appropriate channels to keep them informed.	4.e.2 Document repeated experience of successfully managing events, including identifying speakers, venues, AV and exhibition suppliers and target audiences.
4.a.3 Describes how to select and sustain stakeholder relationships using appropriate channels to keep them informed.	4.p.3 Demonstrates establishing and improving working relationships with relevant regional defence media and communications officers.	4.e.3 Document responses to analysis of the effects of stakeholder engagement, implementing improvements where necessary.
4.a.4 Describes the importance of developing and maintaining good working relationships with relevant regional defence media and communications officers.	4.p.4 Documents experience of successful event management, including identifying speakers, venues, AV and exhibition suppliers and target audiences.	4.e.4 Routinely ensures the co-ordination of presentation and policy.
4.a.5 Describes the resources required to manage events, including identifying possible speakers, venues, AV and exhibition suppliers, and target audiences.	4.p.5 Evidence developing and nurturing reliable contacts with the print and broadcast media (where appropriate).	4.e.5 Evidence application of relevant and maintained contacts in the media and communications industry.
4.a.6 Describes what constitutes reliable contacts with the print and broadcast media (where appropriate).	4.p.6 Routinely applies analysis of the effects of stakeholder engagement.	

TABLE 14.6 *continued*

Understands, responds to and satisfies the communications needs of diverse audiences – clients, government stakeholder groups, partners, media and employees; builds and maintains constructive relationships and balances different demands.		
Describe	**Practice**	**Subject matter expertise**
4.a.7 Describes the benefits of analysing the effects of stakeholder engagement. 4.a.8 Describes the relationships required with other areas of defence and/or other government departments to ensure co-ordination of presentation and policy.	4.p.7 Documents experience of working closely with other areas of defence and/or other government departments to ensure co-ordination of presentation and policy.	

TABLE 14.7 Competence 5: Strategic marketing and strategic communications

Plans, builds and manages delivery of strategies, campaigns and day to day marketing and communications services which are based on audience insight and are effective in getting across defence messages, delivered to the highest professional standards; promotes coherent and consistent defence brandings.		
Describe	**Practice**	**Subject matter expertise**
5.a.1 Describes the defence and single services key messages. 5.a.2 Describes the process of successful marketing and communication planning activity and suggests creative and innovative ideas.	5.p.1 Demonstrates regular implementation of the principles of effective communication across defence. 5.p.2 Applies defence and single services key messages in communications products.	5.e.1 Evidence involvement in the development and implementation of the principles of effective communication across defence. 5.e.2 Devises defence and single services key messages.

TABLE 14.7   *continued*

Plans, builds and manages delivery of strategies, campaigns and day to day marketing and communications services which are based on audience insight and are effective in getting across defence messages, delivered to the highest professional standards; promotes coherent and consistent defence brandings.		
Describe	**Practice**	**Subject matter expertise**
5.a.3 Describes how communication can contribute to changing attitudes and behaviour.	5.p.3 Routinely contributes to marketing and communication planning activity and translates creative ideas into practical application.	5.e.3 Devises and manages strategic marketing and communication planning activity.
5.a.4 Describes how applying audience segmentation principles in developing communication plans and activities.	5.p.4 Applies audience segmentation in developing communication plans and activities.	5.e.4 Evidence how early engagement with strategic-level cross-departmental teams ensured co-ordination of communications plans and activities.
5.a.5 Describes the importance of early engagement with cross-departmental teams to ensure co-ordination.	5.p.5 Documents early engagement with cross-departmental teams to ensure co-ordination.	5.e.5 Evidence management guidance on business cases for strategic communication solutions.
5.a.6 Describes how to build business cases for communication activities.	5.p.6 Builds in-depth business cases for communication solutions.	5.e.6 Evidence involvement in setting clear, measurable objectives for communications plans.
5.a.7 Describes the objectives of any communications campaign.	5.p.7 Applies knowledge of departmental, single service and/or operational objectives to communications campaigns.	5.e.7 Demonstrates routine consideration of political context in making communications choices.
5.a.8 Describes how communication strategy is built on sound evaluation and evidence.	5.p.8 Constructs communications strategies and plans based on sound evaluation and evidence.	5.e.8 Evidence experience in mapping out departmental activities and events in order to develop clear communication themes.
5.a.9 Describes the political context of choosing communication activities.	5.p.9 Demonstrates consideration of political context in choosing communication activities.	5.e.9 Coordinates communications teams in order to devise key messages for relevant audience segmentation.
5.a.10 Describes the importance of mapping out departmental activities and events in support of clear communication themes.	5.p.10 Maps out departmental activities and events in support of clear communication themes.	
	5.p.11 Documents construction of key messages for relevant audience segmentation.	

TABLE 14.8   Competence 6: Evaluation, research, evidence

Gathers and interprets data on the effectiveness of communication strategies, campaigns and services and their impact on audience behaviour and business outcomes; identifies improvement opportunities.		
Describe	**Practice**	**Subject matter expertise**
6.a.1 Describes the critical factors within evaluation and research to enable informing the defence communications agenda.	6.p.1 Presents analysis of market research in order to inform communications and media products.	6.e.1 Ensures evaluation is embedded into communications activity of the team.
6.a.2 Describes the mechanisms to ensure that evaluation is embedded into communication activities.	6.p.2 Evidence where evaluation processes have been embedded into communications activity.	6.e.2 Evidence how sharing research data with other defence stakeholders in communications objectives has influenced strategy.
6.a.3 Describes the dominant media and communications research principles and associated methodologies.	6.p.3 Demonstrates where research principles and methodologies have been employed in defence communications activities.	6.e.3 Evidence application of wide knowledge of the full spectrum of data sources, including academic and commercial solutions.
6.a.4 Describes the processes to collect audience feedback and evaluate the effectiveness of defence communication activities.	6.p.4 Demonstrate where evidence has directly influenced communication strategy and planning activities.	6.e.4 Evidence the commissioning and contract management of research projects, and how the results were shared to inform future communications activities.
6.a.5 Describes how to analyse research data against defined objectives to produce summary reports into communications activities.	6.p.5 Document the analysis of research data against defined objectives to produce summary reports.	
6.a.6 Describes how to measure results against communications goals/objectives.	6.p.6 Demonstrate measuring results against communications goals/objectives.	
6.a.7 Describes the data sources that could contribute to analysing market and/or audience segmentation.	6.p.7 Applies data sources that could contribute to a market and/or audience segmentation.	

TABLE 14.8 *continued*

Gathers and interprets data on the effectiveness of communication strategies, campaigns and services and their impact on audience behaviour and business outcomes; identifies improvement opportunities.		
Describe	**Practice**	**Subject matter expertise**
6.a.8 Describes the components of an effective research brief. 6.a.9 Describes the research conducted in the wider defence community and its impact on defence/ single service/operational communications plans.	6.p.8 Manages research projects against specified objectives and contract management criteria. 6.p.9 Applies knowledge of wider defence research and its impact on DMC and single service communications plans.	

Further reading

BBC (2012) HMS Daring embarks on maiden deployment to the Middle East, News [Online] http://www.bbc.co.uk/news/uk-england-hampshire-16496160 [accessed August 2013].

Defence Media Operations Centre (DMOC) The Defence Communicators' Course [Online] http://www.raf.mod.uk/idtraf/courses/defencecommunicatorscoursedcc.cfm [accessed August 2013].

Ministry of Defence (2007) Media Operations Joint Doctrine Publication 3-45.1, Development, Concepts and Doctrine Centre (DCDC), Crown Copyright.

Ministry of Defence (2011) Getting MoD's Message Out, March [Online] https://www.gov.uk/government/news/getting-mods-message-out [accessed August 2013].

Ministry of Defence (2012) The 2011/2012 MOD Communications Capability Review [Online] https://gcn.civilservice.gov.uk/wp-content/uploads/2012/06/MOD-Communications-Capability-Review-rd-format-1.pdf [accessed August 2013].

Ministry of Defence (2012) Joint Doctrine Note JDN 1/12 Strategic Communication: The Defence Contribution [Online] https://www.gov.uk/government/publications/joint-doctrine-note-1-12-strategic-communication-the-defence-contribution [accessed August 2013].

NATO (2011) Military Public Affairs Policy (MC 0457/2, February)
[Online] http://www.nato.int/ims/docu/mil-pol-pub-affairs-en.pdf
[accessed August 2013].

Naval-Technology.com (nd) Type 45 Daring Class Destroyer, United
Kingdom [Online] http://www.naval-technology.com/projects/horizon/
[accessed August 2013].

Notes

1 Learning the lessons of the 20th century: the evolution in British military attitude to the media on operations and in war, in *War and the Media: Reportage and Propaganda, 1900–2003*, eds M Connelly and D Welch (2004), I B Tauris, London, p 274.

2 I have used 'M&C' as it is the accepted acronym for media and communications within defence. It also reiterates that the majority of such job roles in defence are multi-disciplined, ranging from press management and escorting duties through to social media and public events.

3 NATO defines public affairs as 'the function responsible to promote NATO's military aims and objectives to audiences in order to enhance awareness and understanding of military aspects of the alliance. This includes planning and conducting external and internal communications, and community relations.' From NATO Military Public Affairs Policy (MC 0457/2, February 2011).

4 Referenced by Rid, T and Hecker, M (2009) *War 2.0: Irregular Warfare in the Information Age*, Praeger Security International, Westport, pp 79–100.

5 Such as the Defence Scientific and Technology Laboratory (DSTL) and the Defence Infrastructure Organization (DIO) for example.

6 DDC came into being on 1 September 2014. During the development of the Competence Framework, the organization was known as the Directorate of Media and Communications (DMC).

7 The JMOC came into being at the end of May 2014. Previously it was known as the Defence Media Operations Centre (DMOC).

8 From http://www.civilservice.gov.uk/wp-content/uploads/2011/09/embed-profskills-Apr10_tcm6-36433.pdf [accessed August 2013].

9 From http://www.civilservice.gov.uk/wp-content/uploads/2011/09/embed-profskills-Apr10_tcm6-36433.pdf [accessed August 2013].

10 In April 2014, the Government Communications Network became the Government Communications Service (GCS).

11 Media ops is defined in defence doctrine (JDP 3-45.1) as 'That line of activity developed to ensure timely, accurate and effective provision [through the media] of Public Information (P Info) and implementation of Public Relations (PR) policy within the operational environment whilst maintaining Operations Security.'

12 The Customer Executive Board (CEB) for M&C is attended by senior staff from DDC, the single service media organizations and PJHQ. It is their responsibility to set the requirement for media and communications training conducted at the JMOC ensuring that it meets their needs, as well as deciding which people will attend the courses.

13 There is no single agreed academic definition of strategic communication[s] in either professional or academic circles although it is a term familiar in the military. For the purposes of the DCC, the definition was adopted from the UK's Joint Doctrine Note of 2011, revised in 2012 (see references above) and drew upon the practice of co-ordinated, integrated and synchronized Corporate Communications (see Cornelissen).

14 US Department of Defense (2013) Pentagon spokesman: public affairs must change with times, 25 July [Online] http://www.defense.gov/news/newsarticle.aspx?id=120522 [accessed August 2013].

The evolution of UK public relations consultancies from 1984 to 2009

15

JANE HOWARD CHART.PR, FCIPR

This paper was originally written in August 2008 and updated in 2010 and 2011. Minor edits have been made to the original text for this book to reduce the length.

In 1984, UK public relations (PR) consultancies were showing growing confidence in managing their clients' media relationships.

David Churchill, consumer affairs correspondent of the *Financial Times*, commented on research from AGB Communications, The Growth in Understanding the Role of PR, which found that employing a PR agency brought the advantage of, 'greater expertise and better knowledge of the media than in-house departments.' Marketing directors from the 155 companies surveyed spoke of their 'confidence and belief that the profession of PR has matured.' They saw the PR consultancy's role as creating 'a favourable image'.

The outputs from PR consultancies were not seen to be measurable, but this did not appear to diminish their popularity. Often, PR was described as a subset of an advertising campaign. Total annual fees from the Public Relations Consultants Association's (PRCA) 113 member consultancies were estimated to be £2.5 million in the *PRCA Yearbook* of 1984.

In 1985 aspiring PR consultants were advised by the *PRCA Yearbook* 'to gain some first hand, relevant experience of industry, local government, or law' for a couple of years before applying to join a consultancy. Or, it was conceded, 'many entrants qualify through the secretarial route.' Many existing practitioners had come to PR from journalism.

Anthony Thorncroft, also from the *Financial Times*, provided an external context to the PR consultancy world in saying, 'most companies have never used a PR consultancy; many have little clear idea of what PR can do'.

During the next two decades PR changed from being simply a media specialism to being at the heart of strategic reputation management.

A 2005 report, The Economic Significance of Public Relations, by the Centre for Economics and Business Research Ltd, confirmed this evolution, saying that PR is now 'a vital part of so many organizations. PR is now firmly entrenched in business, government and the charitable sector, represented increasingly at board-level. (It has) developed well beyond traditional media work.'

Evolution of UK PR consultancies

PR consultancies also developed and in 2005 they employed on average around 18 per cent of the UK's 48,000 consultants, contributing about 20 per cent of both the turnover and profit of the PR sector.

The same report said: 'Current combined annual turnover of public relations consultancies, agencies and freelancers is estimated to be £1.2 billion.'

PR Week's 2009 Top 150 Consultancies: 24 April 2009 cited the top 150 PR consultancies in 2008 as employing 7,990 staff, a reduction in total numbers of about seven and a half per cent from the 2005 total. Unfortunately, *PR Week* does not try to estimate total consultancy turnover because of the reporting restrictions arising from the 2002 Sarbanes-Oxley Act.

More up to date information is provided by The Bellwether Report, which is published by the Institute of Practitioners in Advertising and is a market monitor, updated quarterly.

It looks at the PR sector as a whole and estimates total UK annual PR turnover at around £2,430 million to £2,835 million.

All estimates show that PR consultancies have grown and thrived during the last 25 years. In this paper I look at some of the main factors shaping this evolution.

1984–89: The PR consultancy as a source of editorial expertise

A time of consultancy consolidation and specialization in a context of business deregulation, increasing wealth and growing environmental awareness.

In 1985, the FTSE Index of the UK's 100 most highly capitalized UK companies reached 1,000 for the first time and in November the next year, 'Big Bang' deregulated City dealings. British Telecom, British Gas and the electricity boards were privatized and bus companies deregulated. Rules regarding the promotion of professionals, such as accountants and lawyers, were relaxed. Spending on health services grew. Healthcare communications emerged as a specialism and expert financial PR consultancies managed organizations' investor relations and benefitted from the boom in stock market listings.

The *PRCA Yearbook* reported consultancy fees as totalling £25 million in 1985, attributing this to factors including the 'growing complexity of the marketplace, the development of consumer and environmental pressure groups, and the rising demand for information, employer and social legislation.' Consultancies often described their role as being responsible for 'creating the climate of opinion in which the sale can be made'.

A trend was emerging amongst PR consultants that they should not only be disseminating clients' policy, they should also be helping to shape it.

The same publication also described PR companies as having seven main areas of operation: marketing, financial PR, employee, community and government relations, international and, most importantly, media relations, where press coverage was described as the 'backbone' of most PR programmes.

'Single Issue' pressure groups became a feature of daily life and everyone watched closely when Greenpeace re-wrote consumer campaigning rules during the Piper Alpha oil rig disaster, which took Shell so much by surprise.

Exxon Valdez's Alaskan oil spillage demonstrated what impassioned communities could achieve when faced with unresponsive, remote organizations. Formerly, blue-chip companies had imagined them-selves impervious to the agendas of activists and 'citizen power'. PR managers responded with a wide array of crisis and issues scenario planning.

In addition, general public health scares, such as radio-active fall out from Chernobyl in 1986 and bovine spongiform encephalopathy (BSE), commonly known as mad-cow disease, in 1990 galvanized interest and industry groups into communicating more effectively with their customers and business partners.

For the first time, the parent company became identified with its brands and organizations and more accountable for their actions, prompting better communications.

This was a period when organizations recognized that simply issuing literature was not sufficient to maintain their reputation.

However, the tendency was still to give tactical advice, which had not been developed in conjunction with clients' marketing or business plans.

Whilst those in the sector were confident, outsiders often had different views; 40 per cent of the marketing managers interviewed in AGB's Communications survey said that they still saw public relations as the 'poor relation to advertising' and cited uncertainties about the cost-effectiveness of PR as a justification for this comment. When referred to by those outside the sector, this research found that PR was often considered to be the 'promotion of goods by non-advertising means' or 'by subtle means'. It was felt by a majority of respondents that PR had a 'fuzzy relationship to advertising'.

Jim Surguy, Harvest Consulting, explained the marketing sector's perspective on PR consultancies, 'In the early eighties escalating costs for TV commercials made PR activity seem a cheaper, and to some, a more effective medium. So, companies came to appreciate the importance of narrow-casting – reaching audiences through means less all-embracing than advertising. The importance of identifying and communicating to particular target groups become more widely recognized and practiced and this in turn led to a rapid growth in PR consultancies.'

In 1987, Dr Danny Moss of Manchester Metropolitan University set up the first formal PR qualification, a masters degree, at Stirling University. He said, 'There was a view that PR was best taught at postgraduate level. However, until the mid 1990's, when a European PR research symposium was created, most of the theory came from the US'. Public Relations had been taught in American universities since 1922, when the first course was established at New York University.

In 1989 an *Economist* article noted, 'Corporate communications (a term it used synonymously with PR) is now at the same stage in its development as marketing was in the early 1960s. Companies know it's important but are not sure how to go about it or what skills it entails.'

1991–99: PR as part of the marketing mix

PR secures its position as a key element of integrated marketing campaigns. Privatizations, building societies de-mutualizing and the National Lottery launch create substantial PR budgets, which demonstrate returns on investment.

In 1991, Kingston Smith W1 published its first Financial Performance of Marketing Services Companies. Public relations had its own section, confirming its role as part of the marketing mix.

The coal industry, Railtrack, National Power and Power-Gen all privatized. On 14 November 1994 the first draw of the National Lottery took place. Later, our Millennium Bug was much promoted.

Big issue, multi-audience education campaigns became common and PR consultancies joined other marketing disciplines in providing integrated communications. In the 10 years since 1985, the *PRCA Yearbook* showed that the number of PR accounts with annual fees over £1 million rose threefold to 39.

Management of this scale of resource necessitated greater professionalism in project planning, execution and in evaluation. Consultancy Codes of Practice were created, for parliamentary advisers, for health care and for investor relations. The PRCA's Professional Charter complemented that of the IPR, forerunner of today's CIPR.

In 1999 the Consultancy Management Standard (CMS) was launched to improve industry standards, consolidate professionalism and differentiate those companies that attained it.

General business practice was also formalizing processes and standards, with Customer Relationship Management (CRM), Total Quality Management (TQM), Investors in People and ISO 9000 gaining acceptance during this period.

There was a growing understanding that business operated in a pluralist context where communications had to be two-way.

As media channels to consumers multiplied influencing them through advertising was often seen to be disproportionately expensive. PR campaigns became a popular choice because of their cost-effectiveness in reaching and building relationships with a wide range of stakeholder groups.

The impact of big issue PR campaigns often clearly dwarfed that generated by the concurrent advertising programme and budget holders, aided by PR consultancy managers, came to question which marketing discipline delivered the best return on investment.

Jon White, a Cranfield Business School professor, predicted that the 'complexity of the business environment, international developments, changing social expectations regarding economic growth and the role of large organizations will all reinforce the importance of PR tasks in the immediate future.' He was advocating that PR should be, 'an essential part of modern management' and that practitioners should be seen as 'management advisers'. This was the period when 'strategic' and 'management by objectives' became popular concepts with PR consultants.

During this period, PR consultancies began to re-define their roles, beyond media relations towards reputation management.

Kingston Smith's analysis showed that specialists were usually highly profitable and new financial, technology, consumer, lobbying and corporate consultancies were created. 'Perception management' was a popular consultancy service which usually included the analysis and then ongoing management of an organization's internal and external relationships and its business issues.

Established, generalist businesses tended to be less competitive. This was partly due to the shift away from charging clients a mark up for bought in goods and services. Instead, profits had to come from core fee revenues.

Some found they could not charge premium rates for what was perceived to be low-value work. Correctly pricing and executing PR deliverables, 'over servicing', was a recurrent problem, shown in the consultancy accounts analysed by Kingston Smith W1 during this period.

However, for those who could take advantage of it, developing technologies and increasing numbers of media and media channels encouraged more rigorous campaign planning, programmes which had greater impact and results that could change business performance.

In 1993 university status was given to polytechnics, assisting the rapid expansion of degree-level public relations and communications qualifications. Many more PR practitioners were becoming formally educated. In 1999, there were already 18 IPR approved PR courses at 15 institutions and the next year the IPR set up a CPD scheme.

2000–09: More than marketing support: increasing expertise, increasing influence

May 2000 – internet shares fall. September 2001's terrorist attacks were followed by the collapse of Enron, the US's eighth largest company, and WorldCom, the biggest corporate failure then to date. Accountancy and business regulations are tightened. However, growth is re-established until 2007 and the FTSE hits an all-time high in February that year.

Buoyed by general economic growth, quango and government invest-ment where the Phillis Review of government communications had recommended more direct communications to the public, demand for PR campaigns continued to grow. In July 2009 the COI became the UK's largest advertiser. Agencies competed for resource with in-house departments and in both, PR became more than 'marketing support'.

In 2000 the trade association asked 'Is PR part of marketing?' and answered itself:

'Most PR firms claim their services are part of the marketing process... However, some firms, such as political lobbyists or charity workers would claim they are more in the business of promoting a cause of developing an understanding.'

These years see PR consultancy managers grappling with an array of pressures that varied according to the overall business climate. These included problems arising from clients becoming more efficient in buying PR services, of competitive pressures from other consultancies or other marketing disciplines and, difficulties in securing talented professionals who now had in-house careers as options. Appendix 1 shows which business issues were seen to be most important over this period.

Kingston Smith's analysis shows that, for many, the early years were a time for restructuring their PR consultancies with 17 of the top 30 companies, reporting exceptional costs. However, there was still much profitable business to be won.

In 2001 there were more than 84 accounts with fees in excess of £1 million. Many agencies were created, almost all specializing in some way. There were those with traditional expertise and some with new skills for public sector, not for profit and CSR campaigns. Not only did specialists thrive, but the larger consultancies created or invested in a wider range of skills so that their businesses could reflect their clients' organizations.

Often, the consultancy took on the role as interpreter of the external environment which had grown to be much more complex.

Businesses tended to communicate along functional reporting lines and could be inward-looking, so the external perspective provided by the PR consultancy was often valuable.

E-mail to desk was now universal and with it came access to many forms of internet-based communications data which had not previously existed. As with many other businesses, the availability of online intelligence for PR increased exponentially.

This facilitated the consultancy's traditional role as media-intermediary and offered opportunities for wide-ranging corporate advice, the principles of which were much more generally available. 'Comply or explain' the Higgs Review in 2003, told boards, advocating greater disclosure of organizations' governance practices.

By 2006, mainstream media had adopted climate as a newsworthy issue and alongside awareness of a relationship to the environment grew a similar interest in the relationship to the community. This affects organizations, their employees, their products and services.

Reputation reporting became commonplace with consultancies positioning themselves as 'reputation managers'.

The end of this period sees the beginning of a seismic change that continues today in the UK's media landscape. Appendices 2, 3, and 4 chart the declining circulations of UK national, regional and free newspapers; of sales of consumer magazines and the start of the decline in television advertising expenditure.

Consultancies were beginning to find their positions as interpreters of the media landscape challenged by digital businesses. Business would no longer work in a predominantly UK-centric manner and consultancies had to adapt to manage and measure this commentary at the same time as dealing with competitors to their long-established roles of content creators. New specialist skills were urgently needed, and at this time, were in relatively short supply. Consultancies themselves had to adapt quickly to be able to cope with complexities in the external environment.

Further reading

Centre for Economic and Business Research (1995) The economic significance of public relations, Centre for Economic and Business Research, London [Online] http://www.cebr.com/

CIPR, http://www.cipr.co.uk/

Institute of Practitioners in Advertising, The Bellwether Report, London [Online] http://www.ipa.co.uk/

International Monetary Fund (IMF), http://www.imf.org/external/index.htm

Kingston Smith W1 (2001–07) The financial performance of marketing services companies, Kingston Smith LLP, London [Online] http://www.kingstonsmith.co.uk/content/conKsResourcePublication/497

Office for National Statistics (ONS), http://www.statistics.gov.uk/hub/index.html

PRCA (1985 to 2008) *The PRCA Yearbook*, Public Relations Consultancy Association, London [Online] http://www.prca.org.uk/

Surguy, Jim, senior partner, Harvest Consulting, http://www.jimsurguy.com/

UCAS, http://www.ucas.ac.uk/

Appendix 1

TABLE 15.1 Top threats to the PR industry over time

	2001	2002	2003	2004	2005	2006	2007	2008	2009
Economic slowdown	3	1	1	4	3	4	9	1	1
Client commercial pressure	N/A	5	2	1	2	2	2	3	2
Competitors buying business	N/A	9	4	2	7	7	8	5	3
Lack of evaluation	2	3	7	5	4	3	3	4	4
Other disciplines encroaching	N/A	N/A	N/A	8	12	8	7	6=	5
Procurement professionals	N/A	N/A	9	7	6	5	4	6=	6=
Instability of client relationships	N/A	7	6	6	5	6	6	10	6=
Cost of new business pitches	N/A	N/A	N/A	11	9	10	10	9	8
Shortage of skilled consultants	1	4	8	3	1	1	1	2	9
Staff poaching by competitors	6	10	12	12	11	9	5	8	10

SOURCE: PRCA Benchmarking study, March 2009.

NOTE: Each year PR Consultancy CEOs rank the listed 10 'threats' in priority order, with 1 being the most serious and 10 the least serious. The table above shows how perceived business problems change in importance over time.

Appendix 2

TABLE 15.2   Sales of UK newspapers (millions of copies sold)
1983–2008

Newspapers	National newspapers	Regional newspapers	Free newspapers
1983	5,734	2,793	1,555
1984	5,860	2,767	1,638
1985	5,703	2,733	1,846
1990	5,537	2,588	2,023
1995	5,206	2,277	1,648
2000	4,692	2,104	1,562
2005	4,006	1,746	1,526
2008	3,906	1,482	1,695

SOURCE: *The Advertising Statistics Yearbook 2009.*

Appendix 3

TABLE 15.3   Sales of UK magazines 1983–2008

Consumer magazines	Copies sold (millions)
1983	1,638
1984	1,694
1985	1,537
1990	1,239
1995	1,365
2000	1,305
2005	1,328
2008	1,190

SOURCE: *The Advertising Statistics Yearbook 2009.*

Appendix 4

TABLE 15.4 UK advertising expenditure sales 1983–2008

TV	Total advertising expenditure (£m)
1983	978
1984	1,085
1985	1,186
1990	2,004
1995	2,667
2000	3,950
2005	4,097
2008	3,819

SOURCE: *The Advertising Statistics Yearbook 2009.*

PART IV
International

– the impact of
the globalization
of markets on
public relations

What does it take to be a global communications professional?

16

DAVID CRUNDWELL CHART.PR, FCIPR

This paper was originally written in August 2009. Minor edits have been made to the original text for publication.

This essay was first drafted in 2008–09. When reviewing it for publication in 2015 I was intrigued to see that my views haven't changed – only grown stronger.

The original goal was to propose a formula that could be applied by anyone with sufficient experience to help them bridge to becoming a successful global communications professional.

In reaching its conclusion the paper also offered a number of templates that could be applied to understanding the environment in which such a professional operates and enables them to change perspective to build a more global outlook.

It is my hypothesis too that global communicators should not be perceived to be limited by titles. A communicator with Transport for London (TfL) is as 'global' (working in a heavily multicultural city such as London) as is the 'Head of Global Communications' for say IBM, Kelloggs or Coca-Cola.

Why are we here as communicators?

Every organization has some need to be commercial in its outlook – none exist without reason, structure and responsibilities. How those manifest themselves may vary according to local laws or cultural dependencies.

As communicators, regardless of our discipline, our aim is to aid organizations in working more efficiently: to be the oil in the gearbox in both behaviours and professional advice. We must embody the ethos and culture of the organization more than any other area of the business and must frequently act as the moral compass for decision-making.

At every level we should also act as navigators ensuring that the organization avoids pitfalls that would interrupt the growth of the business.

For example, history is littered with individuals vainly trying to avoid a story crossing borders. As legislation and cultures clash with the new premise that the internet is a basic human right, control of information is impossible. This reinforces the need for 'good communication', that demands that we get it 'right first time'.

So what is good communication?

What are we aiming to achieve in our role as professional communicators? Good communication has, for me, seven key elements:

- *Involving*
- *Client driven*
- *Benefit focused (both those that are functional and emotional benefits)*
- *Convincing*
- *True to our brand character*
- *Consistent*
- *Measurable*

Involving: do your communications have humour and touch the emotions? Are they visually arresting, and do they contain the unexpected?

Client-driven: do you know your target and do you understand the social trends that affect them? Can you offer key consumer insights and demonstrate rational and emotional benefits?

Benefit-focused: are your communications relevant and distinctive; do they show single-mindedness? Are they consistent and do they have both a rational and emotional benefit?

Convincing: are your communications credible and honest? Will they build trust, stir interest and consideration – and will they inspire action?

True to brand character: will your communications help maintain the brand's distinctive personality; strengthen the emotional ties between the consumer and the client and will they encourage loyalty?

Will they allow for consistency: can you maintain a high level of executional quality, and still foster a level of long-run continuity? In other words, can you stick with them and own them?

And last but not least:

Measurement: can you achieve both quantitative and qualitative measurement? Can you show change in positive consideration and can you prove behavioural change?

I would argue that those rules above, adapted from those used by a former colleague in the motor industry, are as good a place to start as any.

So what does it take?

At the most basic there are two things a communicator should have: a toolbox of collateral, and the skill and brainpower to use those resources effectively.

What do I mean by toolbox? The hardware to research and create your message, and the technology to publish it. The need for brainpower is more obvious; I do not mean a high IQ, but the brainpower to use the tools at your disposal efficiently.

But alone neither the core elements of a *Toolbox* + a *Brain* are sufficient. The use of tools alone will only give a short-term fix. With just a brain and no channels to communicate through improvement in message delivery is unlikely.

So there must be something else – and the first step to discovering this 'X factor' requires a greater understanding of the world around us.

The psychology of persuasion

Measurement of communications campaigns causes much debate and angst among professionals. As much as quantity, or quality, of coverage is a good thing it is nothing compared to the ability to change 'consideration' for a brand or product. It is better still if we can change attitudes and then behaviours.

Why do we have 'attitudes' in the first place? Research by Sharon Shavitt in 1989 (Individual differences in consumer attitudes and behavior, Association for Consumer Research: Provo UT, 1989) argued that attitudes fulfil four major functions:

- knowledge function, where attitudes contain a limited amount of information about objects, and help us relate to those objects;

- utilitarian function, where attitudes assist us in behaving in ways likely to produce rewards and avoid punishment;

- self-esteem maintenance, where we use attitude to align ourselves with liked objects that can maintain, or enhance, our self-esteem; say as an early adopter of technology;

- social identity function, where our attitudes can provide a way of expressing our personal values and identifying with social groups perceived as endorsing the same attitudes.

The study of attitudes and behavioural change by psychologists began, not driven by any desire to understand the skills required for global communicators, but to assist the world of preventative medicine: discovering how doctors could persuade people to do things they did not want to do.

After understanding why we have attitudes, it is important to have a framework for understanding the factors behind persuasion in creating those attitudes.

William J McGuire of Yale University in 1969 (writing in the *Handbook of Social Psychology*) described five factors impacting persuasion:

- Source: these can differ greatly in attractiveness, power and credibility. The effectiveness of the source divides into two categories: a 'reporting bias' (how much we think the source is likely to be telling the truth) and a 'knowledge bias' (is the source's knowledge likely to make their message accurate?).

- Message: some obviously will have more appeal than others to the audience, but should it be presented as harsh and direct, or balanced telling both sides of the story?

- Channel: the more sensory channels that are targeted, the better.

- Recipient: what level of attention are they paying, what about their personality, IQ and pre-existing attitudes? Does the recipient show the 'third person effect' (Davison, W P (1983). The third person effect in communication, *Public Opinion Quarterly*, 47, pp 1–15), where the recipient feels that the message is more relevant to others than themselves?

- Target behaviour: small changes in actions are a lot easier to achieve than big ones.

Saying it with words, or not

It is clear that a person's physical environment will also affect how they communicate.

An oft quoted example is that of the Inuit and their many words for snow. With snow having a greater day-to-day significance to the Arctic-dwelling Inuit than for almost any other culture, so their language reflects its importance, and need for subtlety.

Munroe and Winters (Cross-Cultural Correlates of the Consonant-Vowel (CV) Syllable) in 1996 showed that language in hot countries differs from that in cold countries.

They suggest that the greater variation in vowels and consonants found in hot countries would have made it easier to communicate over long distances outdoors, while people who live in cold countries evolved a language with more consonant sounds through speaking in sheltered or indoor settings.

Saying things without words is a very well researched area of communications.

Most of this has fallen into seven areas: proximity, spatial positioning, touch, gestures, facial expressions, silence and emotional displays, according to Smith, Bond and Kagitcibasi (*Handbook of Cross Cultural Psychology*, 1996).

This area of study is almost a separate area in its own right, outside the scope of this paper; however familiarity with the standard traits of non-verbal communication and how they differ across nationalities, cultures and ethnic groups is important for a global communicator.

After considering the individual, it is important then to consider how they relate to their organization.

The smell of a place

One of the most approachable and comprehensible gurus of modern business was Sumantra Ghoshal, a former lecturer at the LBS, adviser to global conglomerates and author of *The Individualized Corporation* (1997, written with Christopher Bartlett). His book introduced a means of understanding businesses that provide useful context for a modern global communicator.

When trying to make progress with understanding a business, Ghoshal and Bartlett argued that the most important factor of all is to understand not behaviours, but the influences that exist among the workforce. To do that, managers need first to be able to empathize with their environment; to understand the '...smell of the place...'

As one manager said to them: 'Walk into any office or factory and within the first 10 minutes you will sense the smell of the place. You will sense it in the energy and the hum of the work, you will see it in the eyes of the people, in how they walk and talk. You will sense it in a thousand small details around you.'

In the context of Ghoshal and Bartlett's assertion that businesses need to move from a philosophy of Strategy, Structure and Systems to one of Purpose, Process and People, the 'smell of the place' is core to understanding what holds businesses back.

This ability also links directly into this X factor, beyond the 'toolbox' and 'brains', which we are searching for.

Plotting the future

To understand our stakeholders' future behaviour involves the science of futurology. Knowing what filters in a future study is part of the 'brain power' skill referred to earlier.

Futurology is not new but it is now more scientific. John Smart, one of the world's leading futurologists, founder and president of the Acceleration Studies Foundation said: 'A part of our future appears to be evolutionary and unpredictable, and another part looks developmental and predictable. Our challenge is to invent the first and discover the second.'

To achieve this requires dividing the world into bite-sized chunks. For example: the UK government's 2020 Teaching and Learning Review Group chose to divide future change into five categories: demographic, social, technological, economic and environmental.

The group found that:

Demographics: There will be more over-65s than under-16s in the UK in 2020; people will live, and experience better health for, longer. And we will live in an ever more diverse society.

Socially: There will be a further decline in traditional family structures, in the context of greater diversity of social attitudes and expectations. Gender inequality will continue to decline.

Technology: The pace of change will continue to increase exponentially, bandwidth increases will, combined with the falling cost of hardware, software and data storage, result in near-universal access to personal, multi-functional devices, smarter software and common coding.

Economic: Living standards will be around 30 per cent higher, with more luxuries becoming necessities and a greater proportion of income spent on leisure, household services, sport and culture. Working patterns will become increasingly diverse and organizations will become less hierarchical.

Environmental: Individuals will be expected to take increased personal responsibility for their impact on the environment and they will expect the public and private sector to do likewise.

From a different perspective, the EBRD (European Bank for Reconstruction and Development) has talked of four groups: science and technology, climate change, governance and demography.

The choice of groups will always depend, to some extent, on the raison d'être of your organization.

Once those groups are established however it is then possible to start to map the future for the organization, integrate with the business plan and subsequently devise the communications plan.

The most difficult challenge after this research may be to convince an established culture within an organization that a trend has become mainstream, and is no longer about the future, but about today.

According to research through the Faculty of Business Administration in Newfoundland, once 15 per cent to 25 per cent of a given population integrates an innovation, project, belief or action into their daily life then a trend becomes 'mainstream'.

Innovation and change

It has always been apparent that the future has only one certainty: change itself. As far back as 500 BC, Heraclitus observed, 'Nothing endures but change'.

My own work on change originally from 2001 (in partnership with Cranfield and Aston business schools, and published in refined form in 2009 in the *International Journal of Public Management* (IJOPM), **29** (7)) concentrated on the mindset required for a leading communications director working within the senior management team.

It proved the importance of balancing decisions between three limbs:

- the need still to run the business through a period of change;
- managing the CSR and legacy issues for the company to avoid storing problems for the future;
- and at all times appreciating that every individual who was part of a stakeholder group would be going through their own emotional journey as a result of the changes, and hence appropriate consideration needs to be given for the channel and tone of message.

This emotional journey means that one communications solution for each stakeholder group cannot be guaranteed to work with every individual within that group – one size simply does not fit all.

The successful use of academic study on change, as with futurology, lies as much in the understanding what will work for you in your environment as in understanding why it worked in theirs.

Understanding personalities at work

This brings us to the next element of trying to understand 'what it takes'. Understanding ourselves.

Over 2,000 years ago the Greek philosopher Theophrastus asked: 'Why is it that while all Greece lies under the same sky and all the Greeks are educated alike, it has befallen us to have characters variously constituted?' Theophrastus did not, or could not, answer his own rhetorical question.

Today, we know more. Understanding why the people we are communicating with are different, and internalizing it ourselves, is crucial to appreciating how best to communicate with distinctly different individuals and groups.

The ancient Greeks defined four personality types: the melancholic, the choleric, the phlegmatic and the sanguine. While science has moved on, modern society still recognizes these types.

There are many ways of achieving self knowledge today, some academic, such as the Myers-Briggs models; others like a simpler task-to-process continuum on which one could place oneself and one's colleagues.

Myers-Briggs was designed to identify certain psychological differences, as set out in Jung's 1921 book on *Psychological Types*, and aims to resolve four key dichotomies:

Extraversion – Introversion

Sensing – Intuition

Thinking – Feeling

Judging – Perceiving

Creating 16 different types of basic personality combination, Myers-Briggs is but one measure, and has a number of vocal detractors as well as fans.

There are many other methods of measurement and analysis, including the Minnesota Multiphasic Personality Inventory (MMPI) and its DISC assessment, with DISC standing for:

Dominance – relating to control, power and assertiveness

Influence – relating to social situations and communication

Steadiness – relating to patience, persistence and thoughtfulness

Conscientiousness – relating to structure and organization

Yet despite being frequently criticized over the years Myers-Briggs remains as good a point as any to start some degree of self-analysis and understanding.

Our emotions

In addition to understanding personality type, it is also important to have understanding of emotions.

One of the most well-known studies of emotions was carried out in 1969 by two Americans, Schachter and Singer. Their paper, 'Cognitive, social and physiological determinants of emotional state', contained their formula defining emotion thus: Emotion = arousal × emotionality of thought.

They linked the physical responses of arousal – sweating, raised heart rate and blushing, for example – with the way a person interprets the state of this arousal: and for it to be 'emotion' the individual must define the feelings in emotional terms in order to feel they are in an emotional state.

Understanding of emotion is important, as recent research by Cognosis of 1,600 managers in the UK showed:

- Both rational and emotional buy-in were required to achieve success;
- An ounce of belief was for them worth a ton of understanding; and
- Only 1 in 20 agreed their company's strategy was exciting or inspiring.

As one participant said: 'Leaders must go beyond reason'.

And so what now of our leaders, how do they see the world, what do they want from us as leaders in global operating businesses?

Our leaders – reaching out for the X-factor

Research carried out by Professor John Hunt at the London Business School (2008) showed that of 105 CEOs:

- 70 per cent had a strong bias for introversion;
- they were not happy at being vulnerable;
- had a bias towards tasks rather than people;
- and were biased towards rational arguments and analysis.

This helps us to understand another crucial piece of research in establishing 'what does it take'.

The London Business School had also set out to find what senior executives from global companies, across a variety of industries and geographies, felt were the components of a great global leader of the future.

In 2004 the LBS conducted 100 face-to-face interviews with executives located in more than 20 countries. The result was a table of 39 wide-ranging capabilities divided into three categories: knowledge, skills and attributes.

The conclusion was that 'all their requirements could be summed up as follows: the need for more thoughtful, more aware, more sensitive, more flexible, more adaptive managers, capable of being moulded and developed into global executives' (*Strategy+Business* magazine, issue 36).

To quote the LBS: 'We can teach knowledge, but we need to train people in skills, and we can only develop attributes'. Attributes are the individual qualities, characteristics or behaviours found in leadership itself.

TABLE 16.1   The New Global Business Capabilities

Knowledge	Skills	Attributes
Global macroeconomics	Managing diverse cultures	Unyielding integrity
Global finance	Deadline with ambiguity, uncertainty and paradox	Worldly awareness
Global strategy	Decision-making	Thrive on change
Organization structure and dynamics	Accountability	Judgement and intuition
Competitive microeconomics	Managing performance	Demanding excellence

TABLE 16.1 *continued*

Knowledge	Skills	Attributes
Decision sciences	Project management	Perseverance and tenacity
Global marketing and brand management	Ability to make the complex simple	Adaptability and responsiveness
Sales and account management	Presentation skills	Passionate and persuasive
Technology management	Listening and observation	Curiosity and creativity
Accounting	Network and collaboration	Self-awareness
Human resource management	Teambuilding and networking	Self-confidence to involve others
Corporate governance	Talent assessment	Boundless energy to motivate and energize
–	Interpersonal skills/giving feedback	Judging performance
–	–	Capacity and desire to learn; coachable

SOURCE: LBS, 2004.

Looking at the table in detail, it is obvious that no one will ever be able to offer every capability to their employer. Communicators must not dismiss capabilities just because they do not appear relevant.

A communicator does need to know something about competitive microeconomics for example, even if it is just that it exists, is relevant to performance management and as a result has attributes associated with it.

The final piece of the jigsaw

Looking through this table I argue there is a common thread, which answers our question: what does it take? Empathy.

Empathy is defined as 'the ability to share, understand and feel another person's feeling; the power of entering into the spirit, or feeling, of something: from the Greek "empatheia", passion or affection'.

If you take our toolbox of knowledge and add our trainable skills, we have an automaton, someone who still falls short of having what it takes to cope with the changing world around us.

Add the overall attribute of empathy, however, and we have the ultimate skill set to face the world that global communications professionals inhabit.

Empathy gives a passion, a deep love for the cosmopolitan people-driven world that we operate within.

Empathy, the link to communications

Writing in his book *Coercion* (1999), Douglas Rushkoff saw this link, though without referring to it specifically, when he referred to 'public relations specialists seeking to mirror the conscious and unconscious concerns of their targets in order to change their perception of reality'.

Rushkoff goes on to describe a three-step process to cross-cultural domination. First, learn the dominant myths of the target people and, in the process, gain their trust. Second, find the gaps or superstitions in their beliefs. And third, either replace the superstitions or augment them with facts that redirect the target group's perceptions and allegiance.

Current leading lecturers in public relations also support the concept of empathy, alongside 'skills' and 'attributes' in the context of global communications.

The final test

How does empathy reveal itself in a communicator? Do they check Al Jazeera alongside the BBC or CNN? Does their Twitter feed include journalists and opinion formers from across the geo-political spectrum?

At the time of the selection of the site for the 2012 Olympics, did they research how the competing nations to London attempted to win a global competition?

By searching YouTube for the promotional video that won the London 2012 Olympics ('Proud') one can see a great multi-cultural empathy and awareness.

Communicators who display all three factors are the professionally versatile communicators of today, and will have a role to play tomorrow. Not just in their function, but working in all areas of an organization.

We are all communicators now. The strength of global brands will decrease as individuals exploit the power of information in the modern world to bring identities and personalities to everyone – we all have a face.

Conclusion

'The only true exploration, the only true fountain of delight, would not be to visit foreign lands, but to possess others' eyes, to look at the world through the eyes of others.'

– *Marcel Proust*, Remembrance of Things Past

He wrote this in the early part of the 20th century, at a time when the world of mass media and communications was starting to have a direct impact on individuals' daily lives – it engenders an approach to the world in total sympathy with my hypothesis for leaders in global communications.

Without empathy for one's audiences, and perhaps too a passion for diversity, a global communications professional can never succeed in our gloriously exciting, ever changing, world.

Globalization and national economic development

17

A role for public relations and communication management

PETER L WALKER CHART.PR, FCIPR

This paper was originally written in October 2009. Minor revisions have been made to the original text for this book to reflect developments in media, technology and practice.

Increasing world trade and accelerating economic development occupied the thinking of diplomats and international development economists throughout the 20th century and before. This was a time when, as now, international trade and political power in the world went hand in hand as industrialized economies exploited the raw materials of less developed nations to produce goods for their own and international markets. It is hardly surprising that despite the exploits of individual icons in India, the USA and the UK in the 1930s public relations, as a professional business discipline, played little part in shaping policy let alone being part of the debates on multilateral and bilateral trade and investment programmes.

In the second half of the 20th century the increasing speed of globalization focused the minds of national and international politicians and economists on the issues of how could the countries with emerging economies and less developed nations best develop their economies. What were the obstacles to their economic development? How could these obstacles be overcome? During that time, different development strategies devised in developing countries went in and out of fashion, influenced both by empirical evidence of the success (or more often failure) of grand development strategies, and by the shifting weight of mainstream thinking – particularly in economics. Public relations as a new but internationally established profession was still absent as a voice at the table, as an input to policy thinking and the importance and relevance of the effective communication of those policies and programmes to those most affected. This was and may still be a world dominated by economists and a new breed of international development experts.

At a time when communications and technologies had shrunk the timeframe for transactions, international super businesses had started to expand their markets beyond those of the developed countries. Marketing and branding techniques were refined and adapted to create global brands and to promote market dominance for consumer goods. Public relations was, and is, a fundamental part of those product and business development and globalization strategies with little evidence that countries sought or thought to apply the same strategies and policy thinking to their own economic development.

Twenty-first-century technology has both added a fundamental question that challenges historic thinking and provided effective solutions. The new question to challenge established verities asks, 'what difference does globalization of information in particular make to national economic development?'

Do the same technologies that make globalization an irresistible and irreversible force offer strategic solutions for national economic development?

- in a pull rather than push world – consumers, investors, and business partners can make comparisons and exercise choice at a click;

- the greater the impact of globalization – the more important the smallest community – international development demands local support to be sustainable;
- clear messaging to relevant target audiences is 85 per cent more effective than the generation of awareness.

Big push and virtuous circles

In the first half of the 20th century, internally generated or endogenous growth was the prescription. It was given theoretical coherence and credibility by the structuralist and dependency schools that saw the poverty of developing counties as a symptom of their dependence on developed countries. In order to break out of this 'vicious circle' of dependency, all that developing countries needed to do was to generate their own growth endogenously. Create a 'virtuous circle' of rising output, value-added, and incomes and falling unemployment and poverty.

Considerable research was then conducted into the 'key sectors' of the economy, the activities of which would have a multiplier effect on the rest of the system, accelerating the development process. Hirschman (1958) pioneered theories of backward and forward linkages, based on his analysis of Latin American economies in the 1950s. A 'Hirschman linkage' is said to operate when economic agents are 'induced' to undertake new activities as a result of ongoing economic relationships in the economy. Rasmussen (1957) quantified the importance of different sectors in this regard, in the form of the 'Rasmussen dispersion indices'.

Big push means balanced growth

When analysing both backward and forward linkages, a Rasmussen index value of greater than one, corresponds to an industry with above average linkages throughout the economic system, while a value of less than one suggests the opposite. Empirical work in the

1960s, 1970s and 1990s found that key sectors in terms of both backward and forward linkages were most often found in the manufacturing sector.

Enter the advocates of 'balanced growth' to be achieved by 'big push' policies.[1] They believed that it was necessary to centrally coordinate investment decisions, so that each enterprise was able to benefit from the resulting external economies (Mathur 1964). They claimed that the results of this simultaneous investment programme would be to shift the economy from a low-income equilibrium 'trap' to a high-income equilibrium state (Nelson 1956; Leibenstein 1957). As with the related work[2] on linkages and interdependence, this research focused primarily on the manufacturing sectors, which in part explains the popularity of import-substitution-industrialization (ISI) approaches: it was the development of manufacturing that would create linkages and spur growth throughout the economy.

Market forces

It is a 'no brainer', and easy to understand, why these big push, central direction theories were as attractive to first world bureaucrats as they were to the centralized undemocratic leaders and rulers of the less developed or emerging economies. It was not just the widespread failure of such policies, in combination with the success of export-oriented development programmes that made this kind of thinking very unfashionable, throughout the 1980s.

It became increasingly accepted that planned development of this kind was doomed to failure. Countries should deregulate, open their economies to international competition and allow national development to be directed by market forces, national and international. Globalization of information had changed world politics. Walls had fallen, aspirations and ambitions released, a communication driven internet fuelled pull rather than push society had been born and with it brand power.

At the same time social forecasters like John Naisbitt, who had accurately predicted the patterns of change that would shape the world in the 1980s turned their attention to the paradoxes of globalization.

In his 1994 publication *Global Paradox* he forecast that China, the world's last great communist country, would become the world's largest market economy. The implications of his thesis that, the bigger the world economy, the more powerful its smallest players, were somehow lost to the economists and international development experts and ignored by the public relations profession and professionals throughout the world.

False dichotomy

This change in attitude can be seen in endogenous/exogenous terms: the earlier 'balanced growth' – to be achieved by a 'big push' – stressed the crucial role to be played by coordinated endogenous growth, with 'key sectors' acting as catalysts. Contrast this with the importance of exogenous factors in sustainable growth where exposure to international competitive forces and standards ensures industries must be efficient and profitable to survive, whilst international capital markets allocate investment between global markets efficiently on the basis of accurate price signals.

It may be that too much can be made of what is in reality a false dichotomy. It may be that in order to develop national economies successfully *both* the endogenous and exogenous environments must be supportive. After all the research that supported the 'big push' solutions to national economic ills were based primarily on manufacturing industry. It is hardly surprising that a key element of this exogenous environment – the international financial markets – had a very limited impact upon national development in the 1950/60s. You could not make the same mistake today.

There is also a 'maguffin' in the mix. It takes the issues of national economic development out of the hands of the economists alone. In his Warwick University speech of 2000, President Bill Clinton described it as 'the intensifying process of economic integration and political interdependence, fuelled by an explosion of technology that enables information, ideas and money, people, products and services to move within and across national borders at unprecedented and irreversible speeds'. It is the impact of empowerment through information access.

Reputation – image, branding and developing countries

In this information empowered, market forces stimulated, globalized society is the most important aspect of the exogenous environment facing developing countries: what is their reputation in the international financial markets? Is it possible to consider that a national brand is as much a key element in attracting investment as it is to promoting national manufactured products, stimulating tourism and visitor traffic and establishing political status or respectability?

After all, the argument runs, in the corporate world, reputation or image, has become increasingly important to overall strategy, which seeks to improve, protect and project the corporate 'brand'.

Over the past two decades, ever since the accounting standards put brand values on balance sheets, the concept of branding has become ever more central to all business activities. What exactly is a brand? In essence, a brand is an intangible asset, which can have either a positive or a negative impact on a company, through conveying information on concepts such as trustworthiness, innovation, quality and integrity.

There is more. Consor sees a brand as having two principal areas of value:

- Core Brand Value (CBV) – where a corporate brand can enjoy a royalty rate from which cash flow can be capitalized and value calculated.

- Incremental Brand Value (IBV) – where marketing and other business efficiencies, from distribution to purchasing, travel with the brand and benefit sub brands.

Strip away the jargon and a strong brand enables a company to charge a premium for its product relative to its competitors, whilst a weak brand (negative image) requires the company in question to sell their products at a discount in the market. In effect, a strong brand shifts the demand curve for a company's product upwards, whilst a weak (negative) brand shifts it down.

From concepts to cases

If the link seems obvious, the political and commercial sirens of self-interest are also persuasive. If branding is the driving force for first world businesses why not use it to power emerging economies?

> 'During the last hundred years or so, much of the wealth of rich countries has been generated through marketing – the ability to add attraction to exported brands through country-of origin effect, the increasingly sophisticated techniques of marketing the country itself as a tourist brand, the marketing skills which attract the brightest talent and biggest foreign investments, the acts of marketing coordination which ensure that consistent and attractive messages about the country in general are communicated to the rest of the world through acts of foreign policy and sporting and cultural activities. These skills should now be transferred to poorer countries, thus helping them to graduate from being mere suppliers of low-margin unbranded commodities to brand owners and branded destinations in their own right.'
>
> – *Anholt, S (2003)* Brand New Justice, *p 3*

Clearly, certain countries have a more favourable image than others. But what impact does this have in practice? Does this rather specialized subject relate to the exogenous influences on the development prospects of a nation?

An obvious starting point is the attitude of international investors and the pattern of FDI flows to different countries or regions. Propose Africa or Asia as potential recipients of investment and what images would this conjure up in an investor's mind, regardless of the merits of each individual deal? Would Africa's negative image (or brand) make any potential investment less attractive than a similar investment in the more positively branded region of Asia? It is unarguable that it would.

So, countries with a poor image – negative brand equity – may have a higher risk premium than may be justified, with the result that asset prices are kept artificially low. The opposite is, of course, true for countries with a positive international brand: the demand curve for their financial assets is shifted upwards, with the result that these assets are relatively highly valued. More directly, a multinational corporation looking for a suitable site to build a factory, for example, will also be strongly influenced by the international brand of each country. Again, countries with negative brands will see their developmental options constrained by this exogenous influence.

Can the techniques that measure brand value in business be adapted to the measurement of brand equity in developing countries? If financial standing or ranking is a **Core Brand Value (CBV)** does the same apply to a country's ability to attract high-value tourism or world sporting events?

Two well documented national case studies of planned and managed communication country branding programmes merit consideration.

'South Africa with its – **'alive with possibilities'** strap line and **'rainbow nation appeal'** set out to mobilize popular support in a fractured society and attract world sporting events and investment as the regional headquarters for Africa for many multinationals. This was a planned, systematic and managed communication approach to restoring international credibility, attracting FDI and restoring trade relations to a post-apartheid South Africa. Borrowing heavily on the branding and brand development expertise of Unilever, a national agency (IMC – the International Marketing Council) was established in 2002 to drive the messaging forward throughout the world.

Foreign Direct Investment figures since 2003 and securing high prestige and valued international sports events from the Rugby World Cup, through Cricket to the 2010 FIFA World Cup indicate that, for South Africa at least, tourism and international sports events satisfy both the core brand value and incremental brand value criteria of Consor.

Then there is *Incredible India...* as the coherent presentation of the subcontinent for tourism and destination marketing. Driven by a post '9–11' slump in tourism where visitor traffic dropped to a level too small to measure, an immediate and concerted effort was made to restore confidence and upgrade the offer.

The development of a clear and clever national brand Incredible India as a means of presenting a multi-faceted tourism offering provided the means for securing the buy-in of the totality of the Indian tourism offering from hotels and ground transport to monuments and nature parks. In combination with a systematic and intensive trade relations national road show, a planned and sustained media relations based multi-level communication programme engaged a disparate and diverse population at all levels into embracing the values of the inherent cultural wealth of the subcontinent.

A structured series of international key markets' trade and consumer relations programmes sustained the programme and expanded the tourism market to 2.7 per cent of GDP and 4.2 per cent of total employment by 2004.[3] Taken on its own the Incredible India programme is unlikely to meet the Consor criteria for either Core or Incremental Brand Value.

In 2006 India 'Every Where' was the mantra that launched a revitalized and fast growing technologically and industrially advanced India on the world through Davos and the World Economic Forum. It overshadowed 'Incredible India' and the tourism programme branding initiative. Success as an economic driver, for what is essentially a managed communication programme, can best be judged from WTTC figures for 2009 that show tourism worth 6.0 per cent of GDP and providing employment for 6.4 per cent of the total work force through a period when India's national GDP grew on average by some 8 plus per cent – arguably establishing India's tourism as a core brand value, increasing productivity and increasing value added.

An analysis of national brand values might reasonably suggest that regional – as well as national – effects are at play. Do Asia and India, benefit from the positive brand of the region where the development of certain sectors like IT, have a disproportionately positive impact on a country's brand? Does South Africa suffer from its association with the region's image, reinforced by pictures of poverty and strife above all others in the world media?

In any analysis of these two classic case studies there is one common core element and that is the use of the brand to forge a national consensus and secure 'internal' support and commitment at all levels in society. By contrast, India's national economic brand campaign India Every Where took two years to put together and cost an estimated $4 million but involved just 22 companies in addition to a broad spectrum of government ministries, departments and other organizations.[4]

'Rebranding' emerging economies

Wally Olins (2003) argues that a nation is not a soap powder, but the result of the complex interplay between geography, history, culture, politics and countless other factors. People get rather upset about the very concept of a national brand.

As distasteful as applying branding to a nation may be, it is not difficult to argue that in the highly competitive modern world, a country wishing to succeed may have little choice but to improve its brand image. Framing the argument for the economist says negative image can amount to an exogenous constraint on development. It is imperative to improve the brand so that the demand curve for a country's assets can be shifted upwards – so that a vicious circle can be broken and a virtuous circle created. Indeed, it has been estimated that brand values may account for up to one third of total global wealth,[5] the overwhelming majority of which is in the developed markets. Given that developed countries have successfully used brands to enhance enormously their standards of living, is it not time that developing countries did the same?

According to Professor Nicholas Papadopoulos at Carleton University, Canada, 789 authors have published 766 major papers on 'branding a nation' since the 1950s. So, the answers to two of these three questions ought to be there somewhere.

1 What role, if any, does a country's image – or 'brand' – play in the pricing of its financial assets, and its attractiveness to investors?

   – all the arguments seem convincing and the evidence,
      if circumstantial, appears overwhelming.

2 What factors influence a country's brand, in both a positive and negative sense?

   – here is where it gets more difficult. The PIELLE/ECPGlobal –
      INRA Country Image Study in the 1990s used four distinct
      factors or headings as the basis for research among the
      citizens of 28 countries on their rating of each other:
      - Economic
      - Social
      - Inhabitants/cultural
      - Political

It showed that few countries attributed the same brand values to another – there were few consistently shared perceptions.

What is interesting is that the study indicated that the only consistent factor across all countries is a clear relationship between perceptions of a country as 'having a strong economy' and 'having people that are perceived as trustworthy and keeping their promises'.

By contrast, the same study shows no apparent relationship between a country being viewed as 'one where to spend holidays' and 'one where people would like to work'.

The use of public relations as part of the comprehensive communication management mix in national and international branding and inward investment promotion and economic development programmes is clear. Whether a country can be 'rebranded' and shifted to a more 'virtuous equilibrium' level, the role of public relations practice is less certain than the ability to mobilize and secure internal or national support for the brand concept.

In his recent treatise, *Global Paradox*, John Naisbitt argues that the bigger the world economy, the more powerful its smallest players. His global paradox suggests that in a global economy the values by which judgements are made are global standards but that the nation state is more important than a region or continent. In a nation state, regions, towns and communities become more important than the nation itself.

Against this background and in the light of our research we have concluded that:

1 National branding strategies have an important role to play in mobilizing popular support in a fractured society but these emotional factors have little influence on the global economic judgements that determine international investment and development decisions.

2 National branding strategies related to economic development programmes – privatization, deregulation and inward investment (FDI) – should be narrowly focused and address specialist audience needs – most particularly benchmarking national standards with global regulatory, valuation criteria.

3 A nation's image – brand values – are multi-faceted and can only be promoted and/or protected effectively to specific external target audiences and not as a general approach.

The role for public relations

Any attempt to identify whether public relations is a critical factor in branding a nation and has an impact in the process, is inevitably tied into the difficulties in accurately assessing the real value of national branding or branding strategies and programmes. An objective and informed appraisal of economic development, marketing and brand thinking and case study lessons suggests that:

- Effective national 'branding' must mobilize national support before stimulating international interest and 'external' target audiences.

- An 'holistic' national branding approach conflicts with individual and varying perceptions of national values.

- Existing nation-by-nation perceptions can be reinforced and enhanced through narrow cast, two way communication in investor relations, sectorial export promotion, inward investment promotion, tourism and travel promotion.

- Public relations programmes can most easily and cost effectively tailor information to meet the needs of an audience and match the cross cultural and the time zone response requirements.

- Perceptions of a nation are reinforced by the speed of response to global media with appropriate messaging strategies that are consistent and coordinated – the essence of public relations practice.

No appraisal of the role of public relations in country branding and the promotion of national economic development objectives can be made without consideration of the role of nations themselves in appealing to and communicating with their own diaspora as well as civil society in other countries. Public diplomacy focuses on the ways in which a country (or multi-lateral organization such as the United Nations) communicates with citizens in other societies. Effective public diplomacy starts from the premise that dialogue, rather than a sales pitch, is often central to achieving the goals of foreign policy: public diplomacy must be seen as a two-way street. It is not a new concept – rather one that has been burnished, polished and subjected to a new and significant level of professionalism among diplomats of every nation. Sir Malcolm Rifkind MP, the former British foreign secretary, referred to public diplomacy as public relations for diplomats. It suggests that public relations is public diplomacy for business, professional, commercial, cultural and social interests with a clear, if operationally defined, role in country branding and economic development.

Further reading

Anholt, S (2003) *Brand New Justice*, Butterworth Heinemann, Oxford.

Clinton, W J (2001) New development agenda, address to Warwick University, 14 December/Struggle for the soul of the 21st century, BBC Richard Dimbleby Lecture, December.

Hirschman, A O (1958) *The Strategy of Economic Development: Interdependence and industrialization*, Yale University Press, New Haven.

INRA – ECPGlobal/PIELLE Consulting Group (2000) Country Image Study – an examination of different nations and their inhabitants.

Kolah, A (2005) *Maximising the Value of Licensing and Merchandising*, Sport Business Group, London.

Liebenstein, H (1957) *Economic Backwardness and Economic Growth*, Wiley, New York.

Mathur, A (1966) Balanced vs unbalanced growth: a reconciliatory view, *Oxford Economic Papers*, **18** (2) (July).

Naisbitt, J (1994/1995) *Global Paradox*, William Morrow Inc/Avon Books.

Nelson, R R (1956) A theory of the low level equilibrium trap in underdeveloped economies, *American Economic Review*, **46** (September), pp 894–908.

Nurske, R (1953) *Problems of Capital Formation in Underdeveloped Countries*, Basil Blackwell, Oxford.

Obstfeld, M (1986) Rational and self-fulfilling balance of payments crises, *American Economic Review*, **76** (1) (March), pp 72–81.

Olins, W (2003) Branding the nation – the historical context, *Journal of Brand Management*, **10** (4–5) May.

Rasmussen, P N (1956) Studies in inter-sectoral relations, Thesis/Dissertation, Einar Harks, Kobenhavn.

Rosenstein Rodan, P N (1943) Problems of industrialization of eastern and south-eastern Europe, *The Economic Journal*, **53** (210/211) (June–Sept), pp 202–11.

Stiglitz, J (1992) Comment on 'Toward a counter-counterrevolution in development theory' by P Krugman, Proceedings of the World Bank Annual Conference on Development Economics 1992, pp 39–50.
Whitwell, S (2004) A new way to count beans – Brand Valuation (IFRS-3 for marketers), *The Marketer*, 25 November.

Notes

1 See Rosenstein Rodan (1943) and Nurske (1953), for example.
2 See Naisbitt, J (1982) *Megatrends*, Warner Books, Emeryville CA, and Naisbitt, J (1994) *Global Paradox*, William Morrow Inc.
3 WTTC (World Travel and Tourism Council) economic analysis.
4 Knowledge@Wharton (2006) online journal of business research and analysis, University of Pennsylvania.
5 See Interbrand (2003) The Best Global Brands Annual Ranking, *Business Week*, 4 August.

PART V
Reflections

– an examination
of the fundamental
theories of public
relations and their
application to
modern practice

Is excellence in public relations beyond our reach?

18

RICHARD FLYNN CHART.PR, MCIPR

David Dozier with James and Larissa Grunig developed the *Manager's Guide to Excellence in Public Relations and Communication Management* in 1995 following years of research into how practitioners operated on a day to day basis. The theory of excellence sought to guide the industry into the best practice which would bring benefits to their organizations and help give the practitioners credibility and value within their organizations.

I would like to explore whether there is any evidence today that we are achieving or are even striving to achieve excellence based on this model. I will also consider the relevance of the excellence model today.

I would like to examine the evidence of our day-to-day activities as revealed in the CIPR benchmark surveys (2009 and 2010) and to see where these activities fit within the models of public relations practice developed by the academics and whether they meet the criteria for excellence.

I will also draw on some recent commentaries by industry leaders and examine whether they suggest an approach towards excellence. I will provide some conclusions from the evidence and make some recommendations for the future.

What is public relations?

CIPR describes public relations as 'the discipline which looks after reputation, with the aim of earning understanding and support; and influencing opinion and behaviour. It is the planned and sustained effort to establish and maintain goodwill and mutual understanding between an organization and its publics.'

What are the models of public relations practice?

The models of public relations practice as conceptualized by Grunig and Hunt (1984) are:

- Press agentry/publicity
- Public information
- Two-way asymmetric
- Two-way symmetric

Kitchen (1997) states that Grunig and Hunt accepted that the models are 'inevitably abstractions of reality' and professional practice usually fitted within one or more of these models.

Kitchen suggests Grunig (1992) and his fellow researchers found the press agentry model to be the most widely practised form of public relations reflecting the emphasis placed on media relations.

Dozier, Grunig and Grunig (1995) describe the press agentry/publicity and public information models as those in which the practitioner generates information about the organization and these are distributed using the media or publicity materials. Building strong relationships with journalists can generate good publicity but these methods are one-way communication with the audience using an intermediary and gains or seeks no feedback from audiences. The models which date from the 1900s are still practised today.

The other models developed by Grunig and Hunt (1984) are the two-way asymmetrical and two-way symmetrical models. Kitchen (1997) adapted the characteristics of the models and summarized the two-way asymmetric model as follows:

FIGURE 18.1a   Two-way asymmetric model

Characteristic	Two-way asymmetric
Purpose	Scientific persuasion
Nature of Communication	Two-way imbalanced effects
Communications model	Source to receiver with feedback
Nature of research	Formative, attitude, evaluation
Examples of current practice	Competitive, business, agencies

SOURCE: Adapted from Kitchen 1997.

The characteristics of the two-way symmetric model are:

FIGURE 18.1b   Two-way symmetric model

Characteristic	Two-way symmetric
Purpose	Mutual understanding
Nature of Communication	Two-way balanced effects
Communications model	Group to group with feedback
Nature of research	Formative evaluation of understanding
Examples of current practice	Regulated, business, agencies

SOURCE: Adapted from Kitchen 1997.

These models differ from the others in that they are characteristically two-way communications principally because they seek feedback from the receiver. However in the case of the two-way asymmetric model, no action is taken by the organization on the feedback received while in the two-way symmetric model the organization demonstrates that it has taken the feedback on board and changed as a result.

Feedback from audiences develops conversations but this is used only to continue developing the organization's messaging – asymmetrical. Using the feedback to listen to what is being said and then changing and adapting an organization in response is symmetrical communications, according to Grunig (ed 1992). This sees the organization and audience negotiate and evolve.

Kitchen notes that although Grunig maintains that subsequent studies have shown that examples of all four models can be found being practised today, he admits that most organizations do not appear to practise public relations as a two-way symmetrical function – the model he argued defines the most 'excellent' way of practising public relations – at least not on a regular basis.

What do public relations practitioners do today?

The 2010 CIPR: State of the Profession Benchmarking Survey shows the main functions carried out by in-house practitioners are: media relations, corporate communications, internal communications, communications strategy development, strategic planning, event management and crisis management.

The CIPR acknowledges that the majority of practitioners conduct a wide range of PR tasks.

The survey cites the greatest areas of expected growth for in-house practitioners in the next five years as: online reputation management (73 per cent), strategic planning (51 per cent) and crisis management (43 per cent). It concludes: 'This is undoubtedly due in part to the fact that the financial crisis has led to companies and organizations needing reputation and crisis management services even more than they would in "normal" economic times'.

The results were similar to those in the 2009 survey although its findings were presented incorporating in-house and consultancies views.

The findings in the area of growth were also consistent, though the leading area for growth was described as 'digital PR' followed by reputation management and crisis management. CIPR suggests digital PR is the same as online reputation management (as used in 2010).

While the functions listed in the survey results are not precisely defined, it may be fair to ask whether these are carried out at a departmental or organizational (corporate) level. This may be important in order to accurately position them within the models. For example: do the communications staff develop their communications strategy in isolation from the rest of the organization or in collaboration with other directorates/departments? When citing strategic planning, is this strategic business planning or strategic communications planning? These questions cannot be answered using the survey results.

How do these functions fit within the models of public relations practice?

The main functions as set out in the surveys appear to suggest that in 2009/2010 practitioners were still largely operating within the press agentry and public information models.

This would suggest that little has changed within the industry in almost two decades as Grunig (1992) and his fellow researchers found the press agentry model to be the most widely practised form of public relations reflecting the emphasis placed on media relations and achieving the goal of media publicity. In such practice the communications are characteristically one-way.

The same conclusion could be drawn from CIPR surveys' results in relation to the top areas for future growth ie online reputation management and digital PR as posting information on a corporate website could arguably be seen as coming under both the models of press agentry/publicity and public information and the purpose of the latter in particular is propaganda.

Ironically, in Grunig's research the public information model, which he predicted would be the most commonly practised model, was found to be least common within business organizations but most common in the public sector. The technological developments which have arisen over the last 30 years as a result of the internet may well have changed this scenario and this may be worthy of further research.

The assertion that the internet provides a platform (websites) for propaganda may be harsh and will be discussed here later.

Based on the results of the CIPR surveys 2009 and 2010, it may be fair to assume that either of the questionnaires do not explore whether the profession is already achieving or striving towards the excellence model in its day-to-day activities. That may be something the researchers would like to explore in future surveys.

Is the excellence model relevant today?

In his paper, Excellence theory in public relations, presented to the US Institute for Public Relations and PRSA in 2010, Grunig suggests that the value of Public Relations is based on the quality of relations with stakeholders and its ability to adapt to their needs through the social responsibility considered by an organization in its managerial decision-making.

He says the theory derived principles of how the function should be organized to maximize its value and these can be summarized as through: involvement with strategic management with access to the key decision-makers; to have the function integrated in the management system rather than sublimated to other functions; a symmetrical system of internal communications increased employee satisfaction; and, organizations with excellent public relations valued women as much as men for the strategic role.

He said: 'An excellent public relations function worked with other management functions to help them build relationships with relevant stakeholders.'

That statement is clearly reflected in the CIPR's definition of Public Relations when it states: 'It is the planned and sustained effort to establish and maintain goodwill and mutual understanding between an organization and its publics'.

However it is difficult to see where the institute is trying to get a measure of this in the surveys.

It would therefore be useful to know whether PR industry leaders or experts consider the facets of the excellence theory ie dialogue with stakeholders having an impact on organizational attitudes and business approach as an important part of their practice.

A very useful source for such information, particularly in the absence of being able to undertake personal research on the issue for this exercise is the *PR Week* magazine's Thought Leader Series. In particular the edition published on 16 September 2011 gives a good insight into the experts' opinions.

This special publication focused on Corporate Reputation and used the case study of energy supplier E.ON who had been painted as environmental enemy number one (by some stakeholders) when in 2009 it proposed to build a new larger coal-fired power station on the site of an existing facility at Kingsnorth in Kent. The publication featured lessons learnt from E.ON's head of communications, Guy Esnouf and responses to the case study from a specialist panel mainly drawn from PR consultancies.

While the case study itself is not of particular significance to this discussion paper, many of the comments from the experts are very important to judge the way we (practitioners) operate and their views and conclusions can be linked to the Grunig theories. There is no indication given as to whether any of the experts have academic qualifications or are even aware of the 'excellence theory'.

To summarize Esnouf's situation as set out by *PR Week*'s reporter, Jane Bainbridge: In 2009 the company began discussions with stakeholders on what it dubbed a 'trilemma' – it identified three elements to its communications strategy: the environment, energy prices and security of supply.

The protests over the Kingsnorth proposals were led by environmental groups and were the focus of much media attention. However the company's tracking of stakeholder opinions 'showed virtually no direct link between the coverage and how their customers felt' about the company'.

Despite the coverage many people were not aware of the protests and most could not identify E.ON as the company involved. Customers appeared more concerned about energy prices and estimated bills.

So the company launched an advertising campaign; held a series of local meetings around the country; and drafted in an expert on social media. Their strategy was under the banner of 'Talking Energy' and the central debate was energy conservation.

Esnouf concluded that irrespective of the medium used: 'Conversations (with stakeholders) are always the most important'.

The specialist panel members provided their expert practitioner opinions on the case study and the following are some of the comments made:

'Companies should start conversations with their stakeholders to change their perceptions,' according to **Iain Bundred, Director of Strategic Media at Ogilvy**. He says that all interactions affect how you are perceived by stakeholders and you risk having your brand's reputation destroyed unless you meet their needs.

This could arguably be interpreted as operating a two-way asymmetrical model. This is because the company is actively conversing with its stakeholders and seeking feedback. However, as there is no indication that the company is prepared to change its stance in the light of this conversation so it seems to remain asymmetrical. It could also be seen as the company taking an opportunity to use persuasive techniques to win over the stakeholders to its viewpoint.

Rebecca Reilly, Director, Open Road, suggests that behaviour is more important than content and people are less worried by media coverage of the organization. They are concerned, however, about the way the organization behaves. This seems to suggest a public information model approach with the message being tailored to the needs of individual audiences rather than seeking any feedback.

A consistent message to all audiences across all channels of communication is critical, according to **Charlie O'Rourke, MD, AlMediaComms**. He fears that too much diverse information given to different audiences could lead to the message being misinterpreted 'putting the organization at risk'.

The focus here too is on the message albeit that the press agentry approach is seen as being insufficient. There is no suggestion of gaining feedback or reaching mutual understanding.

Jonathan Flint, MD, Citigate Dewe Rogerson, says: 'This should be a two-way process'. He stresses the importance of listening and of dealing with stakeholders' views and that these should be adopted into an organization's communications plans.

This approach certainly suggests a two-way symmetrical-excellence model approach as stakeholder groups' concerns and views need to be addressed. It does not quite suggest that the company changes its approach or activities.

The age of blogging and social media means that everyone is a journalist with a potential mass audience platform in which to express their views. **Ros Hunt, MD corporate affairs, Cohn & Wolfe,** appears to suggest that an organization has to adapt its style and language to match that of the audience.

Here again the focus seems to be on the message and the tools used to get it across to various audiences and adapting to the audience's personality.

Listening is the key according to **Julia King, MD, Context Europe,** and this includes lending an ear to those who won't necessarily wish to engage in conversation with you. She says it is corporate responsibility to identify the issues that 'will' be important rather than just reacting to the news of the day. She suggests an organization learns more about how to protect and enhance its reputation from 'challenging' audiences rather than supportive ones.

This approach goes beyond conversations and introduces the concept of the company learning from the stakeholders which would appear to be a good fit in the two-way symmetrical-excellence model.

The comments made by the specialist panel members seem to approach for the most part a move towards conversing with stakeholders and in some cases showing that an organization can learn, adapt and benefit from such an approach.

Julia King seems to sum it up in her comment that 'While two-way conversation is the aim, listening is the most important part – this is not the time to push your own message hard. And sadly companies sometimes listen but do not hear.'

From this comment alone one could conclude that excellence seems to be as valid today, if not even more so, than it was decades ago.

Importance of technology in striving for excellence

Larissa Grunig speaking at the US Institute for Public Relations and PRSA 2010 conference hailed the growth of new media and suggested its rise gave organizations the opportunity to build relationships directly with audiences 'with all the principles of excellence'. New media produced the opportunity to open conversations directly with audiences. Blogging and social media gave organizations in turn an ideal opportunity to listen to what people are saying and this information should be gathered within its horizon-scanning activities to help the organization's decision-making processes.

James Grunig suggested many practitioners tend to just dump information into the new media platforms and their corporate websites as a means of publicity or promotion and simply as a way of carrying out communication programmes.

He again stressed the importance of the public relations practitioner being part of the organization's decision-making process. This role is to anticipate and give early advice on decisions being taken that could have an adverse impact on the organization. Where this does not happen the practitioner would end up having to deal with a crisis situation.

'Public relations people need to change and begin to think of what they do more as strategic counselling on issues and less about strictly dealing with the media,' he says.

Conclusions

The CIPR Surveys and the academics agree that public relations is a wide ranging function with practitioners operating within the four models of practice.

There is evidence among the expert practitioners that moving away from reliance on media relations and opening conversations with stakeholder groups is valuable.

The excellence model for public relations practice is not only as relevant today as when it was suggested, but also all the more achievable thanks to new media tools.

Audiences are more interested in the way an organization behaves rather than what it says or what is reported about it in occasional articles in the media.

It is important to continue listening to stakeholder groups so their concerns and views are addressed and fed back into their communications programmes.

We need to ensure the new media is used to have a conversation with stakeholders and not just for posting propaganda.

Recommendations

The CIPR should adopt the excellence model as best practice in public relations and promote it through its courses and CPD programmes.

Future CIPR surveys should seek to examine whether 'excellence' is being practised or strived for within the industry.

Evidence should be sought to support 'excellence' through case studies demonstrating how organizations listen and change as the result of feedback from stakeholders.

We need to ensure that the responsibility for stakeholder communications and engagement is firmly held within the communications function.

Further reading

CIPR (2009) Membership survey: the state of the PR profession, December, ComRes, CIPR [Online] http://www.cipr.co.uk/node/103769 [accessed September 2011].

CIPR (2010) State of the PR profession benchmarking survey, July 2010, ComRes, CIPR [Online] http://www.cipr.co.uk/node/103770 [accessed September 2011].

Dozier, D M, Grunig, L A and Grunig, J E (1995) *Manager's Guide to Excellence in Public Relations and Communications Management*, Lawrence Erlbaum Associates, Mahwah NJ.

Grunig, J E, Excellence theory in public relations, University of Maryland [Online] www.communicationencyclopedia.com

Grunig, J E (ed) (1992) *Excellence in Public Relations and Communication Management*, Lawrence Erlbaum, Hillside NJ.

Grunig, J E, and Grunig, L A (2010) Public relations excellence 2010, Third Annual Grunig Lecture Series, University of Maryland and PRSA [Online] http://www.instituteforpr.org/excellence-theory- 2010/

Kitchen, P J (1997) *Public Relations Principles and Practice*, International Thomson Business Press, London.

PR Week (2011) Thought Leader Series, Corporate Reputation, special supplement, 16 September [Online] http://www.prweek.com/article/1091950/corporate-reputation-september-2011 [accessed September 2011].

The roadmap to excellence in public relations

19

HILARY BERG CHART.PR, MCIPR

This paper was originally written in August 2009. Minor revisions have been made to the original text for this book to reflect developments in media, technology and practice.

The arrival of chartered status for practitioners signifies a critical stage in the evolution of PR. This move to champion the profession will not only support a growing recognition of its role in society, but also demonstrate the personal commitment of many professionals to achieving excellence.

The achievement is a timely one; 48,000 practitioners are now firmly entrenched across the private, public and third sectors. We contribute £6.5 billion to the UK economy (CEBR 2005) and generate significant benefits to the organizations we work for, enhancing reputation and strategic direction.[1]

This is an important development within a *young* profession. While the use of communication to influence public opinion has roots in the Greek and Roman empires (Tench and Yeomans 2006), the emergence of public relations as a profession can be traced to the early 20th century, with its 'formalization' in 1948 through the founding of the Institute of Public Relations. It was the 1970s before scholars made concerted efforts to observe the behaviour of practitioners (Grunig 2001a).

Since then, understanding of its role has varied. A 1999 PRCA survey reported public perceptions ranging from 'manipulative' and 'concealing' to 'black arts' and 'fluffy' (BBC 2001).

Early in my career, misunderstanding was commonplace. Working for Littlewoods in the 1980s, I reported on the annual Miss Littlewood competition for the staff newspaper. Aspiring winners declared their ambition to move into PR, because they 'loved working with people'.

Running a consultancy in the early 1990s, I was interviewed regularly by journalists exploring the 'real world of Ab Fab', comparing practitioners with the BBC's Patsy and Edina,[2] while contemporary media commentary revelled in PR's more radical elements, such as Lynne Franks' conversion to Buddhism and her Native American 're-birthing' sessions for staff (Langley 2007).

The boom in financial PR and the 'booze and schmooze' reputation of the city for liquid lunches and high fees did little for the credibility of the profession (Stern 2003). The 1990s saw the emergence of 'spin' and a government media strategy focused on what political journalist Nicholas Jones (1999) referred to as 'the black arts of campaigning'. This spectre of hyperbole and dubious practice still hangs over the profession.

Cropp and Pincus (2001) talked about 'the field's fuzzy and continually gerrymandering boundaries', describing decades-long confusion over the nature and applications of PR, concluding that the time was right to clarify its role.

For me, the benefit of over 20 years' experience lies in the recognition that both the perception and the reality of the profession are changing. At the start of my career, work was tactical and based on strategic decisions made outside the department, evaluation was minimal – with media coverage translated into 'advertising value equivalents', professional qualifications were virtually non-existent and pay was low. Today that has changed and increasingly, PR is recognized as a necessary and effective strategic management function.

I own yellowing textbooks which place PR firmly alongside advertising as a function of marketing. One text identifies publicity as the outcome of public relations and christens it 'The stepchild of marketing' (Kotler 1984, p 669).

Nowadays, as a lecturer, I present students with alternative relationship models; including the concept of PR and marketing as equal functions (Kotler and Mindak cited in Black 1995). I suggest that while an organization defines its own markets, its publics define themselves. Twenty-first-century PR can manage relationships with a multiplicity of stakeholders, arguably creating the environment in which marketing works best.

Chartered status for individuals will add weight to the aims of the CIPR to '...set the highest standards of professionalism and integrity within the profession' (Taylor 2009). Fellow Adrian Wheeler (2005) describes the industry 'growing up':

'The disorderly market of the past will fade away as clients, consultancies and procurement executives reach a consensus about what consultancies should do and how much it should cost.'

PR professionals will now not only be provided with a clear benchmark of their status. They will also have access to a range of sophisticated techniques to shape the way they practise, share and develop knowledge; contributing towards the growing credibility of the sector.

Indicators of excellence

Ground-breaking work in the 1980s and 90s by Hunt, James and Larissa Grunig, Dozier and other academics, finally created meaningful debate around communications excellence. The focus of this work lies in the Excellence Study, funded by the International Association of Business Communicators (IABC). This resulted in two major projects: Excellence in Public Relations and Communications Management (J E Grunig 1992) and Excellent Public Relations and Effective Organisations (Grunig, Grunig and Dozier 2002). It generated a 15-year programme of research, spanning Canada, the UK and the US, providing a basis for learning in 35 countries.

The findings provide practitioners with information critical to their own professional development and apply to all organizations, globally (Dozier, Grunig and Grunig 1995). While there are critics of this approach, they have yet to develop alternative paradigms or open up their theories to critical debate (L'Etang 2008). This suggests a compelling case for practitioners to use excellence theory as a framework for both personal development and professional counsel.

The study identifies 14 characteristics, differentiating between programme, department and organization, providing a framework in which to consider how PR should work strategically and operationally. It also provides essential insight into organizational cultures within which communication works best.

At programme level, PR must be managed strategically. Meanwhile, at departmental level, there must be a single or integrated PR department, separate from marketing and reporting to senior management, led by a senior practitioner. Critically, the approach to PR must be based on a two-way symmetrical model.

The potential for excellence within the team is defined by knowledge of this symmetrical model and the management role; academic training and professionalism.

'Excellent' organizations reflect the symmetrical model of PR, with a practitioner featuring within what sociologists refer to as the organization's 'dominant coalition'. There is likely to be a complex environment with pressure from activists. The organization will have a participative culture, a symmetric approach to *internal* communications and an organic rather than mechanized structure.

A seat at the table

When conducting communication reviews within organizations, my first move is to investigate whether PR has, in the words of client, John Flamson (2009), Director of Government Office North West, a 'seat at the table'. He says:

> 'Without a direct line to the directorate, and a place alongside strategy development, PR will never fulfil its potential. Its ability to enhance and influence corporate strategy is where the real value lies.'

Organizational effectiveness is greatest when PR has a strategic management role (Grunig 1992). 'Excellent PR' demands attention from managers and fast access to leaders; achieved through a place within the dominant coalition (Black 1995). However, this must be aided by 'high visibility and status throughout his organization' (Dolphin and Fan 2000, p 2).

This approach can be challenging, as internal politics frequently come into play; two-way communication based on openness and inclusion can be compromised when PR becomes part of an 'exclusive' dominant coalition (Pieczka 1996 cited in Tench and Yeomans 2006).

Other factors include the need for stakeholder intelligence to be available continuously. Such information is provided by 'boundary spanners' (White and Dozier 1992, p 91):

> 'Individuals who interact with the organization's environment and gather, select and relay information from the environment to the dominant coalition.'

This role is rarely formalized, however there are exceptions. Working in New York, I found that employees of the Center for Court Innovation (CfCI 2008) used the term 'boundary spanner' without prompting and it appeared in published advice. These individuals saw communications as intrinsic to business planning.

Academics have found that PR can only expand beyond communications if practitioners have *knowledge of business issues combined with good relationships with senior management* (Moss *et al* 2000 cited in Tench and Yeomans 2006).

Nigel Green, Head of PR at Merseyside County Council, was an early role model in this respect, with an open door to the chief executive's office. In 1984 the first ever visit of the Tall Ships Races brought millions of people to Merseyside, then on the cusp of regeneration following the Toxteth riots. The *Liverpool Echo*'s front page headline was 'MR TALL SHIPS' – celebrating not just the event, but the PR professional whose influence made it happen.

As Iceland's Head of PR, I worked closely with the Chief Executive, Malcolm Walker – an entrepreneur who not only has an intuitive grasp of PR but also sees the benefits of its strategic and ethical counsel – on an approach which increased seasonal sales by 34 per cent, saw annual sales rise 9 per cent and changed customer perception from 'dull and boring', to 'open and friendly'. Presenting the company with a Gold *PR Week* Award, judges commented: 'Iceland offers a shining example to other in-house departments of how PR can make a significant contribution to a company's bottom line' (*PR Week* Awards 2000).

Working with another chief executive later in my career I had to wait two weeks for an appointment and our relationship ended when he asked me to send out a press release he had written, which I considered to be inappropriate. A few years later, he was reported in the national press as: 'seeking a face-saving exit from the company.'

PR's boundary spanning role can extend to collecting opinion, economic data and market intelligence. It can communicate information, while using external contacts to pinpoint issues that may have an impact; prioritize the strategic importance of publics; and act as a corrective to business strategy (Gregory 2002).

PR also brings objectivity to corporate decision making (Sung 2007 cited in L'Etang 2008) as practitioners become '... the monitor of public opinion and the conscience and ethical mentor of the organization' (Gregory 2002, p 10). This was the case at the Iceland Group, where PR extended issues management into strategic advice, influencing environmental policy, product stewardship, food integrity and supply chain relationships.

This challenge is being taken up by client Ken Perry (2009), an acknowledged social innovator and Chief Executive of the Plus Dane Group. Having made the bold move of rebranding this social housing provider as a 'Neighbourhood Investor', he is repositioning communications as a strategic force within the organization:

'We may be social housing specialists but everything we do is focused on creating vibrant, sustainable neighbourhoods – in terms of environment, health, education, economy and policy. We can only achieve this by working hand in hand with local people and partners. We see communications as an intrinsic part of business strategy – including real insight into what people's lives are really like, how they feel and what they want.'

Ethical counsel worked successfully for fair trade client, Fishtale. Owner Sarita Adams (2001) says:

'I expected just product launches and press releases. To have my consultant challenging employee welfare with factory owners in the backstreets of Kathmandu helped me make sound business decisions. Later this put me in a stronger position to sell my ideas to journalists and customers.'

Listening as well as telling

Within the struggle to define the role and scope of PR, students are versed in the views of Grunig and Hunt (1984 cited in Heath 2001), whose four models encompass press agentry/publicity, public information, two-way asymmetric and symmetric.

Of these, Grunig (1992) argues that 'excellent' PR departments model more communication on the two-way symmetrical approach than other typologies. He acknowledges, however, that practitioners must act as advocates for their organizations *and* for strategic publics, so that they themselves practise a two-way asymmetric approach.

I describe this as 'listening as well as telling' and a logical step in building effective relationships. In fact, evidence from psychology, interpersonal relationship and systems theory can all illustrate that an actual relationship with publics is at the very heart of PR activity.

Trust is seen as a critical construct in all relationships and in conflicts involving risk (Canary and Cupach 1988 cited in Ledingham and Bruning 2000), therefore relationship management is vital:

> 'Effectively managing organizational-public relationships around
> common interests and shared goals, over time, results in mutual
> understanding and benefit for interacting organizations and publics' –
> Ledingham (2003), cited in Tench and Yeomans (2006, p 157).

Two-way, long-term relationships are at the heart of PR, and are the way to build trust. However, this demands true insight into people. Sandra Palmer, Consultant Director at Corporate Culture (2009), sees this as the key to successful communications, particularly if seeking to change behaviour:

> 'Customer orientation is absolutely critical. Before it is possible to
> change anyone's behaviour, it is important to have an understanding of
> their knowledge, feelings, lifestyles and beliefs. The best communicators

are those who spend time listening, consulting and questioning to gain insight into people's goals, convictions, actions and motivations.'

When promoting a new Community Justice Centre in Liverpool, emphasis was placed on community engagement. This involved the creation of a community reference group to help plan the work of the centre, research into community needs and opinions, and events ranging from open days to surgeries within local supermarkets. Fear of retribution from being associated with the justice system meant that some residents needed alternatives to a public forum. However, internet access was under 10 per cent. People on low incomes responded well when offered Freepost addresses and Freephone lines, and with less than 40 per cent having access to a car, care was taken to organize public meetings on bus routes, in daylight (Porter 2008).

Stakeholder theory demands that management recognizes stakeholder interests, arguing that affected groups should have a role in determining policy (Evan and Freeman 1993, cited in Somerville 2001).

Some publics appear to lack stature, but in reality may be connected to more interested and powerful stakeholders (Tench and Yeomans 2006). Client, South African retailer Woolworths, wished to engage with the wider black community in the years after apartheid, but experienced challenges to traditional communication, including: poor literacy, 11 official languages and eight unofficial languages. Recognizing the environment as a matriarchal society, campaigning on food issues targeted women in the community, who, once convinced of the messages, communicated them widely (Eskinazi 2002).

This need for stakeholder insight also demands expertise within the communications team. According to Corporate Culture Research Director, Belinda Miller (2009):

'Analysis of evidence has never been more important in understanding behaviour. It is really important that communications teams either invest in developing specialist skills or find partners who can provide an objective viewpoint, think laterally and enhance their in-house capabilities to make evidence work harder for them.'

Symmetrical PR is linked inextricably with ethics, and is not accepted universally. Miller (1989, p 45) believes that persuasion and public relations are 'two Ps in a pod', claiming that 'ethically defensible persuasion and ethically defensible public relations are virtually synonymous.' He defines PR as controlling the predispositions and behaviours of publics.

However, belief that the symmetrical approach is the ethical choice and that organizations can 'wreak havoc on their publics by believing it is right for them to "exercise dominion" over their environment' (Grunig 1992, p 42) is widely supported. Kruckeberg and Starck (1988 cited in Grunig 1992, p 42) argue that symmetric PR should 'restore a sense of community' rather than use persuasion to achieve a corporate goal. Pearson (1989, cited in Grunig 1992, p 56) developed an independent theory of symmetrical PR, which he called 'the ideal public relations situation.'

It would be naive to deny practical challenges to this approach. L'Etang (2008) defines a problem in achieving true dialogue between organizations and stakeholders, because the managerial approach to PR is designed to meet corporate objectives. Therefore, strategically, these are prioritized above stakeholder relationships. Furthermore, research has shown that adopting an open and honest credo is not beneficial if the culture of the organization counters it (Serini 1993 cited in Armour 2006).

The internal audience

Symmetry has a clear role to play in *internal* communications and '... is more likely to ensure the smooth day-to-day running of the organization' (Smith and Mounter 2008, p 16).

However, this is not easy to achieve. Morrison and Miliken (2000 cited in Cornelissen 2008, p 199) identify '... powerful forces in many organizations that prevent employees from participation and force them to withhold information about potential problems or issues.' Real life examples are 'fear of negative feedback' and a belief that 'managers know best'.

I have seen few examples of sustained links between PR and human resources. However, such relationships are endorsed by Jayne Phillips, Managing Director at the Plus Dane Group (2009):

'Real innovators are those who give their employees the opportunity to input into strategy, listen carefully to them and respect what they hear. Nobody knows customers better than the people who actually talk to them every day. However, the right mechanisms have to be in place so that communication is both two-way, and as effective as possible.'

The need for strategic skills

Participation in strategic management is the single characteristic distinguishing excellent PR from less excellent practice (Grunig 1991).

PR practitioners have the ability to link their organization to its environment and to support strategic decision making, however this demands a shift from 'technician' to 'manager'. Grunig *et al* (2002 cited in Reber and Berger 2006) conclude that to deal with significant issues, a practitioner needs managerial as well as technical knowledge.

This has implications for recruitment and training, if 'technicians' are to grow into strategic roles. A study into the future of PR (Murray and White 2004, p 21) quotes Simon Lewis, Director of Corporate Affairs at Vodaphone: 'The challenge is bringing the best quality people into the business but also training them.'

Excellence theory argues for a management role for communications, but acknowledges that not all CEOs who value excellent communications have excellent departments, due to a shortage of skilled practitioners and an over-supply of technicians (Grunig 1991).

Arguably, PR is now essential within progressive management – a finding supported by Dolphin and Fan (2000, p 99), who researched communications directors from British industry and the public sector:

'Twenty years ago the proposition that PR might play an essential part in corporate strategy would have been scorned... Today an essential discovery is the extent to which many corporations value the input into their strategic planning from corporate communicators.'

This raises the need for increased skills and standards within the industry – a challenge being met through the CIPR's drive to provide training against benchmarks like professional qualifications and chartered status.

An emphasis on diversity

Alongside skills, it is necessary to consider diversity within PR teams. Grunig (2001b) proposes that excellent teams incorporate people from both sexes and diverse ethnic backgrounds; endorsing the principle of 'requisite variety' (Wieck 1969 cited in Verćić, Grunig and Grunig 1996), arguing that employee diversity enables an organization to interact more effectively with its environment. He adds that PR personnel must be open to learn from people different to themselves.

Dozier, Grunig and Grunig (1995) advise professional communicators to pay attention to the treatment of women and ethnic minorities, as it is proven that organizations which actively support their advancement are more likely to build excellent communications programmes.

In practice, I have found this tenet of excellence is much less evident than others, with many dominant coalitions made up entirely by white males.

While feminist research in the field of PR is extensive, research into the position of ethnic minorities is limited (Tench and Yeomans 2006). Existing studies have found not only wide barriers to the progression of women from technician to manager (L'Etang 2008), but also that practitioners from ethnic backgrounds suffer 'stereotyping, pigeonholing, positive and negative discrimination on the basis of race or colour' (Len-Rios 1998 cited in Tench and Yeomans 2006, p 174).

Nurturing cultures

The subject of excellence cannot be debated without reference to organizational culture. In my experience, this is the overall deciding factor in achieving excellent communications. Interestingly, Dozier, Grunig and Grunig (1995) confirm that a communications department cannot be excellent when the chief executive is not.

Participative cultures provide a superior setting for excellent communications (Dozier *et al* 1995). Here, proactivity is central to decision-making. Practitioners undertake environmental scanning and issues management, generally from within the 'dominant coalition'. Such an approach allows the practitioner to question and influence culture. Excellence theory identifies 12 factors shared by 'excellent organizations', which consider communications in the widest sense; ranging from leadership and intrapreneurship, to social responsibility and a focus on quality.

This is where PR comes into its own, as a drive for communications excellence can impact positively on the organization:

> '...excellent communication management can be the catalyst that begins to make organizations excellent and continues to make them more excellent as time passes.'
>
> *– Grunig (1992, p 17)*

Considering the future

The PR industry has a long way to go in achieving excellence. A survey for the PRCA (2009) shows declining public trust in PR professionals over the last 10 years, some of which has been attributed to recent scandals around MP's expenses and city bonuses. The sector also has a tendency to shoot itself in the foot: many practitioners were dismayed when a PR Week ethics debate, strongly argued by publicist Max Clifford, concluded that 'lying is sometimes necessary' (Crush 2007).

On a positive note, the UK's industry is number two in the world and one of the top three career choices for graduates. Within all management functions, job growth for PR is the highest (Davis 2009).

CEOs value PR, estimating that it brings a 184 per cent return on investment and is 150 per cent more valuable than other departments (Grunig 1991). However, this is only achieved when PR sits within the dominant coalition, and contributes to strategy, as part of a symmetrical communication model. Furthermore, this involves *managers* rather than technicians.

Wheeler (2005) sums up the benefits of chartered status, and the rising profile and credibility of PR:

> 'By 2010 the UK PR consultancy will be recognized as a suit-wearing profession, although probably not literally. All the signs are that the

industry has learnt good lessons from the last decade and is putting them into practice. If we can enhance our knowledge, improve our numeracy and keep our nerve, nothing can stop us.'

There is no doubt that more professional and well-evidenced PR will generate sound results for organizations and the economy. However, the effect on practitioners should also be recognized. Perhaps the last word should go to American football coach, Vincent Lombardi (2009):

'The quality of a person's life is in direct proportion to their commitment to excellence, regardless of their chosen field of endeavour.'

Further reading

Adams, S (2001) *Personal correspondence with owner of Fishtale fair trade mail order company*, June 2001, Liverpool.

Armour, L (2006) The Hobson and Holt Report, *Public Relations Autonomy* [Online] www.forimmediaterelease.biz/armour-paper.pdf [accessed 17 April 2008].

BBC (2001) What's the point of PR?, news, 12 April 2001 [Online] http://news.bbc.co.uk/1/hi/uk/1269079.stm [accessed 12 August 2009].

Black, S (1995) *The Practice of Public Relations*, 4th edn, Butterworth Heinemann, Oxford.

CEBR (2005) PR today: 48,000 professionals; £6.5 billion turnover, summary document, The economic significance of public relations, Centre for Economics and Business Research Ltd, London.

Center for Court Innovation (2008) Communicating the concept of community justice in the United States and the United Kingdom: a comparison of approaches, Leapfrog Public Relations, Liverpool.

Cornelissen, J (2008) *Corporate Communication: A guide to theory and practice*, 2nd edn, Sage Publications, London.

Cropp, F and Pincus, J D (2001) The mystery of public relations: unravelling its past, unmasking its future, in *Handbook of Public Relations*, ed R L Heath, Sage Publications, London.

Crush, P (2007) Ethics debate: the truth hurts, *PR Week*, 28 February [Online] www.prweek.com [accessed 12 August 2009].

Davis, M (2009) The domain of PR, PowerPoint presentation: Advanced Certificate Tutorial, 14 March, PR Academy, London [Online] www.pracademy.co.uk [accessed 8 August 2009].

Dolphin, R R and Fan, Y (2000) Is corporate communications a strategic function?, *Management Decision*, 38 (2), pp 99–106.

Dozier, D M, Grunig, L A and Grunig, J E (1995) *Manager's Guide to Excellence in Public Relations and Communication Management*, Lawrence Erlbaum Associates, Mahwah NJ.

Eskinazi, R (2002) Briefing on PR requirements, marketing department, Woolworths, personal communication, 1 June, Cape Town.

Flamson, J (2009) E-mail correspondence with John Flamson, Government Office North West, 6 August.

Gregory, A (2002) Public relations and management, in *The Public Relations Handbook*, ed A Theaker, Routledge, London.

Grunig, J E (1991) Excellence in public relations and communication management, executive summary/initial data report, University of Maryland [Online] www.iabc.com/rf/pdf/Excellence.pdf [accessed 10 July 2009].

Grunig, J E (1992) *Excellence in Public Relations and Communications Management*, Lawrence Erlbaum Associates, Hillsdale NJ.

Grunig, J E (2001a) Two-way symmetrical public relations, in *The Handbook of Public Relations*, ed R L Heath, Sage Publications, London.

Grunig, J E (2001b) The role of public relations in management and its contribution to organisational and societal effectiveness, speech delivered in Taipei, Taiwan, 12 May [Online] www.iabc.com [accessed 7 April 2008].

Grunig, L A, Grunig, J E and Dozier, D M (2002) *Excellent Public Relations and Effective Organisations: A study of communications management in three countries*, Lawrence Erlbaum Associates, New York.

Heath, R L (2001) *The Handbook of Public Relations*, Sage Publications, London.

Jones, N (1999) *The Sultans of Spin: The media and the new labour government*, Orion, London.

Kotler, P (1984) *Marketing Management: Planning, Analysis and Control*, 5th edn, Prentice Hall International, London.

L'Etang, J (2008) *Public Relations Concepts, Practice and Critique*, Sage Publications, London.

Langley, W (2007) It was all Ab Fab – and then she hit the jungle, *Daily Telegraph*, 25 November [Online] www.telegraph.co.uk [accessed 14 August 2009].

Ledingham, J A and Bruning, S D (2000) *Public Relations as Relationship Management: A relational approach to the study and practice of public relations*, Lawrence Erlbaum Associates, Mahwah NJ.

Lombardi, V (2009) Leader Values, quotes [Online] www.leader-values.com [accessed 8 August 2009].

Miller, B (2009) Personal e-mail correspondence with Belinda Miller, 18 August, Liverpool.

Miller, G R (1989) Persuasion and public relations: two 'Ps' in a pod, in *Public Relations Theory*, eds C H Botan and V Hazleton Jr, Laurence Erlbaum Associates, Hillsdale NJ [Online] www.questia.com [accessed 23 October 2008].

Murray, K and White, J (2006) *Reputation Management: Leading practitioners look to the future of public relations*, Bell Pottinger, London.

Palmer, S (2009) Notes of meeting with Sandra Palmer, 17 August, Liverpool.

Perry, K (2009) Personal e-mail correspondence with Plus Dane Group, 17 August.

Phillips, J (2009) Notes of telephone conversation with Jayne Phillips, 12 August.

Porter, J (2009) Personal e-mail correspondence with Community Justice Centre, North Liverpool, 18 August.

PR Week Awards (2000) In-house department of the year, supplement to *PR Week (The PR Week Awards 2000)*, November, p 13.

PRCA (2009) The reputation of the industry, press release, Public Relations Consultants Association, 26 June [Online] www.prca.org.uk [accessed 12 August 2009].

Reber, B H and Berger, B K (2006) Finding influence. examining the role of influence in public relations, *Journal of Communication Management*, **10** (3), pp 235–49.

Smith, L and Mounter, P (2008) *Effective Internal Communication*, 2nd edn, Kogan Page, London.

Somerville, I (2002) Public relations, politics and the media, in *The Public Relations Handbook*, ed A Theaker, Routledge, London.

Stern, S (2003) The death of PR, *New Statesman*, 20 January [Online] www.newstatesman.com [accessed 14 August 2009].

Taylor, K (2009) Welcome to the website of the Chartered Institute of Public Relations [Online] www.cipr.co.uk [accessed August 2009].

Tench, R and Yeomans, L (2006) *Exploring Public Relations*, Pearson Education, Harlow.

Verćić, D, Grunig, L A and Grunig, J E (1996) Global and specific principles of public relations: evidence from Slovenia, in *International Public Relations: A comparative analysis*, eds H Cuthbertson and N Chen, Lawrence Erlbaum Associates, New Jersey [Online] www.questia.com [accessed 12 October 2008].

Wheeler, A (2005) Knowledge, numeracy and nerve, PR today: 48,000 professionals, £6.5 billion turnover – summary document, CEBR Ltd, London.

White, J and Dozier, D M (1992) Public relations and management decision making, in *Excellence in Public Relations and Communication Management*, ed J E Grunig, Lawrence Erlbaum Associates, New Jersey.

Notes

1   Update: 2013 figures from the PR Census 2013 report a value of £9.62 billion and 62,000 employees, www.prca.co.uk

2   *Absolutely Fabulous*, a BBC sitcom written by and starring Jennifer Saunders, which was broadcast from 1992–96 and 2001–05.

A critical review

20

The four models of public relations and the excellence theory in an era of digital communication

STEPHEN WADDINGTON CHART.PR, MCIPR

This paper was originally written in December 2012. Minor revisions have been made to the original text for this book to reflect developments in media, technology and practice.

This paper examines the four models of public relations and excellence theory. It examines historical criticism and instances where the theories are being challenged by modern public relations practice as a result of digital communication.

Four models of public relations

In 1984, James Grunig and Todd Hunt published the four models of public relations as part of their book *Managing Public Relations*.[1]

TABLE 20.1   Summary of James Grunig and Todd Hunt's Four Models of Public Relations (1984)

Model	Type of communication
1. Press agent or publicity	One-way
2. Public information model	One-way
3. Two-way asymmetrical model	Two-way imbalanced
4. Two-way symmetrical model	Two-way

The model describes the different forms of communication between an organization and its stakeholders.

The first model is publicity or press agent, the second is the public relations information model, the third asymmetric persuasion, and the final one – the two-way symmetrical model – has become accepted as a formal definition of best practice for communication in Western markets between an organization and its audiences.

The excellence theory

The so-called excellence theory[2] developed over the next decade as a result of a research programme commissioned by the Research Foundation of the International Association of Business Communicators (IABC) in 1984. It sought to explore how public relations could evolve from a tactical craft that broadly focused on publicity and media relations to become a management discipline.

James Grunig assembled a team of six public relations academics and practitioners under his leadership. These included his wife Larissa Grunig of the University of Maryland; David Dozier of San Diego State University; William Ehling of Syracuse University; Jon White, a UK consultant, academic and teacher; and Fred Repper, a public relations practitioner.

In the Third Annual Grunig Lecture Series[3] at the Public Relations Society of America (PRSA) International Conference in October 2010, Larissa and James Grunig explained the original objective and motivation of the research team:

> 'We started this project with a simple quest from the IABC Research Foundation which was what is the value of public relations, and can you articulate its value to an organization?'

The first phase of study that led to the excellence theory consisted of quantitative, survey-based research of more than 300 organizations in Canada, UK and US, including a cross section of corporations, non-profit organizations and government agencies.

Survey questionnaires were completed by approximately 5,400 senior executives, public relations practitioners and employees. This resulting qualitative data was reduced through a process of factor analysis into a single index of communication management. The index was used to identify organizations for qualitative research to provide insight into how public relations excellence is achieved in different organizations.

The excellence theory's general theory proposed that the value of communication can be determined at four levels as follows.[4]

TABLE 20.2 An overview of the four levels of analysis proposed by the excellence theory

Programme level – effective organizations must empower public relations as a critical management function.

Functional level – Public relations should be an integrated communication function and separate from other management functions including marketing.

Organization level – effective organizations should base internal and external communication and relationship building on a two-way symmetrical model.

Societal level – Organizations must recognize their impact on other organizations and publics. They cannot be effective unless they are socially responsible.

SOURCE: Adapted from Grunig and Grunig 2008.

The original four models of public relations and vision of two-way symmetrical communications as a model of excellence was reinforced by the subsequent analysis that emerged from the excellence theory. As we'll see, some academics believe this shows Grunig's foresight while others claim that the research team was unduly influenced by the four models of public relations.

Academic criticism

Critical appraisal of the excellence theory isn't hard to find. A critical review together with responses from members of the original research team would be sufficient material for a paper in its own right. A chronological summary of some of the different aspects of academic criticism is outlined below.

Other challenges include ethics, power, propaganda and Western bias. My primary issue with the four models of public relations and the excellence theory is the use of a simple construct that seemingly places an organization or brand at the centre of every diagram, appearing to control communication and relationships. This is not the case in the era of the social web and I would argue never has been.

Applying the excellence theory to organizational communication in an era of digital network communication

It is very easy to get excited about the fragmentation of traditional media and celebrate the upheaval in organization communication created by social media. Digital networks and new forms of digital media are making it easier than ever for organizations to engage with their audiences by creating their own text, images and video and sharing via social networks such as Google+, Facebook, Pinterest and Twitter. But we only get excited about the potential for new forms of digital media to disrupt organizations because so many organizations are wedded to publicity and one-way propaganda as a means of communication.

TABLE 20.3   Academic criticism of the excellence theory

1996	In a paper for the *Journal of Public Relations Research*[i] Michael Karlberg makes the case that the excellence theory is overly concerned with consumers as a primary audience. He believes that the research team missed an opportunity to explore the broader implications of the relationship between an organization and its markets.
1996	In *Paradigms, System Theory and Public Relations*,[ii] Magda Pieczka says that the two-way symmetrical component of the excellence theory is over-idealized. In doing so she attacks the research agenda from which it was developed and the premise of systems theory on which the model is based.
2001	Shirley Leitch and David Neilson challenge the rigid nature of the excellence theory in a chapter written for the *Handbook of Public Relations*.[iii] Their belief is that publics are not fixed categories waiting to be identified but are formed dynamically through the conversation in which they participate.
2011	In *Public Relations, Society and Culture*,[iv] Lee Edwards and Caroline Hodges argue that Grunig's rigid focus on organization theory over-simplifies human behaviour. They suggest that this singular focus on public relations within organizations overlooks the social world in which those organizations operate.

NOTES: i   Karlberg, M (1996) Remembering the public in public relations research, *Journal of Public Relations Research* [Online] http://myweb.wwu.edu/karlberg/articles/RememberingThePublic.pdf [accessed 5 November 2014].
ii   Pieczka, M (1996) *Public Relations: Critical Debates and Contemporary Practice*, Routledge, London.
iii   Leitch, S and Neilson, D (2001) Bringing publics into public relations: new theoretical frameworks for practice, in *Handbook of Public Relations*, eds R L Heath and G Vasquez, Sage Publications [Online] http://knowledge.sagepub.com/view/handbook-of-public-relations/n9.xml [accessed 5 November 2014].
iv   Edwards, L and Hodges, C E M (2011) *Public Relations, Society & Culture: Theoretical and Empirical Explorations*, Routledge, London.

During the October 2010 speech at the PRSA International Conference, Larissa Grunig said:

'The new media that we have today makes it more possible than ever to achieve our goals in terms of relationships with stakeholders. So given today's social and business landscape and the advance of digital and social media, what is still important about the excellence theory?'

The implication of Larissa Grunig's comment is that modern digital media provides the opportunity for excellent public relations practice as defined by the excellence theory.

In this next section I have scrutinized some of the areas where the excellence model is being challenged by digital networks, fragmented media and modern public relations practice.

Communication in digital networks

The jointly sponsored CIPR/PRCA Internet Commission in 2000 foresaw the impact that the internet would have on the media and organizational communication. It recognized how the internet was set to disintermediate all forms of media and that this would necessitate fundamental changes in organizational communication.

The moment that a message is recorded in an electronic form it can be transmitted within a network with ease. The interconnected nature of networks means that if a message resonates with an audience it will be shared and passed from network-to-network. The original creator of the message has no control over how a message passes through a network or how it is modified en route.

David Phillips was an original member of the CIPR/PRCA Internet Commission. He has campaigned tirelessly for the last decade for the public relations industry to wake up to the impact of the internet on organization communication.

> 'The Grunig device of having the equivalent of four models of communication between an organization and its publics has significant limitations. It was conceived in an era of set structures and I think it is showing its age.'

In a paper presented at Bledcom in 2009,[5] Bruno Amaral and David Phillips reported on a research project at the University of Lisbon that investigated how relationships are formed online. The research examined a huge corpus of blog posts and discovered that relationships are formed at a nexus in values. Individuals and organizations that share similar values with other individuals and organizations will naturally converge online.

Amaral and Phillips stopped short of identifying how this convergence took place. Some of it was via hyperlinks but by no means all.

There were lots of connections that were unexplained by network theory. Phillips has continued the programme of study and developed a work in progress called the Lisbon theory.[6]

New models of organizational communication

In *Online Public Relations*[7] David Phillips and Philip Young state that internet technologies have disintermediated not only organizational communication but the entire value chain of commerce:

> 'The context in which an organization can thrive is rapidly moving from its ability to create traditional relationships with publics to its ability to do this in an online world, and mostly via third parties that are beyond its control.'

> 'The presence of information and messages about organizations is spread by and through many devices and platforms that transmit and receive information. Distribution is effected by web crawlers and search engines.'

The point well made by Phillips and Young is that the vast majority of content on the web about an organization is not under its control and the opportunity for engagement is limited. In fact it's not possible for an organization to monitor all the mentions of it online let alone interact in a meaningful way.

The social web is made up of conversations on blogs, forums and social networks such as Facebook and Twitter, accessible in moments in response to a search query. They put publics firmly in control of the reputation of an organization, placing the audience at the heart of the conversation, seemingly turning the four models of public relations and the excellence model theory on their heads.

Memes: dynamic communication

Andy Green challenges the excellence theory's assumption of a neat transactional relationship between an audience and its publics:

> 'I would challenge Grunig's symmetrical model [the fourth model] as it fails to take into account the dynamic nature of memes – it makes assumptions that content is passive, undynamic and inert.'

Memes is a concept conceived by Richard Dawkins in his book *The Selfish Gene* that has come to define the means by which cultural behaviours and ideas are shared. It describes an idea or concept, typically in the form of a piece of content that is replicated and modified through personal communication, increasingly the social web.

Marketing and public relations practitioners strive to generate memes as a means of promoting a brand, product or issue. But devising an idea that is meme-friendly that inspires an audience to develop and share so that it goes viral is as tough as it gets. The internet is littered with failed attempts.

Organizations also need to contend with the issue of the loss of control. Memes as a metaphor of cultural DNA evolve as they reproduce. This is where Green takes issue with the excellence theory. In his view it fails to describe how an idea that is originated by an organization is shared, mimicked and developed by the audience. Everett Rogers explores this issue in *The Diffusion of Innovations*.[8] The relationship between an organization and an audience isn't asymmetrical as Grunig describes. Instead messages are distorted and adapted as it is shared by the audience, as Green contends:

> 'Communicators need to understand that memes are the DNA of communications. You need to understand and respect the power of memes to harness, direct where possible, although not positively control.'

Social media doesn't change anything

Liz Bridgen who leads the MA courses in Public Relations and International Public Relations at De Montfort University responded to a tweet I posted in my search for examples of truly two-way symmetrical communication.

Bridgen encourages students to take a critical view of Grunig and challenged me to consider whether social media changes anything in the relationship between an organization and its publics.

> 'If an organization has a social platform and invites comments from its publics, a symmetrical form of communication, does it conform to Grunig's excellence theory?'

'The answer is clearly no. It is only symmetrical communication if the organization engages but it is unlikely to be a symmetrical relationship.'

The Business of Influence

In *Brand Anarchy*,[9] the book that I co-wrote with Steve Earl, Philip Sheldrake brings a refreshing perspective to organizational communication:

> 'Information and communication technology has laid bare the fact in a way that you can't call anything less than brutal these days. You can't fake it so, to me, reality is the new perception. So you'd better make sure that you build that reality in order to live up to the perception that you'd like others to have of you. Ultimately that's the business of influence.'

In a related article in the *Harvard Balanced Scorecard Report*,[10] Sheldrake says:

> 'No organization is an island. Everything it does occurs within the context of a changing world, in a dynamic interplay with every entity around it. The revolution in information and communication technologies has made this dynamic interplay increasingly transparent, immediate, and global.'

Sheldrake sets out a new model organizational communication as a result of the internet and online networks based on six primary influence flows in his book *The Business of Influence*:[11]

1 An organization's influence on its stakeholders;
2 The influence of stakeholders on each other with respect of an organization;
3 The influence of stakeholders on the organization;
4 An organization's competitors influence its stakeholders;
5 The influence of stakeholders on each other with respect to an organizations' competitors;
6 The influence of stakeholders on the organization's competitors.

FIGURE 20.1 The influence flows between an organization, stakeholders and competitors

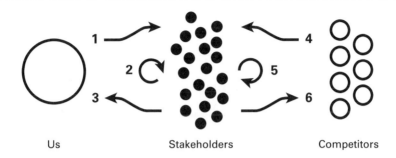

Sheldrake's contention is that the first flow, an organization's influence on its stakeholders, and the corresponding third flow, the influence of stakeholders on an organization, are well understood. This is symmetrical communication between an organization and its publics and it overlays neatly onto the fourth of the four models of public relations. But the internet has made the second flow critical to the management of the reputation of an organization and a market.

Furthermore, stakeholders are using the internet to find each other and thanks to search technology are able to communicate about an organization online. These conversations are likely to be a rich source of insight for an organization if it chooses to listen and are an opportunity for engagement. Technology also makes it easy for an organization to track its competitors and their influence on its stakeholders and vice versa – influence flows 4, 5 and 6.

Switching the axis of organizational communication

Back to Philip Young. I sought out his views on the four models of public relations and the excellence theory after reading *Online Public Relations* and reviewing a post on his thought provoking blog Mediations[12] about his personal view of the theories. Young shares Sheldrake's view that the key to understanding organizational communication lies in an audience-centric viewpoint. He believes that the theories are based on an old-fashioned view of organizational communication:

> 'The organization talks to the audience, listens a bit, talks again, and a lot of public relations theory, especially when written from a media relations perspective, still concentrates on this vector.'

Young's view is that we argue that the most significant conversations are those surrounding the organization and that social media has increased the ability for the audience to communicate with each other:

> 'These conversations are now visible. They are aggregated and are searchable. Grunig sees the main path as up and down, from organization to audience and back, but the most significant discourse is left to right among the audience.'

Grunig continues to make the case for the four models of public relations and the excellence model. He responded to the claim that the internet disrupts his model in a paper, Paradigms of global public relations in the age of digitalisation:[13]

> 'For most practitioners, digital media do change everything about the way they practice public relations... Rather, the new media facilitate the application of the principles and, in the future, will make it difficult for practitioners around the world not to use the principles.'

Conclusion

The four models of public relations and the excellence theory aren't wrong but they are idealistic and as Sheldrake shows are showing their age in an era of internet-driven network communication, and are insufficient to explain the modern business of public relations.

Few organizations truly engage with their audiences as Grunig *et al* describe in the four models of public relations and the excellence theory but are locked into one-way forms of communication or imbalanced two-way asymmetrical communication.

Grunig's intention in developing the four models of public relations and excellence theory was to set out how public relations should be practised. It has been idealized by academics and practitioners. That's not a flaw or fault in the theory. I'd argue that this is recognition of the breadth and rigour of Grunig's work.

The increasing adoption of social media and the shift to integrate social technologies into organizations puts audiences at their heart and calls for a reappraisal for the four models of public relations and the four levels of analysis proposed by the excellence theory.

The four models of public relations and the excellence theory were milestone texts in the project to professionalize public relations and shift away from propaganda and persuasion. But the four models of public relations and the excellence theory have signification limitations but then they were both conceived in a pre-social web era of well-defined organizational structures and modes of communication.

It is important to recognize that these are models. As such, no organization can expect to conform to them precisely. However they are important as a means of helping students and practitioners understand the flow of communication between an organization and its publics.

I've stopped short of proposing how the four models of public relations and the excellence theory might be developed. I'll leave that to far more learned and wiser minds than my own. That said my view is that the models must take an audience, consumer-centric or influencer viewpoint and consider their impact on an organization rather than vice versa.

This is after all the business of public relations.

Notes

1 Grunig, J E and Dozier, D M (2002) *Excellence in Public Relations and Communication Management: A study of communication management in three countries*, chapter 8, Routledge, New York.

2 Grunig, J E (1992) *Excellence in Public Relations and Communication Management*, chapter 11, Routledge, New York.

3 Grunig, L and Grunig, J E (2007) The Third Annual Grunig Lecture Series, PRSA International Conference.

4 Grunig, L and Grunig, J (2008) Excellence theory in public relations: past, present, and future, in *Public Relations Research, European and International Perspectives and Innovations*, eds A Zerfass, B van Ruler, and K Sriramesh, VS Verlag für Sozialwissenschaften.

5 Phillips, D and Amaral, B (2009) A proof of concept for automated discourse analysis in support of identification of relationship building in blogs, BledCom [Online] http://www.academia.edu/465376/ A_proof_of_concept_for_automated_discourse_analysis_in_support_ of_identification_of_relationship_building_in_blogs [accessed 5 November 2014].

6 Phillips, D (2011) Online trends and the Lisbon theory, Leverwealth blog, (November) [Online] http://leverwealth.blogspot.co.uk/2012/11/ online-trends-and-lisbon-theory.html [accessed 5 November 2014].

7 Phillips, D and Young, P (2009) *Online Public Relations: A practical guide to developing an online strategy in the world of social media*, Kogan Page, London.

8 Rogers, E M (1962/2003) *The Diffusion of Innovation*, 5th revd edn, chapter 8, Simon & Schuster International, New York.

9 Earl, S and Waddington, S (2012) *Brand Anarchy*, Bloomsbury, London.

10 Clark, P W and Coffey, J L (2011) Balanced scorecard report, Harvard Business Publishing, **13** (4) [Online] http://hbr.org/product/balanced-scorecard-report-july-august-2011-vol-13-/an/B11070-PDF-ENG [accessed 5 November 2014].

11 Sheldrake, P (2011) *The Business of Influence*, John Wiley & Sons, Hoboken NJ.

12 Young, P (2009) It's excellence Jim, but not as we know it, Mediations blog [Online] http://publicsphere.typepad.com/mediations/2009/12/ its-excellence-jim-but-not-as-we-know-it-grunig-revisited.html [accessed 5 November 2014].

13 Grunig, J E (2009) Paradigms of global public relations in an age of digitalization, *Prism Journal* [Online] http://www.prismjournal.org/ filcadmin/Praxis/Files/globalPR/GRUNIG.pdf [accessed 5 November 2014].

INDEX

Note: The index is filed in alphabetical, word-by-word order. Numbers within main headings are filed as spelt out. Acronyms are filed as presented. Page locators in *italics* denote information contained within a figure or table; locators as roman numerals denote material contained within the preliminary pages.